Pieter Desmet & Steven Fokkinga

Emotions BY DESIGN

Using the **SCIENCE** *of emotions to create beloved* **PRODUCTS & SERVICES**

BIS

Contents

Preface

When was the last time a product sparked a deeply positive emotion in you?

Was it when that sleek countertop appliance transformed your kitchen into something magazine-worthy? Or when your new noise-canceling headphones finally silenced your chatty coworker? Or perhaps when you found your moldy old retainer in a box of keepsakes, unleashing a flood of childhood memories? While your example might differ, we'd be willing to bet that it involves a product that is extraordinary for its striking appearance, incredible functionality, or personal significance.

When we posed this question during one of our workshops, we received an answer we hadn't anticipated. A participant came forward, placed a black pencil on the table, and declared, "I feel deep admiration for this pencil." We looked at the pencil. Nothing happened. Sensing our confusion, he set down another pencil—identical in size and color, but with a round barrel instead of hexagonal. It promptly began to roll and tumbled off the table. When a pencil hits the ground, he explained, the lead core breaks and the pencil becomes useless. A hexagonal barrel is just as pleasant to hold—but it never tries to make a run for it. Since he used pencils for most of his writing and drawing, that minor difference mattered enormously.

This example, although simple and somewhat peculiar, is profoundly revealing. It illustrates two crucial insights about emotions and products. First, it shows how emotion is *subjective*: the same thing can evoke very different feelings in different people. What may be of great concern to one—the shape of a pencil—leaves another indifferent. The passionate euphoria of a young fan at her favorite band's concert stands in stark contrast to the boredom and mild despair experienced by her chaperoning dad. For anyone in product development, subjectivity presents what seems like a challenge at best, and, at worst, a dead end. How can anyone predict and influence how people will feel about products, if human emotions are so personal and unpredictable?

But the pencil example also reveals a second insight, which will take center stage throughout this book. Even if you do not personally identify with the pencil owner's emotions, at least you can follow his reasoning. If you worked at an angled desk every day, you would probably have similar feelings about the two designs. This shared recognition shows that emotions are not random or irrational: their causes and effects follow rules, and these rules are the same for every human. The rules have evolved over millennia to help us respond appropriately to what is happening around us.

Consider an emotion that is as relevant today as it was thousands of years ago: fear. Fear comes in many forms, but it is always induced by some kind of *danger*. The emotion of fear is subjective only in that people perceive different things as dangerous. For a little kid, that thing might be a mean-looking neighborhood dog. For his mother, it might be the towering stack of unpaid bills by the front door. But both will react in similar ways: by becoming more alert, seeking protection, or reaching out for help. In other words, even though the ingredients of the emotional stew might differ, the way they cook is always the same.

Science has provided us with an increasingly clear picture of what is going on in the kitchen. After a period of relative neglect in the first half of the twentieth century, when emotion was considered a topic unbefitting a serious scientist, emotion research began to flourish. In the 1980s, work in the fields of psychology, neuroscience, and anthropology joined together to unravel the mystery of what emotions are, how they work in our brains and bodies, and how they influence our behaviors and preferences.

So, what is an emotion, according to science?

Emotions are functional states arising from cognitive appraisals of events in relation to personal needs and values, which generate specific action tendencies and physiological changes that prepare the organism for adaptive responses to environmental challenges and opportunities.[1]

Don't worry if that sentence doesn't make any sense right now. We'll unpack it throughout the book, showing how each part can be leveraged to design products people will love.

Emotional Design

It is perhaps most helpful to start with what emotional design is *not*. It is not a special class of products that stand out for their fanciness or exclusiveness. Every product evokes emotions. Some products have a greater chance of being beloved (or loathed) because they play a more prominent role in people's lives. But if a 30-cent pencil can arouse a profoundly positive emotion, any product can.

1. There are several schools of thought within emotion science. Some perspectives complement each other, while others fundamentally disagree on key points. Our models and approaches are grounded in the *functionalist perspective* of emotion, spearheaded by researchers like Magda Arnold (e.g., 1960), Richard Lazarus (e.g., 1991), Nico Frijda (e.g., 2007), and Ortony, Clore, and Collins (1988). The definition of emotion presented here is a distinct expression of this perspective. A related perspective describes *basic emotions*, which, while also rooted in functional thinking, maintains a stronger focus on biological universals (e.g., Ekman, 1999; Izard, 1977). Other influential perspectives are the *dimensional* (e.g., Russell, 1980; Watson & Tellegen, 1985), *constructionist* (e.g., Averill, 1980; Barrett, 2006), and *somatic* (e.g., Damasio, 1994; James, 1948; Lange, 1922) approaches. Each of these perspectives offer valuable insights into the nature of emotions, though they sometimes arrive at different conclusions about how emotions function and what they fundamentally are.

Emotional design is also not a specific aspect or feature of a product. It is not the icing that you add after all the serious cake requirements have been fulfilled. Instead, it is a set of guidelines that help you understand the kind of cake you are making and how you should balance the ingredients. Every aspect of a product, from its functionality and usability to its appearance and cultural meaning, is experienced by the human emotional system. This system evaluates to what extent these diverse elements, as a whole, fulfill or frustrate the user's needs. For example, a smartwatch might have the most advanced health sensors, but if its interface makes everyday tasks unreasonably complex, users will experience disappointment rather than delight. Similarly, a meal-planning app might offer impeccable functionality and ease of use, but if it fails to understand users' cultural food preferences or dietary values, it will create an emotional disconnect that undermines its practical benefits.

This brings us to what emotional design *is*: an *approach* that asks you to study, understand, and anticipate people's emotional responses so you can design products that make sense and are fantastic to use. This approach does not in any way devalue the importance of product aspects not traditionally associated with emotion, such as technology or usability, nor does it promote the practice of spuriously attaching emotions to a product through marketing or storytelling. Instead, it considers every significant event that occurs between product and person, from first look to final use, and offers concrete steps to produce the most effective and enjoyable results from each of those interactions.

The Focus of This Book

A pencil is the epitome of a mass-produced consumer product: inexpensive, widely available, deceptively simple—try making one yourself!—and something you pay little attention to (until you desperately need one and can't find one). Many of the cases presented in this book focus on consumer products, partly because they work well as concrete examples, partly because that is our domain of expertise. However, the approaches in this book apply to any designed object, service, or system that people use to fulfill a need or solve a problem—apps, packaged foods, government services, interiors, electronic devices, transportation systems, etcetera. Although each application comes with its own set of requirements and constraints, the fundamental link between emotions and design decisions is the same. Airports can be frustrating to navigate, and so can websites; cars can evoke nostalgia, as can hotel services; offices can inspire workers, but so can apps.

We have aimed to make this book both insightful and applicable to anyone involved in the development of products, services, and systems—whether you are a designer, architect, engineer, market researcher, brand manager, or strategy consultant. We have seen time and again how an emotion-focused approach can create a shared language across disciplines that puts humans at the center of the conversation. The rudiments of this language are already known to each of us, thanks to our lifelong experience of emotion. This book aims to further develop this shared language by enriching it with scientific discourse and weaving it into the vocabulary of product development.

The structure of the book reflects our dual goal: to make the theory accessible and enjoyable to read, and to provide actionable methods, models, and examples that enable you to put the theory into practice. The body of the text is intended to be a casual read containing everyday examples and a minimum of jargon. We have interspersed the text with product case examples that bring the theory to life. These examples come from three complementary sources: existing products and services that showcase the principles of emotional design, inspiring student projects, and cases from our own consultancy practice in which we experienced first-hand how these principles translate into real-world impact.

Each chapter also provides what we call *design opportunities* or *research opportunities. Research opportunities* introduce practical methods for understanding users' emotional experiences that you can weave into user research and market research. *Design opportunities* demonstrate how to apply relevant insights in design and innovation work. Most chapters conclude with a *theoretical deep dive*, that provides a more detailed analysis of the chapter's underlying psychological concepts for those interested.

This book is divided into eight chapters; each introduces an approach to emotional design. We have been developing them over the past twenty-five years, during our research and teaching at Delft University of Technology, the Netherlands, as well as through our Rotterdam-based consultancy, Emotion Studio. The chapters are largely self-sufficient and can be read separately from one another. However, since the earlier chapters introduce some concepts that reappear later in the book, we recommend reading the book from beginning to end for a more comfortable reading experience.

The book includes a section called *Tools & Techniques*, which brings together the instruments, measurement scales, and step-by-step guides referenced throughout the book. Think of it as a practical toolkit you can revisit whenever you put these approaches into practice.

Pieter Desmet & Steven Fokkinga

1

FUNDAMENTAL *Needs*

For over twenty years, we have been teaching an industrial design graduate course titled *Design & Emotion*. We begin each course by asking the new students to bring a product that fills them with joy. The classroom is pretty small, so this assignment invariably makes it look like a design exhibition—or a garage sale, depending on who you ask. The products are as diverse as the reasons that students bring them. Piyali brought a potato peeler that was so comfortable to use that she bought a second one for her mother back home. G-Young brought her beloved Polaroid camera, which allowed her to share photographs instantly with the people she met on her travels through Africa. Maurizio displayed a Lego brick that transported him back to his childhood bedroom. And Chi brought a nose-shaped pencil sharpener that never failed to spark conversations when she used it in public.

We assign this task to encourage our students to ponder the link between products and emotions. Over the years, the exercise has provided us with hundreds of product examples and the stories behind them. We began to wonder whether this massive set of carefully chosen, joy-inducing products might reveal some of the secrets of good product design. Just as a medical researcher studies a large sample of healthy individuals to identify commonalities in their lifestyles or habits, could we discover universal qualities that make these products so delightful? Might there be a discernable pattern in their forms, colors, or materials that produces joy? Could we find similarities in usability, functionality, or character?

The answer to these questions was a resounding no. The dataset includes as much of the ugly as it does the beautiful. We found durable products as well as disposable goods, one-of-a-kind gems, and mass-produced commodities. Some products solve unique problems, while others seemingly have no purpose whatsoever. Apparently, very diverse (even opposing) product qualities can elicit positive emotions in people.

How solid is this finding? Our data collection method wasn't exactly scientific. For one thing, design students are hardly your typical product users. They are often drawn to odd or extraordinary products. And they also perceive everyday things differently because they understand what goes into making them.

Yet, we have repeatedly encountered identical findings in our scientific research with the broader population. There is no fixed set of product attributes that universally triggers positive emotions. For instance, in a study that measured the emotions of Japanese and Dutch consumers as they viewed images of different car models, we found that the same car model could evoke completely different emotions in the two groups. The Fiat Multipla, infamous for its rather unique design (see image 1.2), exemplifies this phenomenon. Some of our participants found the car repulsive and outrageous; others found it delightful and even

1.1 What joy looks like, one product at a time

inspiring. Even more strikingly, these differences did not follow any apparent logic. They cut across genders, age groups, and cultures—a female Japanese octogenarian was just as likely to love (or hate) the Multipla as a 25-year-old Dutch man.[1]

1.2 An acquired taste

This apparent lack of structure presents us with a significant challenge. The ultimate goal of our research is to help practitioners create products that evoke positive emotions. To do this effectively, we need to predict which design decisions—materials, shapes, colors, features, and so on—will trigger specific emotions. But how do we make such predictions when there is no way to detect any systematic relationship between emotions and existing products? This seeming absence of underlying structure in our findings was deeply unsettling—enough to make even the most dedicated researcher question their career choice.

Fortunately, there *is* a structure underlying these emotions. We were just looking for it in the wrong place. The structure doesn't reside in a product's outward physical properties but rather in the inner life of the users who experience them. To reveal that structure, we must turn away from products for a moment and focus on what truly gives people joy.

The Jars of Joy

What is the essence of joy?[2] Although this familiar feeling may seem quite basic, at second glance, it harbors an enormous richness. Consider how diversely it is expressed. Joy can make a person listen intently to a story, jump around uncontrollably, or quietly sit back in an armchair. Sometimes, joyful moments are carefully planned; other times, joy takes us by surprise. Joy can be experienced alone in a room or at a stadium with thousands of others. And there is as much variety in the causes of joy. It can be sparked by receiving a long-awaited promotion, parachuting out of an airplane, being visited by a childhood friend, or taking the first sip of beer on a hot day. Joy is found in major achievements, social engagements, and simple pleasures. Essentially, we are faced with the same question as before: what is the common factor underlying these diverse events? Why do *all* these situations make people feel good?

1. Desmet (2003).

2. For the time being, we are using "joy" as a synonym for "positive emotion" or "feeling good." In Chapter 6, we unpack positive emotion and reveal its many variations.

This time, the answer is simple. These things bring joy because they fulfill our needs.[3] Sometimes, the need is concrete and conscious, as when you want to have lunch and are glad you've found a good sandwich shop. At other times, needs are subconscious and not actively pursued, as when you bump into a childhood friend, have a nice chat about old times, and walk away feeling uplifted. In each case, those feelings of joy tell you that something about the situation has fulfilled some relevant and important need you have—whether you are aware of that need or not.

Basically, we say that people enjoy things because they want them. You would be excused for finding this explanation so obvious as to be practically meaningless. Are we just substituting "want" for "need"?

No, because it helps us understand something new. Saying that "people enjoy getting what they need" shifts your attention away from the outside world, the realm of objects and events, to people's inner worlds, the realm of goals and wishes. Unlike outside—where there is an endless jumble of things that can evoke joy—on the inside, there is structure and clarity. People need many different things in life, but these needs can be identified and clustered. Furthermore, although people may have different goals and wishes on the surface, deep down everybody wants the same things.

Let's imagine the spectrum of human needs as a collection of jars. The fullness of each jar represents how well the corresponding need is satisfied at the moment. Some experiences drain the jars; others fill them up. Consider the universal need for meaningful human connection. A businesswoman traveling alone for weeks may notice that the contents of her "human connection jar" are getting unpleasantly low. But if she returns home and spends the whole weekend with her family and friends, the jar can be refilled to the brim.

If you picture needs as jars, emotions are the level gauges of the jars. An emotion signals how full a particular need jar is at that moment. Positive emotions indicate that a relevant need jar is adequately filled; negative emotions alert you when a jar is running low. Emotions are especially sensitive to sudden changes in a jar's level. Running into an old friend, for example, might abruptly fill your friendship jar, causing you to feel joy. Saying goodbye to a good friend who is moving abroad might drain that jar, making you feel sad. These emotional signals are essential because, although you have many needs, you can only be aware of a few needs at a time. Without emotions, you would have to consciously check the level of all your jars all the time—an impossible feat.

3. Throughout this book, we will use the word "need" to refer to any concrete or abstract thing a person may need, want, desire, or pursue. In Chapter 3, we will home in on the differences between types of needs.

1.3 How full are your jars?

How many jars do you need to attend to? We stated that each moment of joy reveals that a certain need was fulfilled. Does that mean you have a uniquely corresponding need jar for every single activity that brings you joy? If so, your need pantry would be stocked with thousands of jars. There would have to be one for dancing, one for visiting museums, one for paragliding, one for sampling cupcakes, and so on. That's a lot of jars to keep track of!

Fortunately, this is not the case. Your collection of need jars fits neatly onto a single shelf, because it represents needs that are more general than the activities that fulfill them. For example, dancing and paragliding can both satisfy the *need for physical activation:* the need to energize the body through movement or physical activity. In the same vein, visiting museums and sampling cupcakes can both fulfill the *need for sensory experience:* the need to engage the senses with rich or pleasurable stimuli. And these needs can be further grouped. Both physical excitement and sensory experience be clustered under the broader *need for stimulation*: the need to seek out new and extraordinary experiences (see diagram 1.4).

Clustering cannot go on indefinitely. If you clustered all human needs into a single "superneed"—a *need for good things,* for example—you would lose all nuance and usefulness. Therefore, we stop clustering at the level where needs are not tied to any particular context or activity, but which still captures the essential variety of things that people need in life. We have dubbed the needs at this level *the fundamental human needs.*

All specific needs can ultimately be clustered into the fundamental needs. There are two important implications here. First, the set of fundamental needs is *finite.* Unlike the limitless number of specific needs that people have—the need for a chocolate sundae or the need to have a good discussion with Marie—it is possible to list, discuss, and evaluate all the fundamental needs. This is especially helpful in the design process, as it allows the designer to understand all the things a user might want in a situation and, therefore, how to improve that

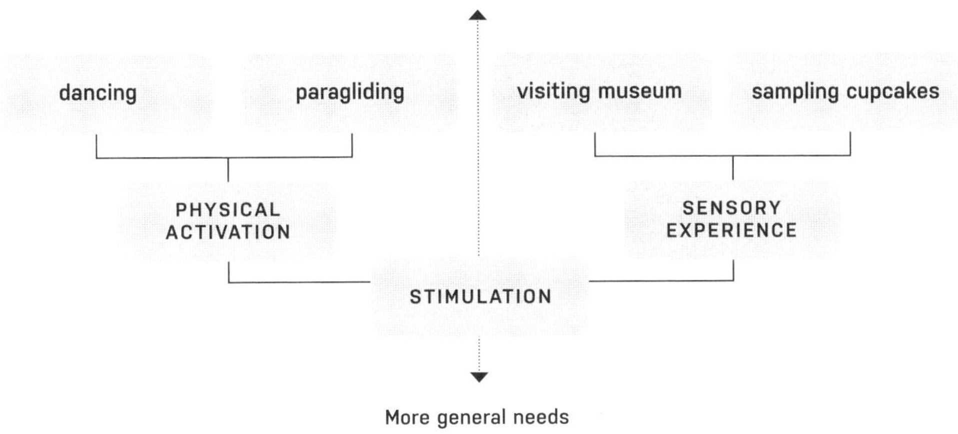

1.4 An example of need clustering

situation. Second, these fundamental needs are *universal*. Regardless of culture, age, or lifestyle, every human ultimately wants the same things. This doesn't mean that everyone fulfills their fundamental needs in the same way, of course. One person may satisfy their need for stimulation by jumping out of an airplane, while another might get that stimulation by solving the Sunday crossword. The universality lies in the fact that every person needs *some* kind of stimulation.

What, then, are these things that every person requires and desires? While there may not be a consensus among psychologists, there is considerable overlap in what are considered the most common human needs. After studying the literature and applying different sets of universal needs in several research projects, we have compiled a list of thirteen fundamental needs that hits the sweet spot between comprehensiveness, detail, and applicability for design. Thirteen jars every person needs to attend to. At the end of this chapter, we discuss the theoretical underpinnings of our overview of needs. But for now, let us explore these universal needs through a thought experiment.

The Island of Needs

You are part of a small group of people who get shipwrecked on a desert island. After the initial shock has worn off, the new islanders unanimously point to you as their leader. In return for this "privilege", you are responsible for organizing all the resources and activities on the island, and ensuring every person's needs are fulfilled. As you look into the throng of hopeful faces and receive some questioning looks, you wonder, "Which essential things do I have to provide to turn this bunch of washed-up survivors into a happy and thriving community?"

1. Security – First you must ensure your islanders are safe from harm. When a potential food source is discovered, you must determine that it isn't poisonous. Anyone who climbs a tree or a cliff has to be extremely careful, as a broken limb or nasty cut can mean a death sentence now. More than just *being* safe, people also need to *feel* safe. To achieve this, you keep fires burning through the night as a mental safeguard against the sinister shadows and strange sounds coming from the jungle.

In the "real" world, humans need to protect themselves from a lot more than just physical threats. They want financial security – a dependable job, a predictable cost of living, and a thriving economy. They want to live in a safe neighborhood and in a country that is free from political unrest. Those who enjoy these securities tend to take them for granted; take any of them away, however, and they will inevitably experience worry, sleepless nights, or worse.

2. Stimulation – The need for Security prompts you to become a very protective leader, so you decide that everyone should stay in the camp unless doing otherwise is strictly necessary; food choices should be restricted to the handful of items that are undoubtedly safe; and swimming, running, and climbing are prohibited. Almost immediately, your citizens feel smothered and bored. They want to explore the island, experiment with new food combinations, and compete to see who can climb the highest tree. In short, they need stimulation, variety, and fun.

In our world, there are entire industries devoted to quenching our never-ending thirst for stimulation: films, books, restaurants, holiday resorts, and amusement parks are different formats that address this common, basic need. But stimulation doesn't need to be served on a platter—it can just as easily be found in jobs, hobbies, and personal relationships.

3. Fitness – Every person has a body that needs to be fed, exercised, and rested. This means your islanders need food and water for nutrition, shelter against the scorching sun and tropical storms, and a daily regime of physical activity to keep fit. After physical effort, people need rest and recovery, so you have the group make beds and chairs.

Physical well-being has become one of humanity's most vigorously pursued goals. People follow healthy diets, join gyms, hire personal trainers, and make multi-day visits to retreat centers, all to achieve and maintain their fitness. As much as this has to do with being and looking healthy, it also has to do with *feeling* healthy—healthy enough to tackle the challenges that life presents and the goals we set for ourselves.

4. Competence – Much labor is required to survive on a desert island, and because you want everyone to do their fair share, your islanders need to be put to work! But there is another reason to give every person something to do. In the Middle Ages, some European poets and painters portrayed a utopian land of plenty in which roasted partridges flew straight into people's mouths, the skies rained fine wine, and no one ever had to work. To the toiling peasants at the time, this may indeed have sounded like a perfect world. However, as most people nowadays recognize, the pleasure of doing nothing will eventually run out at the end of a long, lazy holiday.
People naturally want to test their skills, exercise their abilities, master challenges, and accomplish things.

In modern society, people can experience competence when they perform a function, such as doing their job or maintaining their space. They can also satisfy this need in their free time by playing games, engaging in sports, and pursuing their hobbies.

5. Autonomy – Although you are the undisputed leader of the island, you should not assume you have the license to dictate every action and decision your followers make. Throughout childhood, every person develops the need to make their own decisions and find their own way of doing things. This means your islanders will be significantly happier if they can choose their tasks and how they carry them out. Autonomy is ultimately also about identity—people want the freedom to be themselves and

express their personalities. In daily life, people express who they are through the activities they undertake in their free time, the people they spend time with, the clothes they wear, and the products they surround themselves with.

6. Relatedness – You want to maximize the chances that a passing ship will detect your presence on the island, so you task one person with going up to the highest peak to keep a signaling fire burning. Because the climb is long and arduous, this person's stores of fresh food and water can only be replenished once a week. Pretty soon, that solitary islander will start craving human contact.

In all walks of life, people require meaningful and mutually beneficial relationships to thrive. These can be found in romantic relationships, familial bonds, friendships, and relationships with close coworkers and neighbors. Relatedness starts with the urge to share thoughts and experiences with others. People also fulfill this need by caring for others and feeling that they are cared for in return. Lastly, people want to be consoled during hardship and share their happiness when times are good.

7. Community – In addition to relationships with individual people, each islander also wants to be in good standing with the group at large. You must make sure that every person feels included in the community. As social beings, humans rely on group support for much of their happiness. This need to belong is strong enough for people to willingly change their behaviors, beliefs, and even logic to conform with the group. A well-known experiment from the 1950s saw participants promptly give wrong answers to simple questions if others in the group—who were secretly in cahoots with the researchers—did so.[4] The need for Community is also satisfied by much larger, more abstract groups. People can feel a sense of belonging to a city, a sports club, a nation, and a cultural heritage. They

4. In Solomon Asch's conformity experiments, participants were shown a card with a single vertical line, followed by another card with three lines of varying lengths. They were asked to identify which of the three lines matched the length of the original line—a straightforward visual comparison task where the correct answer was easy to identify. When confederates (individuals secretly working with the experimenter) unanimously gave incorrect answers before the real participant's turn, many of the real participants conformed by providing the same wrong answer (Asch, 1951).

express group membership through clothing, symbols, customs, rituals, and celebrations.

8. Recognition – As time goes by, the islanders become specialized in various fields. Some fish or hunt, others cook, build, or clean. Although everyone works hard, some people attract more praise and attention than others. You notice how these distinctions gradually create an informal social hierarchy, with certain roles gaining higher status in the community. To keep everyone happy, you have to make sure that those with less popular or visible contributions also feel appreciated and are able to maintain their standing in the group.

Every person wants to be liked, respected, and acknowledged for what they do and who they are. This applies just as much to the first grader returning home with their school report as it does to the veteran scientist hoping for a Nobel Prize. In modern society, recognition is often acquired after receiving some status symbol—be it a job promotion, academic degree, or public praise. Yet despite these outward markers, the core need remains deeply personal. Although some people go to great lengths to become famous, others are more than content if they are acknowledged by the few people closest to them.

9. Morality – One of the islanders cannot adjust to life on the island and becomes depressed. Unable to work, he depends on the efforts of others to fulfill his needs. Some group members argue that because he doesn't contribute, he isn't entitled to receive an equal share of the limited supplies. Other people strongly oppose this position and argue that he deserves just as much food, and additional care, because of his condition.

Although people differ in their moral judgments—what constitutes a fair distribution of resources, for example—they universally want to see their morality reflected in their environment. This is why people can get upset about events that have nothing to do with them, like seeing a dog mistreated in the street or reading about a fraudulent banker who received an exorbitant bonus. People also want to see their moral values reflected in their own actions—they become unhappy if they are unable to keep a promise or cannot fulfill their responsibilities as a parent or spouse.

10. Impact – Over time, you see your island society develop. Systems have been set up that provide a continuous supply of food and water. People have cooperated to build homes for each other. Every member contributes in their own way to the daily needs of the community. When the islanders think back to their first day on the island, they are proud to see how far they have progressed.

People want to see that they influence and contribute to the world around them. This is perhaps most apparent in tangible legacies—people derive great pleasure from building things or putting structures and artworks "out there" into the world. But the need for Impact can be equally fulfilled by intangible things: scientific achievements, political movements, or even a great new cheesecake recipe. Impact can also be felt through smaller things, such as persuading a colleague to adopt your project idea or teaching a child to tie their shoelaces.

11. Ease – As the island society becomes more sophisticated, the hassles and frustrations of survival that plagued your early days have largely been addressed. The islanders are more efficient at their tasks and no longer have to work all day. They can spend their spare time relaxing and engaging in leisure activities. People need to balance challenge and stimulation with tranquility and comfort.

One of the hallmarks of modern society is the enormous amount of convenience it has produced: nearby supermarkets provide a one-stop-shop for all our daily needs, navigation systems take the complexity and stress out of reaching a new destination, and easy-listening music and mood lighting help us relax after a long workday. Periodically, people even pay good money to make their lives as easygoing as possible by taking all-inclusive vacations.

12. Beauty – As the years pass, you notice your islanders spending more time on seemingly non-essential activities. They arrange shells in patterns around shelters and transplant flowers from around the island into the community's main square. Eventually, they build a bench at the western edge of the island, positioned for the most stunning sunset view. Each evening, islanders gather there, finding a contentment that practical provisions alone cannot provide.

In our world, the need for Beauty is equally fundamental but infinitely more varied. People decorate homes, visit museums, and travel to witness natural wonders. While what humans find beautiful varies significantly across cultures—from Japanese minimalism to ornate Middle Eastern arabesques—our need to experience beauty is universal. Anthropologists have yet to discover a culture that does not create objects that go beyond functionality to please the eye. People can feel discomfort when beauty is absent from their surroundings, leading them to personalize sterile spaces or seek natural beauty during breaks—illustrating that people don't just appreciate beauty; they need it in their lives.

13. Purpose – Let's assume that you have successfully fulfilled all the needs discussed so far. As a result, your island community is healthy, close-knit, and productive. Is that all there is? Not coincidentally, this is precisely the question that pops into the heads of people who become aware of the final fundamental need: Purpose. Even though their lives are relatively good, after a while, the islanders may start to ask, "What are we doing here? How much longer will we be on this island?"

People want to feel that there is a purpose to their lives and that their actions have meaning. How and where people find meaning largely depends on their beliefs and preferences. Some people find it in their job, their family, or their friendships. Others find it in religion, politics, or charity work. Regardless of the source, people universally want to see purpose in what they do and experience. For the mental well-being of your islander it may be wise to start building a raft.

How People Juggle Needs

Like the islanders, every single one of us is engaged in a daily balancing act to fulfill the thirteen fundamental needs. To flourish and be happy, a human being has to make sure that none of their jars go empty. People need their lives to be stimulating, secure, purposeful, and so on. Specialization won't help you in this process—you cannot overfill a few jars and hope that will make up for some of the empty ones.[5] Being accomplished at work doesn't compensate for an absence of warm relationships, and being extremely healthy does not substitute for a lack of purpose in life. But with only so many hours in a day, people constantly have to prioritize which needs to focus on.

To further complicate things, filling one jar sometimes prevents the filling of another. Consider the need for Community versus the need for Autonomy. You are likely a member of a several social groups—a family, a company, a religion, a sports club. The need for Community inclines you to conform to the norms and practices of these groups. At the same time, your need for Autonomy urges you to act in ways that set you apart from the group and make you an authentic individual.[6] These needs are not always in conflict, but there are times when you have to trade one off against another.

Fortunately, things are not quite as daunting as they seem. People can usually choose how they satisfy each fundamental need. If one option becomes unavailable, they can look for another. For example, if starting a family prevents a passionate paraglider from pursuing her hobby every weekend, she could look for an equally stimulating activity closer to home, like organizing murder mystery weekends or learning how to juggle.

People also don't have to do thirteen separate things to satisfy each need individually. Most activities will fulfill more than one fundamental need. Imagine that every day before work, you buy a pastry at a small bakery down the street. You thoroughly enjoy this daily pursuit, so you must be satisfying some fundamental needs in the process. Obviously, the pastry keeps you from starting the day hungry. But that could not possibly be the whole story; otherwise, a dry cracker at home would elicit the same amount of joy. So, which other needs might you be fulfilling during your morning ritual? You like the familiar routine of starting each day the same way (Security), you enjoy doing things at your own pace and leisure (Autonomy), the bakery always has a variety of delicious pastries to choose from (Stimulation), you might have a nice chat with the shop owner (Relatedness) who knows you and appreciates your patronage (Recognition), the

5. This point was convincingly presented in a paper with a telling title: "It's not just the amount that counts: Balanced need satisfaction also affects well-being" (Sheldon & Niemiec, 2006).

6. See Hornsey and Jetten (2004) for an overview of how people balance their need for Community and Autonomy.

bakery is in the neighborhood (Ease) where you feel at home (Community), and you like to support the local bakery instead of shopping at the supermarket (Morality). Before you've even made it to work, you've added to the jars of eight fundamental needs with a single activity.

One important note is to avoid automatically associating specific activities with certain needs. For instance, it can be tempting to link the need for Competence directly with professional activity. But people without a vocation are not destined to feel incompetent. Volunteering at a community center, learning how to change a bike tire, or getting better at playing darts in the local pub are all ways to fulfill the need for Competence outside paid work.

For the same reason, merely knowing which activity a person enjoys isn't enough to tell which needs it is fulfilling. Take cooking, for example. Of three people who enjoy it, one might relish the precision of neatly laying out ingredients and following a recipe to the letter (Competence), another might enjoy the freedom of experimentation with personal recipes (Autonomy), and a third might love cooking together with others while catching up on the day (Relatedness). Before figuring out how to link a person's needs to their activities, you must get to know more about that person.

Fundamental Needs in Detail

Please take a moment to read and reflect on the overview of the thirteen needs provided in *Tools & Techniques* (pages 231-233). A simple yet effective way to explore them is to think of an activity you enjoy and look for the need or needs that activity fulfills for you. You can try this for a few of your favorite activities. Try not to stop at picking the most obvious need met by the activity. Instead, dig a bit deeper to reveal the variety and multitude of reasons you enjoy it.

The overview also introduces a new concept: *sub-needs*. Sub-needs are more specific expressions of each fundamental need. Exploring the sub-needs can help you better understand the fundamental need they fall under. In some cases, sub-needs are components of the overall need. Physical comfort, physical activity, and rest are all necessary parts of meeting the need for Fitness, for example. In other cases, sub-needs are possible manifestations of a fundamental need. For instance, expressing your views is a common way of fulfilling the need for Autonomy. Of course, not everyone engages in self-expression, and alternative ways to fulfill the same need do exist. Therefore, sub-needs are not necessarily universal, although they are still high-level and widely recognized. Reflecting on sub-needs and generating new ones is an effective exercise to deepen your understanding of fundamental needs.

Bringing Needs to the Design Space

Now that we have completed our detour into the sources of joy, need jars, and a desert island, it is time to return to the world of products and services. Our freshly gained insights into the human psyche will help clarify what emotional design is and how it can be created.

Earlier, we discussed the fundamental link between emotions and needs: emotions are the level gauges that keep track of how fully our needs are being met at a given moment. A person has a positive emotion when a need is fulfilled and a negative emotion if a need goes unmet. In the domain of design, this principle forms the first law of emotional design.

THE FIRST LAW OF EMOTIONAL DESIGN

A product only evokes a positive emotion if it fulfills a genuine user need

Designing for emotion is essentially designing for needs. Before you can arrive at joy, you must first navigate the complex maze of human needs. Fortunately, the overview of fundamental needs provides us with an excellent map, helping us to evaluate existing products and design better ones.

When Products Meet Needs. . . and When They Don't

Products and services interact with people's fundamental needs in different ways. Some needs are clearly fulfilled, others are unaddressed, and some are even hindered. Mapping these interactions helps us understand in what ways a product serves its users and where opportunities for improvement may lie.

Fulfilled needs are those that a product helps satisfy. Some products are designed with a particular need as their central focus. In design discourse, this is often described as "the job the product is doing." This can be a single need, like a smoke detector (Security), a TV remote (Ease), or a water gun (Stimulation). In other cases, a product may fulfill multiple needs at once, like a fitness tracker that supports both Fitness and Competence. Beyond their primary function, products can fulfill additional needs in certain situations, or that fulfillment may come as a side-effect of use. For example, while a racing bike primarily supports Fitness (working the body and staying in shape), it may also support Competence (becoming a better rider), Stimulation (enjoying speed), and Morality (reducing one's carbon footprint).

Compromised needs are the needs that are blocked or hindered by the product, either unintentionally or as part of a trade-off. Naturally, designers don't set out to prevent users from meeting their needs, but it can happen. For example, designers might put a wide range of features in a banking app to fulfill the user's need for Autonomy, but inadvertently make the app so complex that it winds up compromising the need for Competence. This case could be resolved through a clearer, more intuitive interface. In other cases, the compromised need is the consequence of an unavoidable trade-off.[7] For example, high-heeled shoes are considered elegant in many fashion cultures, but they can come at the cost of convenience (compromising the need for Ease) and lead to foot problems (compromising the need for Fitness).

In addition to unfulfilled and compromised needs, there can also be those that go *unaddressed*: needs that a product doesn't engage with, positively or negatively. For instance, a smartwatch that tracks health data but offers no social features leaves the need for Relatedness untouched.

The Need Profile

A *need profile* is a simple framework that lists the fulfilled and compromised needs of a particular product or service by order of relative importance and degree of fulfillment (or unfulfillment) in a specific context. Each need comes with a short explanation of how the product interacts with it. This format can help you analyze the ways an existing design serves its users and discover opportunities for improvement, as well as spark new design directions. The insets on pages 29-30 show two examples of need profiles.

Both examples begin with a brief user scenario or user story. This step is essential for understanding which needs are likely to come to the fore. The context in which a product is used plays a key role in determining which fundamental needs become most relevant.

Next, the fulfilled and compromised needs are listed in order of relevance, each with a brief explanation. For example, Ease and Autonomy are Simon's most important fulfilled needs, while Stimulation, Security, and Competence play a secondary role. This hierarchy helps clarify which aspects of the user experience deserve the most attention when evaluating or improving the design.

Getting specific about both the product and user scenario helps to make need profiles more effective. For instance, rather than creating a need profile for "headphones," it is much more insightful to create one for "noise-canceling headphones used while commuting on public transport." This level of detail ensures that your analysis reflects the real-world context where these emotions and needs arise. If we had instead chosen to analyze "headphones used while running,"

7. We'll explore trade-offs between needs extensively in Chapter 5.

different needs would have emerged, or the same needs would have appeared in different positions of importance. Factors like physical activity, setting, and intent of use all influence which fundamental needs become most salient in that situation.

The two example profiles also illustrate the importance of defining the product scope—the boundary that determines what you consider part of the product and not part of the product. In the headphones case, we did not include the different types of content people could listen to through headphones. Otherwise, we might also have included needs like Competence (listening to training podcasts) or Recognition (listening to motivational programs). Deciding the scope is especially important when it comes to multipurpose products like smartphones, which are so versatile they could potentially fulfill any need. In such cases, it may be better to analyze the individual applications on the device.

The car-sharing service case highlights that need fulfillment is always relative to a benchmark situation, which is typically the user's situation before using the product or service. In this case, Elena compares the car-sharing service with her previous situation of owning a car. That comparison pushes her needs for Ease, Morality, and Community to the top of the analysis. However, had she previously not owned a car, other needs could have come to the fore, such as Autonomy (being more mobile) and Stimulation (the joy of driving), while Morality could even become a compromised need (sharing a car is less sustainable than not driving a car at all). You may also have noticed that Ease appears in both the "fulfilled" and "compromised" needs lists. That's no mistake. Products often touch on the same need in different ways; sometimes, a need is fulfilled it in one respect and frustrated in another.

Developing need profiles is an inspiring and insightful mental exercise, especially for teams. Creating them deepens conversations, challenges assumptions, and often brings new perspectives on a product's potential to light. Having a need profile is an excellent way to begin using fundamental needs as sources of inspiration. They lend structure to your intuitions and can surface design opportunities.

At the same time, it is important to realize that this type of analysis is mere speculation unless grounded in an understanding of real users. Remember: you cannot reliably infer which needs are fulfilled solely from the activity. You can make informed guesses, but you can never be entirely sure. To move from assumption to insight, you need to know more about the person behind the product. In the upcoming chapters, we'll introduce user research techniques that can help you uncover rich, real-world insights into user needs and emotions.

If you are looking to get started immediately, you can use the freely available Fundamental User Needs Scales (see *Tools & Techniques*, page 234). This pair of questionnaires measures the fulfillment and compromise of the thirteen fundamental needs in the context of design, which can support the creation of truly data-informed need profiles.

NEED PROFILE 1
Noise-Canceling Headphones

Scenario: Simon is a 34-year-old marketing consultant who commutes by train four days a week. These journeys are his mental buffer between work and home. This is his time to gather his thoughts, listen to music, or enjoy some quiet. The train is often noisy and crowded, so he uses noise-canceling headphones to create a sense of personal space.

Scope: This profile focuses on the headphones as a physical product, specifically the noise-cancellation feature and its role in shaping the user's environment during public commutes. Listening content, such as music or podcasts, is excluded to keep the focus on the core functionality.

Fulfilled Needs

Ease – By silencing the background noise of the train, the headphones help Simon feel more at ease during his commute. They reduce the mental load of filtering out distractions, creating a more peaceful experience.

Autonomy – The headphones allow him to shape his own space in noisy settings. He decides what he hears—and what he doesn't.

Stimulation – The immersive sound experience makes music and ambient sounds more vivid and enjoyable, adding a layer of richness to a routine part of the day.

Security – The headphones offer a psychological buffer from the outside world, especially in crowded or overstimulating environments.

Competence – The quiet environment allows Simon to gather his thoughts and mentally prepare for the workday ahead, helping him feel more in control and ready to perform.

Compromised Needs

Relatedness – Wearing the headphones can make Simon less approachable, potentially missing out on spontaneous chats or friendly gestures from fellow commuters.

Morality – In shared public spaces, the use of noise-canceling headphones may be perceived as antisocial or self-absorbed, creating a minor conflict with his desire to be considerate of others.

NEED PROFILE 2
Car Sharing Service

Scenario: Elena is a 29-year-old freelance designer. Until recently, she owned a small car for weekend trips, client visits, and grocery runs. The car sat unused most days yet still required maintenance, insurance, and a parking permit. Six months ago, she sold it and switched to a car-sharing service, which allows her to book nearby vehicles through the app whenever she needs one. This conscious lifestyle shift was driven by her desires for convenience and a more sustainable lifestyle.

Scope: This profile focuses on the core service: short-term, app-based access to shared cars. It includes booking, maintenance coverage, and the ability to drive when needed. It excludes ridesharing with strangers or long-term leasing.

Fulfilled Needs

Ease – Elena no longer worries about car maintenance, insurance, or finding a parking spot. Booking a car now takes less time and mental effort than managing ownership.

Morality – The shift to sharing rather than owning aligns with her values. She feels better knowing she's reducing her environmental impact.

Community – Knowing that the cars are shared within her neighborhood gives her a small sense of connection to others who've made similar lifestyle choices.

Security – The fact that the cars are maintained and insured by the company gives her peace of mind, especially when driving longer distances or at night.

Compromised Needs

Competence – The app can sometimes be finicky, and she occasionally feels uncertain about how to handle issues like reporting damage or refueling. With her own car, she had a routine.

Ease – Although the service alleviates many burdens associated with ownership, it introduces new ones: cars are not always available nearby, and last-minute bookings can be stressful. Sometimes, she misses the simplicity of just grabbing her keys and leaving.

DESIGN OPPORTUNITIES: FILLING THE JARS

The overview of fundamental needs is a powerful source of design inspiration, even when you have zero user data, because it draws from something profound: the pool of universal needs that underpin human well-being. The following design opportunities illustrate how to use fundamental needs to explore, stretch, and enrich your design ideas right away without prior user research.

Design Opportunity 1. Needs as Design Seeds: The first opportunity is to use this collection of fundamental needs as a creative tool. The approach is simple: when ideating concepts, take the list of needs and ask, "What would the design look like if it tried to fulfill the need for [X]?" Here, X can be any of the thirteen fundamental needs, no matter how unlikely the match might seem. What would a suitcase look like that fulfills the need for Community? A hotel service that satisfies the need for Impact? A shopping app for Morality? The question may be straightforward, but the answers might take you in unexpected directions. Products don't have to be limited by the needs they were originally designed to address. Perhaps an alarm clock could foster Relatedness by connecting people with loved ones, or a treadmill could support Purpose if each run contributes to a social cause. When you've run out of ideas for one need, simply move on to the next. The process can be repeated for all thirteen needs, each one offering a fresh spark of inspiration.

The value of this opportunity lies in stretching the frame: using needs as starting points for creative inquiry. To illustrate, we present thirteen chair designs (see inset on pages 33-35), each fulfilling one of the fundamental needs. They show how even the simplest product can, in principle, address every fundamental need.

Design Opportunity 2. Going Deep with a Single Need: The second design opportunity is, in a way, the opposite of the first. Instead of jumping from need to need to spark creativity, you choose one and sink your teeth into it. You explore its different forms, meanings, manifestations, and expressions. Whereas the first opportunity focuses on creative divergence, this one emphasizes conceptual depth.

Each fundamental need can take numerous forms. Earlier in the chapter, we introduced the concept of sub-needs, which are more specific expressions of each fundamental need. Autonomy, for instance, can be about having freedom of choice but also about expressing your identity or resisting control. Morality can be about doing good but also about living in line with your values or seeing those values reflected in the world around you (see *Tools & Techniques*, pages 231-233). These sub-needs are a great starting point for further exploration. Looking more

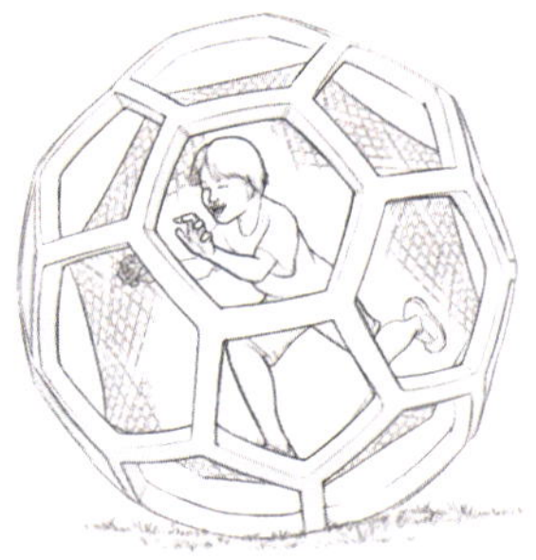

1.5 Goedzak by Simon Akkaya / 1.6 Link by Gina van der Werf

closely often reveals nuances, and those nuances can guide design in unexpected directions.

This kind of inquiry often begins with an observation. You might notice a situation where a particular need is under pressure or entirely unsatisfied. Or you might simply be drawn to a fundamental need as a source of inspiration.

Two of our students followed this approach to complete their graduation projects—each in their way. The first project is *Goedzak*.[8] (see image 1.5). Simon began with a fascination for Morality. He explored how design can encourage altruistic behavior, and ended up inventing a humble garbage bag. When you have items you no longer need but that still work, the *Goedzak* offers a dignified way to pass them along. You simply place them in the bag and leave it on the street. The transparent front reveals the contents; the yellow stripe signals intention. People walking by can take what they like, and whatever remains is collected by charity shops. Rain or shine, the bag keeps everything clean and dry. Using *Goedzak* seems like a small act, but it satisfies the need to do good (Morality), to see that good done (Impact), and to avoid unnecessary hassle (Ease).

The second project is *Link* (see image 1.6). Gina set out to design an exercise device for children who are blind or have low vision. She noticed that all the existing solutions, such as stationary bikes, focused on safety and exercise but ignored the very thing that makes play feel like play: Stimulation. She explored the joy of physical movement and designed *Link* to bring that experience back. It's a person-sized sphere that children can move by walking or running inside of it—freely, safely, and without needing to be led. The enclosed form protects them from collisions, while the movement offers a joyful sense of speed and control. *Link* supports the need for physical exercise (Fitness) and safety (Security). More importantly, it restores the spark of Stimulation and the freedom of Autonomy—two needs often missing from existing solutions.

8. The name "Goedzak" cleverly plays on a double meaning in Dutch. Literally, it translates to "good bag." But "goedzak" is also a colloquial word for a kind-hearted and selfless person.

A CHAIR FOR EVERY NEED

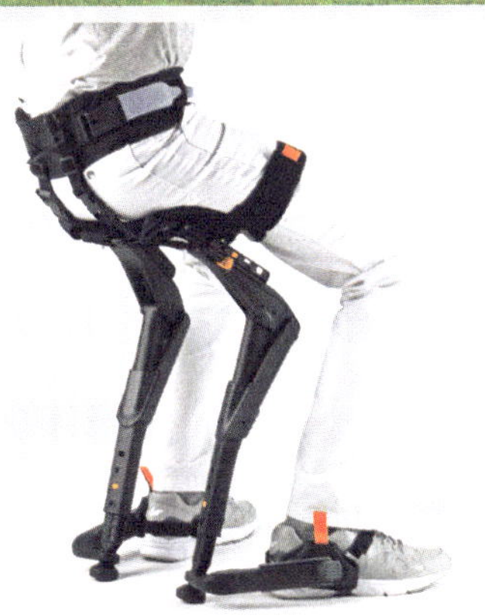

Body Chair (Autonomy)
A six-meter-long, rice-filled cushion that adapts to your body. Shape it however you want to sit—the chair follows your preferred posture, giving you complete control over your seating experience. By Kirsi Enkovaara.

Harp Chair (Beauty)
This sculptural object turns sitting into an artistic experience. The design was inspired by the curved bow of a Viking ship. Its woven rope seating creates striking optical patterns, blurring the line between furniture and art. By Jørgen Høvelskov.

Folding chair (Community)
The humble folding chair transforms any space into a meeting place. Its uniform design creates equality among users, while the shared ritual of setting up chairs builds instant group bonds.

Chairless Chair (Competence)
A wearable support system for professionals who need to move and sit frequently. Healthcare workers, engineers, and lab technicians can rest anywhere while staying mobile and efficient. By Carl Stahl GmbH.

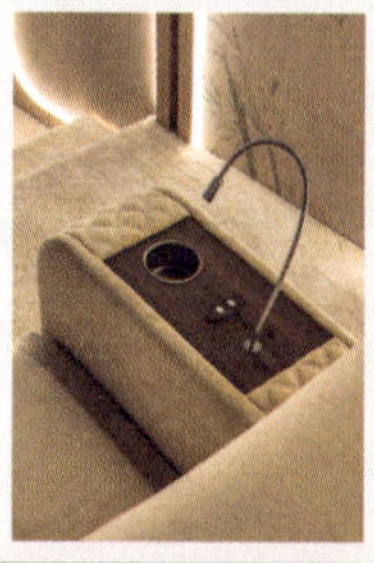

Luxor Tech (Ease)
This is the ultimate comfort chair, with near-horizontal reclining, a built-in phone charger, cooled cup holder, and massage function. Designed to make you never want to get up. By Vismara.

Kneeling Chair (Fitness)
The kneeling chair follows your body's natural movements. Its tilted seat reduces lower back pressure and relieves neck and shoulder tension through better posture. Original design by Peter Opsvik.

Terra! (Impact)
An outdoor chair that needs time to grow. You cover the cardboard frame with soil and grass seeds, then wait as nature develops your creation. The result is both a living mark on the landscape and a comfortable garden chair. By Studio Nucleo.

Chubby Chair (Morality)
3D printed from recycled fridge plastic, this chair shows its origins through visible imperfections and varied colors. Instead of hiding recycled materials behind perfect finishes, it celebrates sustainability openly and proudly. By Dirk van der Kooij.

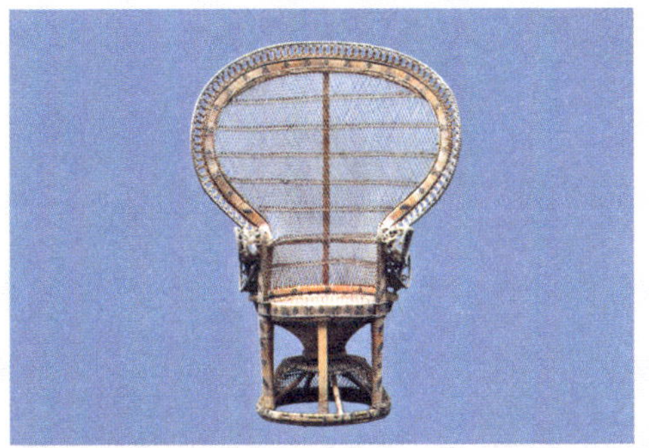

Stitch and Wooly (Purpose)
This chair arrives incomplete, requiring you to finish it through stitching and embroidery. The time-intensive process and personalized result create deep satisfaction and ownership. By Susanne Westphal.

The Peacock Chair (Recognition)
Originating in the Philippines and popularized globally in the 1960s–70s, this throne-like chair frames you with its towering fan-shaped back. Adopted by celebrities and activists, it commands attention and signals status.

The Courting Chair (Relatedness)
This Victorian-era dual-seat design positions you for intimate conversation with another person. The S-shape creates perfect distance—close enough for you to whisper secrets, separate enough to preserve propriety.

Hush Pod (Security)
A felt cocoon that wraps you in soft enclosure, temporarily shielding you from the outside world. You can open or close the cocoon to match your need for psychological safety. By Freyja Sewell.

KU DIR KA Rocking Chair (Stimulation)
This chair makes sitting an engaging balancing act. Because only four of the ten chair legs touch the ground simultaneously, you can change orientation with subtle weight shifts. By Paulius Vitkauskas.

THEORETICAL DEEP DIVE

Modeling human needs

The following four questions allow for a deeper dive into the theoretical foundations of human needs by reviewing their definitions and examining the assumptions that they have been built upon.

What exactly is a need?

We bet that you were able to comprehend this chapter without a proper definition of the word "need." While most of us have an intuitive grasp of what constitutes a need (because we are constantly affected by their presence), if we want to explain further the assumptions underlying our overview of fundamental needs, the first step is to establish exactly what we are talking about. Psychologists and other researchers have defined needs in several ways, typically by framing it in terms of their area of study.[1] A popular definition in biological and evolutionary frameworks is that need is "a drive for things that people require to survive." This definition works well to explain basic things, such as food and security, but fails to explain why people seek out more complex things, such as acknowledgment from others. You could ultimately explain such needs by lumping them in with the concept of "survival," but you would have to make so many assumptions and mental leaps that you would lose the simplicity that you started with. A second definition among psychologists is that needs are "the goals people set for themselves." This meaning implies that people know their needs and can list everything they desire. The problem with this definition is that many needs are not deliberately pursued or even entirely conscious. Take friendship: although everyone has a need for Relatedness, most friendships don't start by you looking at another person and deciding to become friends. Instead, friendships emerge organically from meeting many different people and forming bonds with those we gravitate to or click with.[2] A third definition, also from psychology, is that needs are "the things that people require to thrive and be happy." This association was actually proposed by Aristotle in the 4th century BCE, and has only recently been revived through *positive psychology*, which studies the determinants of human well-being.[3] In this view, needs fulfillment adds up to increasing happiness—the more needs you fulfill, the happier you become.[4] We subscribe to the last definition because we believe it is the best and simplest explanation, and because it fits best with our overall aim to create products and services that make people feel good and bring out the best in them.

Why are there thirteen fundamental needs? Does that number have any significance?

It doesn't. Since the early 1900s, psychologists of all types have been assembling sets of basic needs—and no two sets are equal. The psychologist William McDougall proposed twelve human instincts in 1908,[5] while thirty years later, his colleague Henry Murray arrived at no less than twenty needs.[6] Recent need models are more economical, such as Abraham Maslow's hierarchy of needs[7] (five), Cognitive-Experiential Self-Theory[8] (four), or Self-Determination Theory[9] (three). How can there be such a discrepancy? We will let renowned need theorist, Abraham Maslow, answer this.

"The number of drives one chooses to list depends entirely on the degree of specificity with which one chooses to analyze them. The true picture is not one of a great many sticks lying side by side, but rather of a nest of boxes in which 1 box contains 3 others, and in which each of these 3 contains 10 others, and in which each of these 10 contains 50 others, and so on."[10]

In other words, the number of needs you regard as basic depends on how specific you consider them. Recent theorists favor a short list because they adhere to the scientific principle of parsimony (also known as Occam's Razor): explain as much as possible with as little as possible. In this case, that translates to "explain as much of human behavior and emotion with as few needs as possible." An additional advantage of short lists is that they are more easily tested and validated.

Some exceptions to the rule of simplicity are need models from applied fields like organizational psychology. One example is Martin Ford and C.W. Nichols' Taxonomy of Fundamental Human Goals, which contains twenty-four needs.[11]

The purpose of our set of thirteen needs isn't to propose a scientific agenda or prove the "basicness" of certain needs—it is to inform and inspire designers to find new avenues of product relevance. This purpose requires a list of needs that is short enough to maintain comprehensiveness but long enough to preserve detail and richness.

Are all the fundamental needs equal? Is there no hierarchy?

Several scientific theories propose a hierarchy of needs. Of these, the most famous is probably Maslow's hierarchy of needs. Maslow states that there are five fundamental needs, each occupying a single level on a vertical hierarchy (which

1.7 Maslow's hierarchy of needs

later proponents represented as a pyramid). In this ranking, people must satisfy lower needs (found at the bottom of the vertical scale), such as the needs for food and safety, before addressing higher needs, such as morality and creativity. At the same time, Maslow found that fulfilling higher needs produces "more profound happiness, serenity, and richness of the inner life."[12] A different type of hierarchy is represented in root need models, which propose that there is a single need from which all other fundamental needs are derived. Examples of root needs are self-preservation (in terror management theory[13]), belonging (in core social motives theory[14]), and self-interested gain (in behavioral economics[15]). A third type of model—dynamic need models—proposes a system of needs that compete—pursuing one need can make it harder to fulfill another need. For example, cognitive-experiential self-theory[16] posits four needs that require constant balancing. Lastly, there are models that propose that there is no hierarchy among fundamental needs. An example is self-determination theory,[17] which postulates three needs that must be fulfilled independently.

In line with the last type of model, to us, the thirteen needs are independent and equally prominent. Why have we chosen not to impose a hierarchy? Although it seems plausible that people naturally prioritize certain needs over others, the assumption becomes questionable when faced with its many exceptions. For instance, the idea that people don't start fulfilling their "higher" needs (with reference to Maslow's hierarchy) until they have satisfied "lower" ones is inaccurate. People are perfectly capable of seeking opportunities for creativity and morality without being healthy or having a good social life (both of which rank somewhere in the middle of Maslow's scale). Sometimes, people even sacrifice the gratification of lower needs in the pursuit of higher ones—people deprive themselves of food to look more attractive or engage in extreme sports that jeopardize their safety for the sake of stimulation, for example.

We also don't subscribe to the idea that fundamental needs inherently constrain each other, as proposed by dynamic need models. Fundamental needs don't always compete for fulfillment—they can coexist or even reinforce each other. However, when considering specific, contextualized needs, we fully agree that needs often compete and clash. We discuss this in detail in Chapter 5.

Why are these needs fundamental?

The scientific debate about which needs are fundamental to human life has not yet been resolved—if it ever can be. Nevertheless, there is considerable and increasing consensus about the needs that should be included. Our set of thirteen fundamental needs was based on six need typologies: Deci and Ryan's self-determination theory,[17] Sheldon and colleagues' factors of well-being,[18] Ryff's determinants of psychological well-being,[19] Ford and Nichols' taxonomy of fundamental human goals,[20] Schwartz's human values typology,[21] and Rokeach's human values typology.[22] One of our papers discusses need typologies and the origin of the thirteen fundamental needs in more detail.[23]

1. Pittman and Zeigler (2007).
2. In Chapter 3, we will argue that goals are a subset of needs.
3. Seligman and Csikszentmihalyi (2000).
4. Tay and Diener (2011).
5. McDougall (1908).
6. Murray (1938).
7. Maslow (1987).
8. Epstein (1992).
9. Deci and Ryan (2000).
10. Maslow (1987, p. 8).
11. Ford and Nichols (1987).
12. Maslow (1987, p. 57).
13. Pyszczynski, Greenberg, and Solomon (1997).
14. Fiske (2004).
15. Miller (1999).
16. Epstein (1992).
17. Deci and Ryan (2000).
18. Sheldon et al. (2001).
19. Ryff (1989).
20. Ford and Nichols (1987).
21. Schwartz (1994).
22. Rokeach (1973).
23. Desmet and Fokkinga (2020).

2

MICRO *Emotions*

As much as we enjoy working with design students, with their fresh perspectives and endless creativity, we equally value our collaborations with industry partners, who bring the excitement of real-world impact. Companies regularly approach us, drawn to our emotional design methodology. They are eager to discover how it might reveal opportunities overlooked by traditional market research. These collaborations usually focus on products that people naturally associate with emotions. Think hotels crafting memorable stays, pastries evoking childhood nostalgia, and cars that become extensions of personal identity.

Then came an unexpected call from a young research manager at a multinational corporation in an entirely different sector. His domain? The world of soaps and detergents—products that, until then, had never been part of our conversations about emotional design. Despite working in a highly traditional industry, he wanted to explore new approaches. He was encouraged by the sales increases emotional design had generated in other fields and wondered if it could achieve similar results for his category. During our first meeting, he showed us one of their premium laundry detergent tablets. By objective measures, it performed on par with its main competitor—same cleaning power, similar price point. Yet their competitor's product consistently outsold theirs. His team had already tried several formula adjustments and packaging refinements without success. Now, he was ready to explore uncharted territory. "Could the difference," he asked, "be explained by emotions?"

The challenge sparked our professional interest but also a touch of apprehension. On one hand, up until that point, our research had reliably shown that all products and services evoke emotions. On the other hand... *laundry detergent*? We expected that our usual method—asking consumers to use a product for some time and then measuring their emotional responses—would not yield meaningful insights, especially since we would be comparing emotional responses to products that don't really seem to differ that much. Traditional research approaches, such as interviews and focus groups, seemed equally ill-suited. After all, how long could we expect people to sit in a room and genuinely discuss their emotions about laundry detergents before the conversation became forced or artificial?

We opted for a different approach: this time, we would capture emotions *in the moment*. We visited twelve consumers at home and observed their entire journey with the product—from the moment they took it off the supermarket shelf until they tossed the empty container in the bin. We asked them to share every feeling they experienced while using the detergent, along with how strongly they felt it and what had triggered it. Then, we mostly stood back, noting their emotional journey without leading or prompting. Afterward, we sat down with the participants to delve into their journeys in greater detail. Some were amused by our extraordinary interest in what they considered a mundane household chore,

2.1 An emotional roller coaster

but none shied away from sharing their innermost laundry feelings.

Back at our office, the data we had collected covered an entire wall. The results took us aback: there was a blind spot in our thinking. Despite our theoretical understanding that all products evoke emotions, we underestimated how emotionally invested people are in this everyday household task. Laundry pods are far from emotionally neutral. These consumers had experienced an average of 28 emotional moments during the product journey, resulting in 340 events to dissect. The diversity was equally striking. We had anticipated seeing emotions commonly associated with consumer products, such as satisfaction and confusion. However, we faced a kaleidoscope of emotional responses—guilt, disgust, fascination, hope, and virtually every other emotion imaginable.

Our initial concern about turning up empty-handed had proven unfounded. But in a twist of irony, we now faced the opposite problem. There were simply too many emotions, and none of them stood out as singularly important or defining. We decided to narrow it down to the most prominent emotions—those that the users had felt most intensely. That restriction yielded a more manageable list of around thirty emotions. However, we soon realized that we had lost something essential. The new overview was fragmented and distorted; it no longer represented the nuanced consumer experiences we had witnessed in the field. The elimination process had retained certain emotions that were intense but insignificant while excluding others that, although mild, were vital to understanding the broader product experience.

The breakthrough came when we realized that we had been fundamentally misunderstanding emotions up until that point. We had been on a quest for grand emotional moments, assuming these to be the centerpiece of product experiences that drive consumer decisions. But that is not how emotions work. Instead, most of them stay under the radar of people's awareness, subtly influencing their thoughts and behaviors without them even realizing it. In this chapter, we show how we made sense of the laundry detergent data and advised our client. Before proceeding, we need to take a brief detour to explore the nature of emotions and how they surface in our day-to-day lives.

Beyond the Peaks: The Rich Terrain of Everyday Emotions

How many emotions does a person typically experience in a single day? Let's conduct a thought experiment: reflect on the emotions you felt yesterday—both the positive and the negative. What comes to mind? Perhaps you felt frustrated when you got stuck in traffic or amused by a friend's text message. You might recall around four to ten emotions. Perhaps your list is shorter or longer, but you get the idea: in a single day, people seem to experience a handful of emotions.

In reality, your list represents only a fraction of all the emotions you experienced yesterday. You actually experienced *hundreds of emotions*. That may be difficult to believe a day later, but if someone had kept track of every emotion as you experienced them, that is the number you would end up with. A 2015 study did just that: the researchers recruited more than 11000 participants and sent them prompts at random intervals to report how they were feeling in the moment.[1] The participants could select from eighteen emotions or report no emotion. The researchers found that people experience an emotion in 90% of their waking hours.

Your brain is constantly processing information about what is happening and how you are responding emotionally, often without you realizing it. For example, you may experience slight irritation when you cannot find your keys, a brief moment of satisfaction when you sip your morning coffee, or a pang of nostalgia triggered by a familiar scent. Most of these daily emotions are subtle and short-lived *micro emotions* that blend into the background of the conscious mind and fade soon after they are experienced.

Of course, you occasionally experience strong emotions—you graduate, your daughter speaks her first word, you drop your phone in the toilet. People usually think of such events when asked to recall a specific emotional moment. You might define these as *emotion archetypes*. Because these are the ones you remember best, you live under the illusion that they represent the majority of your emotional experiences. In reality, emotional archetypes are the exceptions, the rare and isolated peaks in a vast landscape of mostly mild experiences. You recall the peaks,

1. Trampe, Quoidbach, and Taquet (2015)

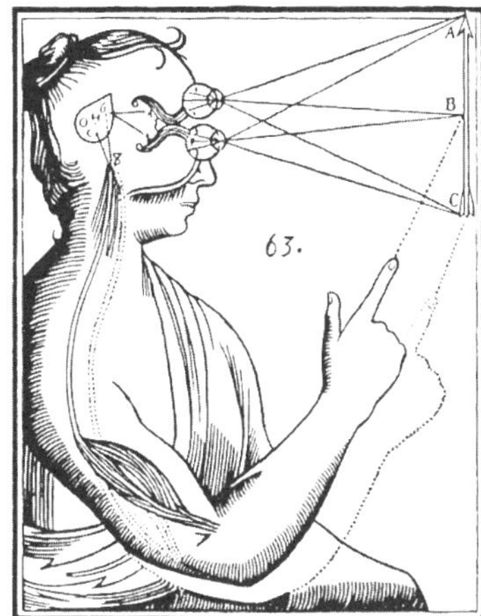

2.2 Descartes' mind-body dualism / 2.3 Mr. Spock: "I fail to see the logic in your actions"

but you typically forget the countless subtle hills that surround them.
Just how important are micro emotions? Why would they be worth capturing and analyzing if they fade from memory so quickly? Let's ask Mr. Spock.

From Vulcan to Human: Why Pure Logic Without Emotion Fails Us

For centuries, philosophers and scientists have debated the relationship between mind and body. The traditional view, known as mind-body dualism, posits that the rational mind operates independently of the emotional body—that reason and emotion are fundamentally distinct processes. This perspective shaped not only philosophical thought but also decades of popular culture. Consider the iconic Mr. Spock from *Star Trek*, whose ability to suppress all emotion supposedly made him the most rational being on the ship.

In the late 20th century, neuroscientist Antonio Damasio championed a radical alternative: the human emotional system plays an *essential role* in rational decision-making.[2] People depend on their emotions to guide their judgments about others, situations, and the best course of action at any given moment. While philosophers from Aristotle to Hume had long argued that emotions are crucial for good judgment, Damasio added compelling neuroscientific evidence through his studies of patients with brain injuries.[3]

2. See his bestselling book *Descartes' Error* (Damasio, 1994).

3. The earlier proponents of the insight that emotion and reason are interconnected include ancient Greek philosopher Aristotle, who argued in his Nicomachean Ethics that emotions, properly educated through virtue, are essential for practical wisdom and ethical decision-making; 17th-century philosopher Baruch Spinoza, who argued that active emotions accord well with reason; 18th-century philosopher David Hume, who declared that reason "is, and ought only to be the slave to the passions"; and 19th-century psychologist William James, whose work on emotion and bodily changes directly influenced Damasio's concept of emotions.

Damasio studied individuals with damage to the prefrontal cortex—the region of the brain responsible for both abstract thinking and emotional processing. He observed that although these individuals retained their intelligence and memory, they struggled immensely with making sound decisions. Why? Because they had lost the ability to process emotions. One patient was a previously successful finance professional who, despite maintaining his financial knowledge, could no longer make sound judgments about deals and money. Stripped of his emotional guidance system, this once prudent financier had turned into a reckless gambler.

Why do people need emotions to make good decisions? Because humans simply don't have the mental bandwidth to rely on reasoning alone. The capacity of people's conscious attention is astoundingly limited. One recent study found that just one-millionth of a percent of all the information the human brain receives actually reaches a person's awareness—about the equivalent of a single drop of water in 100 Olympic swimming pools.[4] This is where emotions come in: they act as beacons to direct your focus to what matters most at that moment.

Your emotional guidance system has a memory. Rather than evaluating every new situation from scratch, emotions draw upon a rich store of past experiences. Damasio's crucial insight was that these emotional memories are not stored in our conscious minds, but in our bodies. To describe this phenomenon, he introduced the concept of "somatic markers" (from the Greek *sōma,* meaning body). Somatic markers serve two crucial functions in decision-making. First, they collect and store lived emotional experiences as bodily sensations. Second, they retrieve and reawaken these emotions when the person faces similar situations again.

Let's look at how this unfolds. Imagine you regularly visit a local café for your morning coffee. Over time, minor annoyances begin to accumulate—perhaps your coffee is regularly delayed, your order gets mixed up, or the environment feels too noisy. These micro emotions add up and become embedded as somatic markers. You may not consciously recall each minor irritation, but the next time you consider going to that café, you feel a subtle reluctance. That hesitation is your somatic marker speaking: a bodily trace of previous emotional experiences.

This mechanism is more sophisticated than it might seem. Your brain is constantly looking for patterns in a dynamic sea of impressions. It's entirely possible that the common denominator isn't the café at all but rather the service of a specific barista or—you never know—your own morning grumpiness before that first coffee. When making decisions, your mind unconsciously

4. A recent study from the California Institute of Technology (Zheng & Meister, 2025) quantified the speed of human thought at approximately 10 bits per second, while people's sensory systems receive around one billion bits per second. These findings align with earlier studies that suggest that every person is exposed to thousands of stimuli every second, but only become aware of those that their brain deems important enough to enter consciousness (e.g., Dehaene et al., 2006; LeDoux, 2012).

2.4 Steam, pleasures, and the occasional frustration

weighs negative experiences against positive ones to create an overall sentiment that guides your choices.

Without somatic markers, people would have to consciously weigh every single option and consequence for even the smallest decisions. That includes not only major decisions, such as whether to relocate to another city, but also everyday decisions, such as what to have for breakfast or whether to take the bike or the car. That never-ending torrent of costs and benefits would overload our cognitive capacities and quickly lead to decision paralysis. Damasio illustrates this with a striking example. At the end of a consultation, he asked his client to choose between two dates for their next appointment. A decision that should have taken seconds turned into an ordeal. The patient spent nearly half an hour listing reasons for and against each option, considering previous engagements, proximity to other events, and even potential weather conditions. In the end, Damasio could take no more and decided for him.

Contrary to Vulcan philosophy, humans don't make better decisions by suppressing emotions. In fact, without emotion people cannot make decisions at all! Everyone needs a well-functioning emotional system that provides the right somatic markers at the right times. The truly logical approach, it turns out, is not to deny your emotions, but to embrace them.

In short, somatic markers perform two key functions. First, they accumulate emotional experiences as a rich collection of bodily sentiments towards everyday people, things, and situations. Second, when you encounter a new situation, these stored feelings spring up instantly. Somatic markers are responsible for the "gut feelings" that guide your decisions and behavior before you've even had time to think things through.

The Invisible Emotional Lives of Everyday Things

"Are you emotional about everyday products and services? Hands up if the answer is yes." When we pose this question during lectures for non-students, most hands stay down. That reaction is typical—most people don't think of themselves as being emotional about the things they use. They might name a few exceptions, as our students in the previous chapter did: a cherished heirloom watch that connects them to a loved one, a spa visit that brings deep relaxation, or a social media platform that delivers moments of both joy and frustration. But beyond these outliers, people tend to assume that everyday products and services play neutral roles in our lives.

The 340 emotional moments we found in the laundry detergent project tell a *very* different story. When you consider just how many products and services people interact with on a daily basis, it becomes clear that human lives are filled with a continuous stream of micro emotions. These emotions unfold from dawn to dusk; they are fleetingly subtle. While we rarely remember them, Damasio's work shows they are not lost. They accumulate in the body as somatic markers, shaping your preferences and driving your future choices. This insight is captured in the second law of emotional design.

THE SECOND LAW OF EMOTIONAL DESIGN

A product evokes a constant stream of micro emotions that drive user behavior

This law offers a clear direction for designers. By capturing micro emotions throughout the product journey—as we did with the laundry detergent—designers can detect emotional patterns that usually go unnoticed. This approach works well for products that typically stay under the radar– phone chargers, park benches, digital payment services, and, indeed, laundry detergents. But it's equally useful for products and services that evoke more overt emotional responses. Subtle emotional interactions can have a powerful influence on user preferences and behavior, making them essential considerations in the design process.

From Satisfaction Scores to Emotional Journeys

When the research manager asked us to measure the emotions evoked by his laundry detergent, he didn't quite know what to expect. But his question also didn't come out of the blue. His company had already conducted research to determine customer satisfaction for their product and that of their competitor. Most organizations use this kind of market research to improve their products or services. If you've recently stayed at a hotel or ordered a meal for delivery, chances are you received a short survey afterward, asking for your evaluation. These surveys typically use simple feedback questions. One common example is a satisfaction rating on a scale from one to seven, where one means "completely dissatisfied" and seven indicates "completely satisfied." Another popular metric is the Net Promoter Score (NPS), which asks users to rate how likely they are to recommend the service to a friend or colleague on a scale from zero to ten.[5]

There are several reasons these straightforward questions are so popular. For starters, they're quick and easy to answer, which is especially important given that consumers are rarely compensated for their feedback. They allow teams to track customer satisfaction over time or compare different products. Ultimately, if your primary concern is whether customers will buy your product again, it seems efficient to boil down all those micro emotions into a single score. After all, they either buy the thing again or they don't, right?

So why bother delving into the complex realm of people's micro emotions when a single metric seems to tell you all you need to know? We think it is essential for three reasons:

- ***Most products are "meh"*** – True, once in a while, some new product revolutionizes the market and gets showered with praise. Other times a product is so pointless or cumbersome it becomes the butt of public ridicule. By and large, however, new products and services land somewhere in between. On a seven-point scale, they hover between a four and a five. The differences get even smaller when comparing similar products such as phone plans, streaming services, or, in our case, laundry detergents. A product manager once bemoaned, "How am I supposed to make strategic decisions when our scores differ by only 0.02 points?" These kinds of metrics offer little guidance on what actually matters to your customers.

- ***A single score makes different products look the same*** – Imagine two dating apps that both score +48 on the NPS scale. That tidy number can hide what might be dramatically different experiences. One app might have a delightful interface, while the other might have a more active and relevant community. These call for entirely different strategies. One may have stronger future potential, while the other may better serve a niche segment. Yet the NPS score alone tells you nothing about these crucial differences.

5. Each respondent is classified according to the score they give. Scores from zero to six makes them a "detractor," from seven to eight a "passive," and from nine to ten a "promoter." The NPS is calculated by detracting the total percentage of detractors from the total percentage of promoters, resulting in a score from -100 to +100.

- ***Feelings, not numbers, drive decisions*** – Most importantly: metrics don't tell you *why* people feel the way they do. They offer no clues for potential improvements. How do you turn a three into a four or a five into a six? Should you add new features or refine existing ones? Is the issue related to the packaging, the user interface, or the customer service? Which needs are left unfulfilled? Without a view into the emotions behind the scores, it's impossible to answer these questions, reducing innovation to little more than guesswork.

Sometimes, organizations try to get around these limitations by adding a text box to their survey and inviting customers to explain their scores. People often leave those blank or write only a few words. And even when someone does provide a thoughtful answer, there's a deeper issue: they simply cannot recall their micro emotions after the fact. That's not a flaw in effort—it's just how memory works. As noted earlier, micro emotions unfold in the moment, often outside of conscious awareness. They register in the body as somatic markers, which are not available for recall afterward.

When people are asked to report how they felt during a prior experience, they don't have the ability to access a detailed log of emotions. Instead, they reconstruct a story that seems plausible, based on a handful of remembered moments and how they feel at the moment they are answering. This process is further skewed by psychological biases, such as recency bias (where more recent events carry more weight) and negativity bias (where unpleasant moments are easier to recall than pleasant ones). And because people are unaware of these biases, they often respond with complete confidence, despite the likelihood they are getting the story wrong. Nobody does this intentionally, of course. It's just the nature of human memory.

How to Catch an Emotion

The next question is: how can you, the designer, tap into that constant stream of micro emotions? The main challenge is that these emotions are inner states: real to the individual but invisible to others. Simply put, nobody can see into another person's heart. It's a bit like tuning into a radio signal—if you don't get the frequency just right, you miss the message. This led us to develop the *Micro-Emotion Scan*, an approach to capturing emotions as they unfold. It allows us to observe people in their natural environments and document their stream of micro emotions while interacting with products or services.

The method is straightforward but powerful. We accompany participants as they use a product and ask them to share their emotional responses in real time without filtering or analyzing them. The procedure unfolds over two phases.

2.5 PrEmo in action

In the first, we focus solely on capturing each emotion as it arises, noting its intensity and what triggered it. Only after they complete the entire product journey do we sit down with the participants to discuss their experiences in more detail. This separation preserves the natural flow of emotions, unclouded by interpretation or discussion.

A key element of the approach is making it easy for people to express what they are feeling without disrupting their experience. Subtle emotions often fade within seconds, and putting them into words can be surprisingly difficult. To address this, we developed *PrEmo*, a set of cartoon characters expressing 14 distinct emotions: seven positive (such as joy and pride) and seven negative (such as sadness and fear). Participants simply point to the character that best matches what they're feeling in the moment (see image 2.5). The *Tools & Techniques* contains a section that explains how you can use PrEmo in your own research (page 235).

In the theoretical deep dive at the end of the chapter, we will explore various techniques for measuring emotions and explain why self-report, when properly structured, offers the most complete and nuanced picture of emotional experiences. Compared to other methods, such as physiological sensors, brain imaging, or facial expression analysis, it provides more meaningful insights into how people actually feel when using products and services.

Emotions in the Laundry Room

Let's look at what this approach revealed in the laundry detergent study. After capturing and analyzing twelve respondents' emotional experiences with our client's laundry detergent—the "pod"—using the Micro-Emotion Scan, we repeated the process with another twelve respondents for their competitor's product—the "tablet" (see product descriptions below). This enabled us to make a direct comparison of the emotional journeys evoked by both products. The result is what we call an *Emotion Map*.

Each Emotion Map visually represents the customer journey, showcasing the collective emotional responses of all respondents, arranged along a timeline. This timeline is divided into usage stages, including storing the product, opening the package, and discarding the waste. Positive emotions appear in the upper half; negative emotions in the lower half. The distance from the baseline indicates intensity: the further away, the more strongly the emotion was felt.

Because we didn't direct participants or prompt specific reactions, each emotional journey was unique. Even so, we observed a remarkable level of consistency in the kinds of emotions people experienced. Pages 62-63 show the Emotion Maps for both products. Take a moment to explore them—they offer a visual snapshot of the emotional landscape we uncovered.[6]

Two Laundry Detergent Products

Both products are from premium brands and cater to the high end of the market.[7]

- ***Pod:** A detergent pod that consists of compartments with differently colored liquids. The pods come in a sturdy plastic pouch covered in glossy blue colors and silver foil. The information on the packaging emphasizes that the product offers technologically advanced washing results and scent release.*
- ***Tablet:** A white pressed-powder tablet with green detailing wrapped in thin transparent plastic. The tablets are packaged in a cardboard box that opens lengthwise to reveal the tablets neatly stacked in a grid. The packaging features several claims highlighting the product's environmental friendliness.*

Five Principles for Mapping Emotions

Rather than discussing the Emotion Maps step by step, here we highlight five principles that emerged from this case and the many other cases in which we have studied people's emotional responses in detail. They reflect recurring patterns, the subtle but powerful dynamics that often go unnoticed in traditional research.

6. An Emotion Map also captures hundreds of respondent statements. These do not fit into the visual timeline but are of equal consequence to the insights and design recommendations.

7. For confidentiality reasons, certain details of the brand, product, and packaging visuals have been subtly altered.

1. The Sequence of Emotions Matters

The emotional impact of a product isn't only about *which* emotions it evokes but also *when* they occur. Emotions don't happen in isolation. They unfold as a sequence, each one coloring the next.[8] A minor frustration early in the journey can be forgiven if it's followed by moments of delight. But a single irritation at the end can cast a shadow over the entire experience. That's why it's essential to look beyond individual touchpoints and consider the emotional rhythm of the whole journey—how feelings rise and fall from start to finish.

Both products were appreciated for their fragrance. But how the fragrance was released over time made all the difference. The pod's scent built gradually from when users opened the packaging to when they took the wet laundry out of the machine, and finally, when folding their clothes. This created a steady rise in positive emotions throughout the journey. The tablet, in contrast, opened strong: its scent was most noticeable when the box. was opened but faded during use. The result? A promising start that gradually became disappointing, leading to a less satisfying overall experience. Even though both products smelled good, the emotional sequence left users with very different impressions.

2. Real Environments Reveal Real Emotions

To understand how a product truly feels to use, you need to see it in context. Emotions are shaped by the user's surroundings, habits, and constraints. A feature that works well in theory can cause irritation if it clashes with how people actually go about their day. That's why the Micro-Emotion Scan is conducted in people's personal environments. It allows us to capture emotional responses that would be missed in a lab or interview setting, responses triggered by multitasking, limited space, distractions, or shortcuts that are part of everyday routines.

Many participants handled their laundry while doing other tasks. They're folding a finished load, scrolling through messages, or trying to stop a toddler from climbing into the laundry basket. The tablet worked well in these situations: its box opened easily with one hand and stayed upright on the counter. The plastic pouch of the pod, in contrast, required two hands to manage. Users found it awkward and unstable, especially when multitasking. These may seem like minor details, but they disrupted the user's flow, causing micro-frustrations.

8. See the Theoretical Deep Dive at the end of Chapter 4 for a comprehensive discussion of how sequential emotions influence each other.

3. Users Experience the Product as a Whole

Companies often develop products across departmental silos—formulation, packaging, branding, graphic design, and so on. Decisions that work well from their respective standpoints can feel disjointed when translated into a whole product. Emotions cut right through these artificial boundaries. They reveal what users actually care about. Their concerns may be very different from the aspects the company has invested most of its effort into developing. Users don't experience separate components; they react to the product as a unified, unfolding experience. Emotion Maps help reveal emotional disconnects, showing where the parts don't add up to a coherent whole and where the overall experience can become more fluent and aligned.

Users responded positively to various aspects of the pod. They appreciated the sleek, high-tech graphics on the packaging and found the pods friendly and approachable. But taken together, the combination felt mismatched, as if the packaging and the product inside belonged to different brands. The tablet made a very different impression. Its package design was simpler and more understated, which users found initially underwhelming. But within the product's sustainability narrative, the packaging, product, and messaging all felt consistent. This sense of coherence made the overall experience more satisfying, even though none of the individual elements stood out on their own.

4. Small Emotions Can Have a Big Impact

Strong positive emotions can turn users into fans, while strong negative ones can ruin the whole experience. Even so, emotional intensity alone doesn't always tell you what matters most. A burst of confusion might feel intense in the moment, but if it's resolved quickly, it might not overshadow an overall positive experience. Meanwhile, mild emotions, if they occur repeatedly, can shape the overall experience. That is why it's important to look beyond emotional peaks and pay attention to the smaller emotional moments that accumulate over time.

Several users felt confused about where to place the tablet in the washing machine. Confusion was one of the most intense negative emotions we recorded. People described feeling frustrated, even embarrassed, as they tried to figure it out. But once they understood it, the issue quickly faded into the background. For most, it was a one-time problem that didn't affect their overall product experience. By contrast, a few minor

annoyances—such as needing two hands to open the pouch of the pod—were less intense but happened repeatedly. These small friction points had a more lasting impact on the emotional journey.

5. Thoughtful Design Can Transform Negative Moments

Some product journeys include moments that are inherently unpleasant. For example, some people find ironing extremely tedious and will inevitably experience negative emotions while doing it. When such moments cannot be avoided, you can try to soften their impact. When users sense that a brand makes an effort to ease the burden—through clear communication, thoughtful design, or even a touch of humor—it changes how the product is perceived. It doesn't eliminate the negative, but it makes the experience feel more human.

Detergents are required to display regulatory warning labels, for example "Do not ingest" and "Avoid eye contact." The pod's packaging presented these warnings with a scattering of icons and small-print text, making them feel forced and unintelligible. The tablet's packaging took a different approach. Its warnings were clearly worded and accompanied by well-designed graphics. This didn't make the warnings pleasant, but it did make them feel intentional and considerate. Users noticed the difference. The design didn't remove the negative, but it signaled genuine care, making users feel reassured and respected.

2.6 Comparing individual Emotion Maps

RESEARCH OPPORTUNITY: CONDUCTING A MICRO-EMOTION SCAN

A Micro-Emotion Scan is an inquiry into all the emotions that emerge during a product or service journey. It can be applied to virtually any interaction—doing the dishes, buying shoes, drinking coffee, visiting a doctor, or going to the movies. Unlike traditional research methods that rely on post-experience recall, this approach captures emotions as they naturally unfold, preserving the subtle feelings that would otherwise be lost to memory. The method is best seen as a collaboration between the interviewer and the participant. The participant engages in the activity as they would normally while staying mindful of their emotional responses and expressing them in real time. The interviewer follows along, creating a detailed record of all emotions as they emerge. The procedure is flexible and can be adapted to fit your needs and resources—but it works best when guided by six core principles, which are detailed in *Tools & Techniques*, pages 236-238.

DESIGN OPPORTUNITIES: USING EMOTION MAPS

After creating an Emotion Map and distilling key insights, the next step is to identify opportunities for improvement. The Emotion Map provides a complete overview of how people feel as they move through the product journey, making it a strong starting point for innovation. Of course, a complete product development strategy also takes into account factors such as market opportunities, technological advances, and cost constraints—which we don't cover here. Instead, we focus on four design opportunities that can be directly informed by emotional data. In the laundry case, each one led to a concrete design recommendation, which we explain on the next page. Pages 59-61 show other examples from everyday products and services that show how these strategies can be applied more broadly.

Design Opportunity 1. Address the Emotional Lows: A natural first step is to address the most negative emotions. When feelings such as frustration, confusion, or impatience present clear opportunities for emotional improvement, the fix is obvious: a small tweak in packaging, a clearer instruction, or a more intuitive interaction. But not all negative emotions point to simple solutions. If the Emotion Map doesn't clearly indicate where to focus, it can be helpful to compare maps across similar products. If the same issue appears everywhere, it may be a category-wide challenge or simply unavoidable. Even then, recognizing the low points gives you a place to start.

Design Opportunity 2. Don't Lose the Good Stuff: When redesigning a product, it's natural to focus on what needs fixing. But in doing so, it's easy to overlook what already works well. Positive emotions deserve just as much attention, especially because improvements in one area can unintentionally eliminate positive aspects you weren't aware of. It's also important to be specific: for instance, do users want this exact opening mechanism, or would they be just as happy with another mechanism that has the same qualities?

Design Opportunity 3. Turn Liking Into Loving: Some features don't spark strong reactions but still generate moderately positive emotions. This "liking" often represents untapped potential. How can you transform "liking" into "loving"? The Emotion Map can help identify moments when users are mildly pleased. With a better fit, clearer communication, or a small twinge of delight, these features can carry more emotional weight and become true highlights of the experience.

Design Opportunity 4. Introduce New Moments of Joy: The Emotion Map shows what people already feel, but it can also help you identify opportunities to introduce new moments of delight. A thoughtful detail or playful touch can turn a neutral interaction into an emotionally engaging moment.

Redesigning the Tablets

The four opportunities led to the following design proposals in the detergent project.[9]

1. ***Address the Emotional Lows:*** The tablet's innovative package opening mechanism puzzled users at first. The design was unfamiliar, and several participants were unsure how to open the box correctly. Although the confusion faded once they figured it out, the initial experience triggered frustration. We addressed this by adding a simple visual cue to clarify the opening motion, reducing confusion without changing the packaging structure.

2. ***Don't Lose the Good Stuff:*** Users appreciated how easily the box containing the laundry tablets could be opened and closed with one hand, especially when multitasking during household routines. Since we were also exploring a packaging redesign, we made sure to preserve this single-handed usability in all new concepts, ensuring that a seemingly small strength was not lost in the process.

3. ***Turn Liking Into Loving:*** The packaging for the tablet included information about its environmental benefits, which users valued. However, the claims felt abstract and hard to relate to. We revised the messaging by adding concrete comparisons. For example, we showed how one box saves the CO_2 equivalent of a 20-kilometer car ride, making the impact easier to grasp and more emotionally resonant.

4. ***Introduce New Moments of Joy:*** The tablet package included a fragrance card to preview the product's scent since the tablets themselves were sealed. Some users misinterpreted the card as a wardrobe freshener and enjoyed using it that way. We embraced this reinterpretation by redesigning the card to resemble a small item of clothing, adding a subtle cue to encourage this second use, and turning a functional component into a small moment of delight.

9. For confidentiality reasons, we won't share our specific recommendations for the Pod. Instead, we show how the research insights could improve the competing tablet. This also highlights how even well-performing products benefit from emotional design improvements.

DESIGNED TO TRIGGER MICRO EMOTIONS

1. Address the Emotional Lows

Apple MagSafe connector
Introduced in 2006 with the MacBook Pro, Apple's MagSafe connector used magnets to securely attach the power cable, allowing it to detach easily when pulled. This design reduced the risk of laptops being pulled off surfaces, enhancing safety and user convenience.

Tupperware's airtight seal
In 1946, Earl Tupper introduced the Wonderlier Bowl with a "burping" lid inspired by paint cans. It eliminated leaks and guesswork in food storage—turning a common kitchen frustration into a daily moment of tactile satisfaction.

Philips Philishave
Philips launched the Philishave in 1939, marking the debut of the first rotary electric shaver. Designed to offer a safer and smoother alternative to straight razors, it redefined the shaving experience by alleviating the discomfort and risk associated with traditional methods

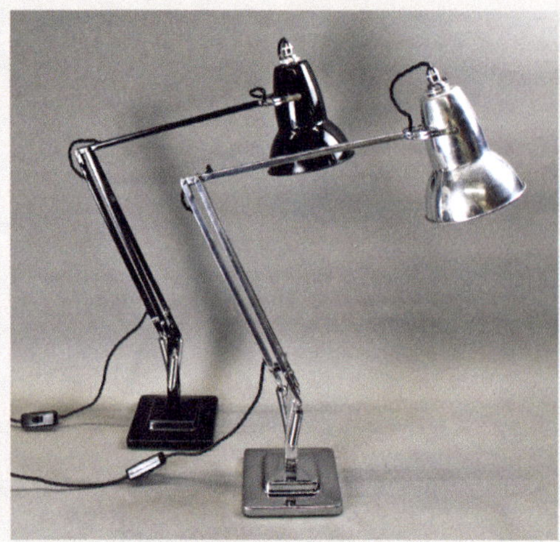

Anglepoise lamp

British engineer George Carwardine designed the original Anglepoise lamp in 1932, introducing a balanced-arm mechanism that allowed for unparalleled adjustability. Despite numerous updates over the years, its signature spring-and-lever system has remained intact, preserving the intuitive movement that continues to captivate users.

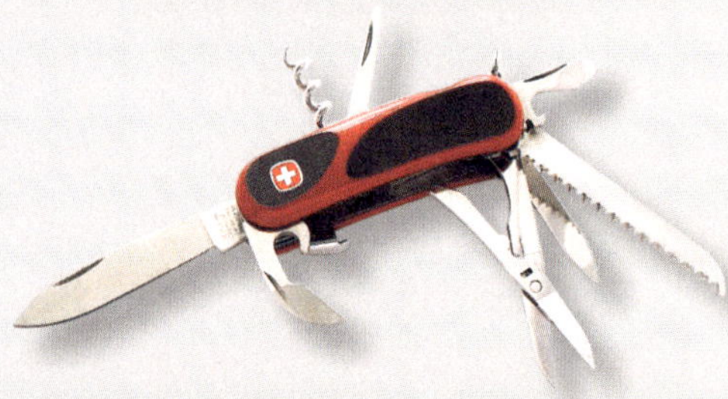

Swiss Army Knife

First produced in 1891 by Victorinox, the Swiss Army Knife has evolved in function and material content but not in feel. Its iconic red handle, folding snap, and familiar weight have remained, preserving the tactile qualities that users trust and enjoy.

LEGO Interlocking Brick System

On January 28, 1958, the LEGO Group patented the stud-and-tube interlocking brick design, revolutionizing the construction toy industry. This design allowed for a stable and versatile building, and its enduring compatibility has preserved the tactile and imaginative play experience for generations.

3. Turn Liking Into Loving

Braun SK4 record player
The device was designed by Hans Gugelot and Dieter Rams in 1956. Rams proposed replacing the original metal lid with clear acrylic—a novel material at the time. This turned the act of playing records into an engaging experience and earned the nickname “Snow White’s Coffin.”

Google Doodles
The first Google Doodle, a stick figure for Burning Man in 1998, was a quirky inside joke. It grew into a beloved feature that honors global events and cultural moments—turning a blank search bar into a tiny cultural stage.

4. Introduce New Moments of Joy

Nintendo 64 Rumble Pak
Released in 1997 for the Nintendo 64, the Rumble Pak introduced haptic feedback to console gaming. The subtle vibrations made explosions, collisions, and action feel real—giving players a whole new way to experience games through their fingertips.

Volkswagen Beetle flower holder
When Volkswagen reintroduced the Beetle in 1998, they included a small vase on the dashboard—a nostalgic nod to the car's 1960s heritage. While serving no practical purpose, this feature allowed drivers to personalize their space, adding a whimsical touch to the driving experience.

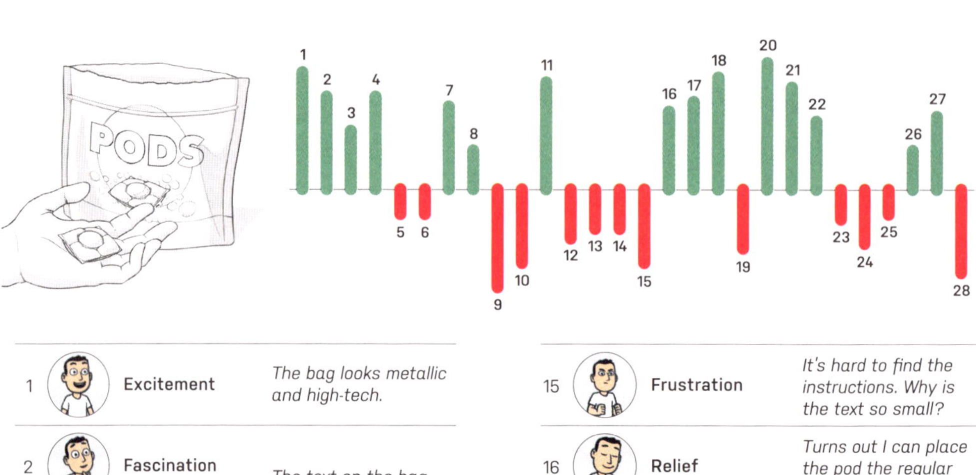

1	Excitement	*The bag looks metallic and high-tech.*
2	Fascination	*The text on the bag mentions new technologies.*
3	Desire	
4	Satisfaction	*Opening the bag is straightforward.*
5	Dissatisfaction	*The edge of the bag is frayed. Did I open it wrong?*
6	Confusion	
7	Delight	*The bag releases a nice scent. Not too strong.*
8	Desire	
9	Disgust	*The back of the bag shows unfriendly warning symbols without explanation.*
10	Worry	
11	Delight	*The pod looks familiar, friendly, and powerful.*
12	Confusion	*These pods don't match the bag. Where is the high-tech factor?*
13	Dissatisfaction	
14	Boredom	

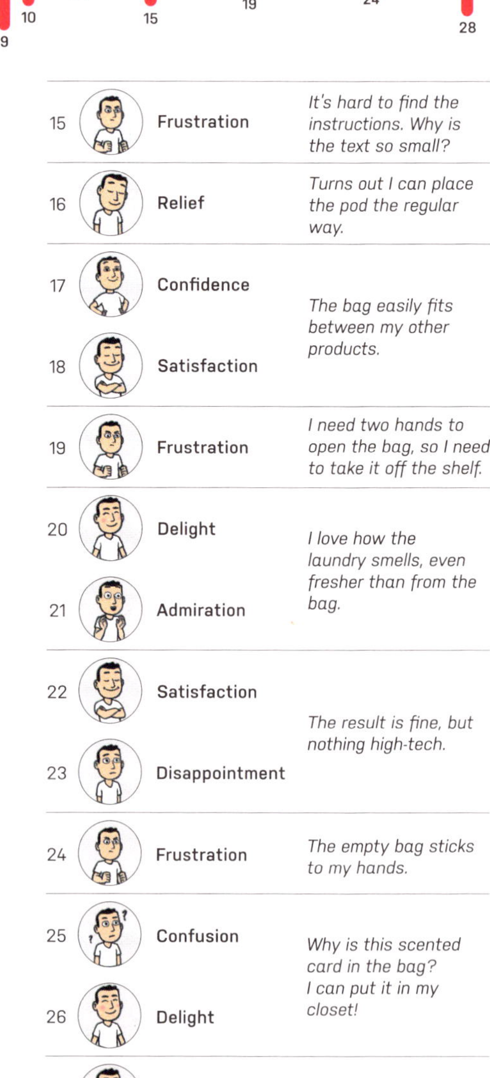

15	Frustration	*It's hard to find the instructions. Why is the text so small?*
16	Relief	*Turns out I can place the pod the regular way.*
17	Confidence	*The bag easily fits between my other products.*
18	Satisfaction	
19	Frustration	*I need two hands to open the bag, so I need to take it off the shelf.*
20	Delight	*I love how the laundry smells, even fresher than from the bag.*
21	Admiration	
22	Satisfaction	*The result is fine, but nothing high-tech.*
23	Disappointment	
24	Frustration	*The empty bag sticks to my hands.*
25	Confusion	*Why is this scented card in the bag? I can put it in my closet!*
26	Delight	
27	Satisfaction	*It's easy to dispose of the bag but I feel bad for wasting plastic.*
28	Shame	

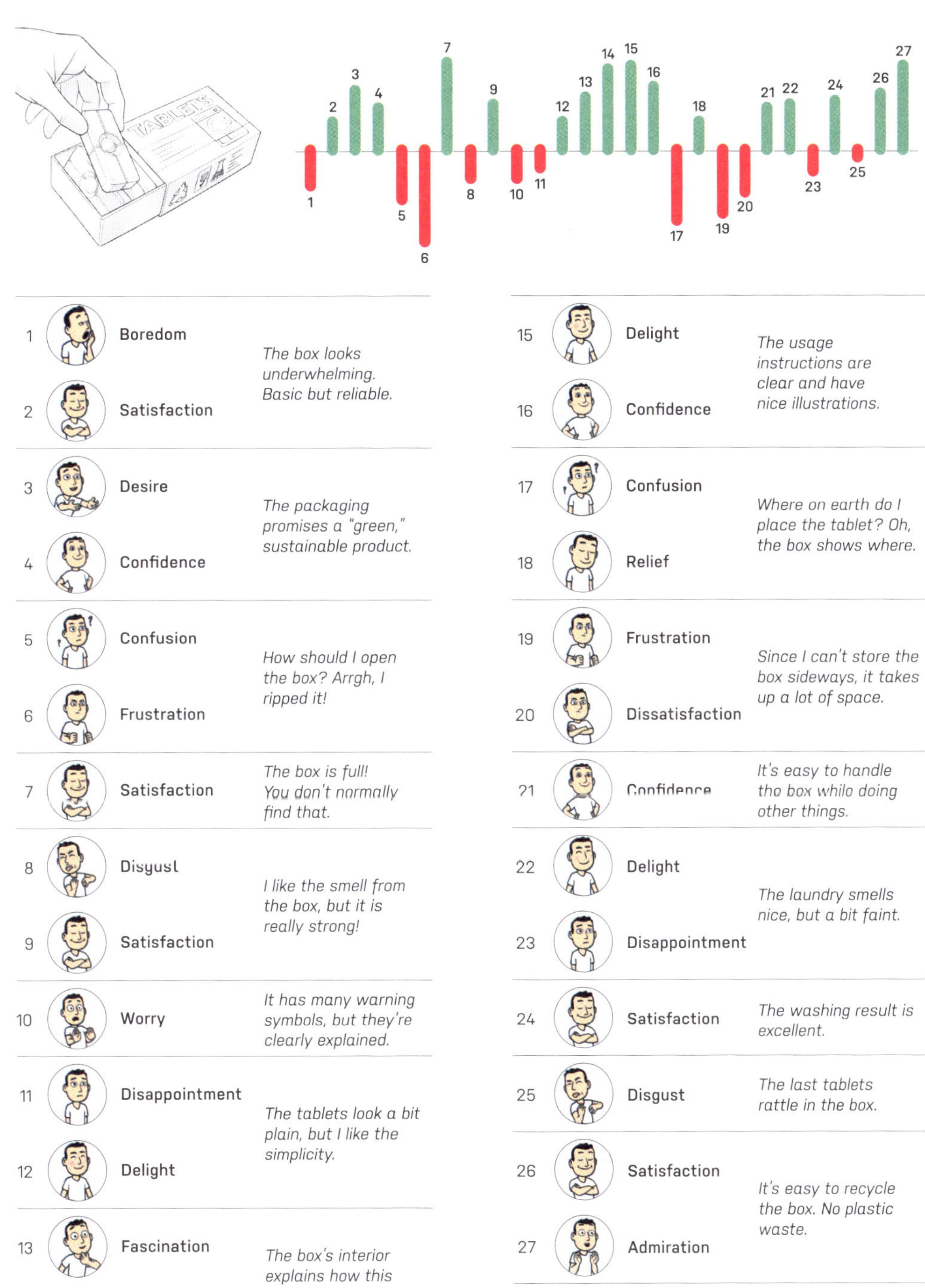

2.7 The Emotion Maps of the pod and the tablet

THEORETICAL DEEP DIVE

How Emotions Are Measured

Why don't you use more advanced or objective measurement techniques than just asking people about their emotions?

This is a question we often get. The underlying assumption is understandable: we rely on self-reporting simply because it's easy or low-tech. And yes, self-reporting is straightforward and requires minimal equipment. But these are not the main reasons we prefer it. To explain our preference, we need to unpick the threads of emotion and look at what it is made of.

Psychologists describe emotion as a "multi-componential phenomenon," meaning that it consists of several interconnected elements. These components, taken together, constitute emotions, yet none of them on its own fully captures what an emotion is. You cannot directly observe an emotion in its entirety, but you can measure its individual parts.[1] Each offers a different entry point into a person's emotional state. What follows is a closer look at these components, including their contribution to the emotional experience and how researchers attempt to measure them in practice.

Behavior

Imagine someone walking down a street by themself. In one scenario, they are feeling content and serene. Picture how this state affects their gait and behaviors—perhaps they stroll along at a leisurely pace, gaze wanderingly, and pause from time to time. Now, visualize a second scenario in which this person is frightened. They might hasten their pace, glance around nervously, and avoid stopping at all.

All emotions influence people's actions in one way or another. But it is good to realize that emotions are not hardwired to cause specific behaviors. They create *behavioral tendencies*. For instance, anger might lead someone to shout, lash out, or stamp their feet, but they could just as well mumble, withdraw silently, or not react at all.[2] How people act out their emotions is subject to factors related

1. Mauss and Robinson (2009) provide a comprehensive review of the measurement of different components of emotion.

2. The behavioral tendencies of emotions are discussed in detail in Chapter 6 (for positive emotions) and Chapter 7 (for negative emotions).

ANGER	INDIGNATION	RESENTMENT
ANNOYANCE	DISSATISFACTION	FRUSTRATION
CONTEMPT	HATE	DISGUST
BOREDOM	RELUCTANCE	SADNESS
DISAPPOINTMENT	PITY	LONELINESS
REJECTION	HUMILIATION	LONGING
ENVY	JEALOUSY	GUILT
REGRET	SHAME	EMBARRASSMENT
FEAR	STARTLE	WORRY
ANXIETY	DISTRUST	DOUBT
NERVOUSNESS	INSECURITY	DISTRESS
DESPERATION	CONFUSION	SHOCK

AMUSEMENT	SCHADENFREUDE
SENSORY PLEASURE	SERENITY
RELIEF	SATISFACTION
EUPHORIA	HAPPY-FOR
LUST	AFFECTION
TENDERNESS	ELEVATION
GRATITUDE	WORSHIP
ADMIRATION	MOVED
PRIDE	DETERMINATION
FASCINATION	POSITIVE SURPRISE
INSPIRATION	AWE
EXCITEMENT	HOPE

2.8 The Emotion Typology (https://emotiontypology.com)

to cultural background, personality, present company, ongoing activity, and even the time of day.

How is behavior measured?

The short answer is: carefully, but rarely. Apart from certain academic studies, the behavior of respondents is seldom used as an entry point to infer their emotional states, for the reason we have already pointed out: there is no reliable connection between emotion and behavior. Emotions may create behavioral tendencies, but people differ in how they turn these into observable behaviors. Observing behavior may play a supporting role in emotion research, however. For instance, skilled interviewers see how an interviewee reacts to pick up clues about how they might be feeling, but those hints will always require careful verification.

Expressions

Humans are social beings who constantly broadcast their state of mind, with the face serving as the primary channel. A person's face contains over forty muscles—far more than necessary for basic functions such as eating and speaking—enabling it to display a vast array of expressions. People frown when annoyed, widen their eyes when surprised, and smile when happy. These facial expressions are mostly automatic but can also be intentionally exaggerated, suppressed, or even faked.

How are expressions measured?

A common approach in emotion research is having a trained human observer or a computer interpret respondents' facial expressions (see image 2.9). If done right, the advantage is that the respondent can describe their emotions without interruption. However, whether "doing it right" is possible depends largely on the application. Interpreters are trained on coding systems that associate certain facial expressions with emotions (the most popular being FACS[3]). These systems typically show images of actors making exaggerated versions of emotional expressions. As one might expect, if interpreters are asked to categorize new images featuring similar expressions, the accuracy rates are quite high (with humans slightly outperforming automated systems). But the accuracy drops dramatically when interpreters are shown spontaneous expressions of emotions,[4] which are precisely your focus here. Another issue is that coding systems only include facial expressions for a few "basic emotions" such as joy, anger, and fear. But, as this chapter demonstrates, even something as mundane as laundry detergent can elicit nuanced and complex emotions including shame, relief, and disappointment, which lack predefined expressions.

Autonomous bodily processes

Emotions influence several involuntary bodily processes, including hormone production, heart rate, blood pressure, sweat production, respiration rate, and muscle tension. You may have observed this phenomenon in yourself: you get sweaty palms when you are nervous, or your heart rate skyrockets when you are angry. And the butterflies in your stomach when you are in love can be attributed—albeit far less poetically—to gastrointestinal activity.

How are autonomous bodily processes measured?

Some autonomic bodily processes, such as hormone levels or gastrointestinal activity, are too invasive or complex to measure outside a lab setting. Other metrics, including heart rate, skin temperature, and sweat production, are more practical to use. These metrics have fluctuating numerical values which, when plotted, resemble the squiggly lines produced by lie detectors that you have probably seen in the movies. These data streams are analyzed by an algorithm or a person to infer when someone is experiencing an emotion. Like facial expression measurement, this approach has the advantage of not interrupting the person during the activity. Many people also like the idea of capturing hard (numerical) data that comes directly from the body instead of relying on interpretations of facial expressions or feelings. However, there are also some significant drawbacks to consider. During measurement, the respondent needs to be connected to sensors, which are set up and monitored by a technician (see

3. Facial Action Coding System by Ekman and Friesen (1978).

4. This was shown experimentally by Dupré et al. (2020).

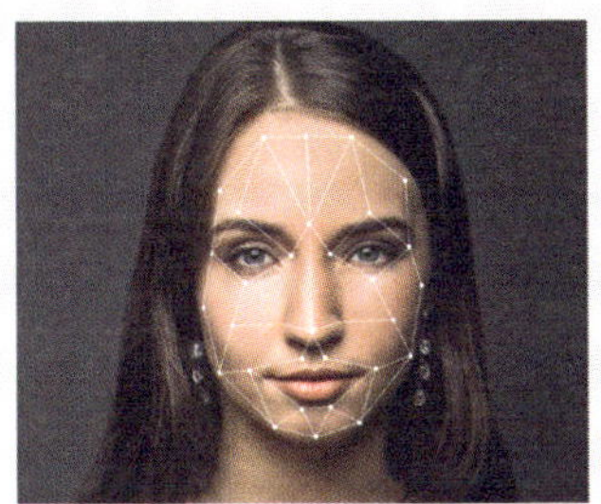

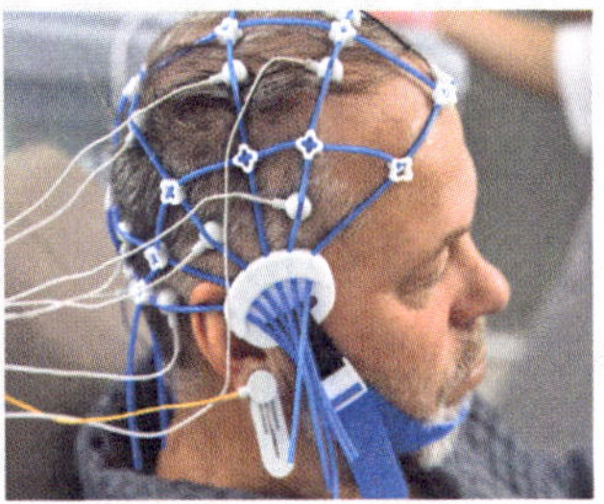

2.9 Facial expression measurement / 2.10 Physiological measurements / 2.11 EEG

image 2.10). Fortunately, the hardware has become smaller and less invasive over the years, making it viable for research in people's homes. Second, the simplicity of the data means it carries less meaning than other measures. While these measures can distinguish between certain emotions, including joy, contentment, sadness, and fear, they typically fail to differentiate between emotions that are more similar, such as fear, frustration, and anger. Third, physiological processes are influenced by many other factors, particularly physical activity. Therefore, respondents should typically remain still and be shielded from distraction during measurement. Lastly, and crucially for the present purposes, physiological data tends to be quite "noisy." The signal measured has to be strong to be detected. In other words, the sensors can only pick up on emotions of a certain intensity but won't detect most micro emotions.

Brain activity

The brain is at the core of emotions. It enables the nervous system to process emotional information and offer an appropriate reaction. Neuroscientists are far from understanding exactly what happens during an emotional episode—they cannot measure the content of thoughts and emotions. They can observe which brain regions show increased or decreased activation over time, however. Through these observations, they have found patterns linking particular brain activations with certain emotions. This is not as straightforward as brain region one lighting up for emotion X and region two for emotion Y. Instead, scientists compare the activation of many different brain regions and run complex statistical pattern-recognition tests to infer the emotions of a test subject.

How is brain activity measured?

The use of neuroimaging techniques to infer emotion has seen a significant uptick in recent decades due to the technology becoming more accessible. There are several methods of measuring brain activity, which differ substantially. The two most common are Electroencephalography (EEG) and Functional Magnetic Resonance Imaging (fMRI).

EEG uses electrodes placed on the scalp to measure the electrical fields produced by brain activity (see image 2.11)v. In commercial applications, these electrodes are typically integrated into a cap worn by participants. EEG offers excellent temporal precision (millisecond accuracy) but poor spatial resolution, making it difficult to pinpoint exactly where in the brain the activity occurs. Additionally, it can only measure activity in the brain's surface areas. These limitations mean EEG typically cannot identify specific emotions, only related phenomena such as alertness, relaxation, or general emotional valence (positive/negative feeling). EEG is, by far, the most popular method because it's less expensive and can be used outside a lab setting.

fMRI measures blood flow changes associated with neural activity. Its primary advantage is excellent spatial resolution—it can map activity throughout the brain with millimeter precision. The trade-off is lower temporal resolution: while EEG captures thousands of data points per second, fMRI takes one measurement every few seconds. The practical constraints are significant: fMRI is expensive, requires specialized knowledge, and forces participants to lie motionless inside a large machine during measurement. Consequently, fMRI is mostly used for passive tasks such as reading, observing images, or watching videos.

Neuroimaging has high-tech appeal and suggests the possibility of "reading minds." Some companies even claim that neuroimaging is the only way to truly understand people's thoughts and feelings, untainted by interpretation and social desirability filters. At the same time, companies often pair neuroimaging with interviews or surveys to make more sense of the captured data. Wherever the truth lies, its practical constraints make it much less suitable for most research in product and service innovation. fMRI is predominantly applied in marketing and advertising, where participants can observe content while remaining stationary. While the technology continues to develop, portable devices that can accurately detect specific emotions during everyday product interactions remain in the future.

Feelings

Feelings are the subjective part of emotions—what an emotion feels like to the person experiencing it. Feelings are a person's awareness of the effect that an emotion has on their body, their thoughts, and their perceptions. These include inward sensations (guilt can feel like a knot in your stomach, for example, or love like you are levitating) and outward sensations (in the way that fear can make time crawl or happiness seems to make the whole world smile with you).

How are feelings measured?

Measuring feelings means relying on respondents to interpret and communicate their emotions. People cannot directly convey their emotional states. Instead, they have to translate them into words or actions. This method, known as self-report, can be applied in many ways. Respondents might select a piece of music, a color, or a line from a poem to convey how they are feeling. The most common approach, however, is to use descriptors in the form of labels such as "happy" or "nervous" or, more recently, emojis.

The main advantage of self-report is that it yields a rich and contextualized account of the respondent's emotional state. If respondents are adequately prepared and asked the right questions, this method is able to capture emotions of any type, force, and duration—including micro emotions. Self-report does present some challenges: the need to report emotions interrupts the flow of experience; the quality depends on participants' emotional awareness;[5] and some people may be reluctant to share certain feelings. However, in our experience, these challenges can be addressed through thoughtful research design and participant selection.

Conclusion: what works best for product experience research?

It may be clear from this review which method we favor for our research—but hopefully also why. We believe that self-report provides the most detailed and nuanced insight into people's emotions. Emotions are inherently subjective experiences uniquely tied to an individual's perception and internal processes. While facial, physiological, or neurological measurements might provide data that gives a more objective impression, they fall short of capturing the full complexity and nuance of emotional experiences. They might identify the presence of an emotion, but they often lack the context and subtlety that can be gained through self-reporting. Self-report certainly has its limitations and warnings, but in most situations, these can be overcome by applying the guidelines provided in this chapter.

5. About 10% of people have alexithymia, a condition that limits emotion recognition. See Ricciardi et al. (2015).

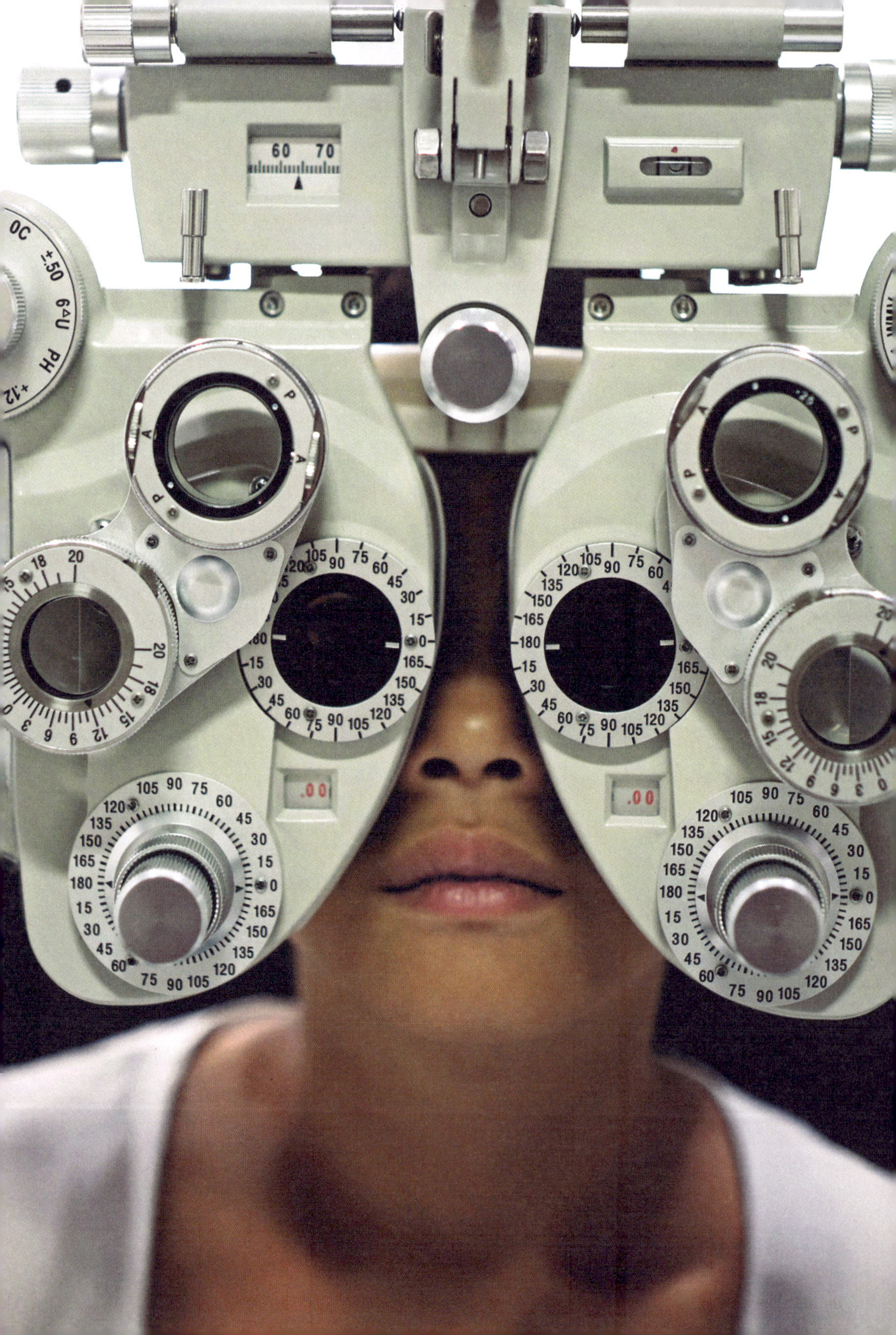

3

SPECIFIC *Needs*

An estimated 25 million[1] children around the world use a wheelchair not just for basic mobility, but as a gateway to independence and participation. Although it's hard to picture now, in the early 2000s, most children's wheelchairs were little more than scaled-down versions of adult models (see image 3.1). Children aren't miniature adults, though. The designs had no sensitivity for how children behave, imagine, and express themselves, leaving little room for play or personality. They were adequate but joyless. And that mattered. Because for a child, a wheelchair isn't just for getting from A to B. It's a component of how they develop, socialize, express who they are, and experience the world.

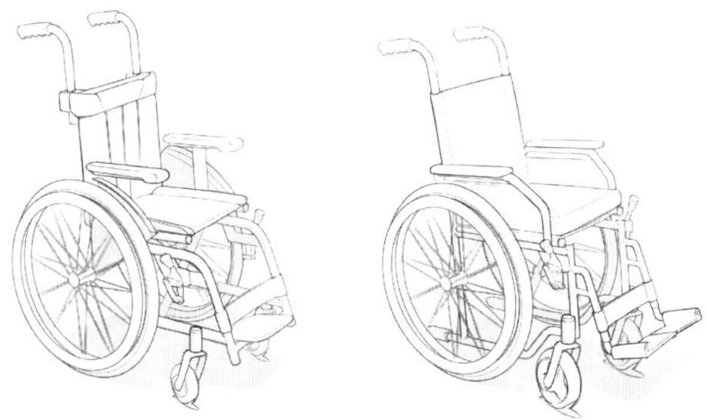

3.1 Children's wheelchairs in the early 2000s. Not bad—not great

Frustrated by the limitations of existing designs, a Dutch foundation supporting children with disabilities[2] issued a challenge: could our students design a truly child-centered wheelchair for children aged six to twelve? Eva, one of our master's students, eagerly took it on. Her goal was clear: transform the entire emotional experience of using a wheelchair. She wanted to create a design that *sparks joy*. In line with the approaches presented in the previous chapters, she began by interviewing children from the user group, as well as their parents, mapping their emotional responses to six existing models (using PrEmo, as described in Chapter 2). She uncovered a rich palette of emotional responses ranging from contempt to admiration and from boredom to fascination. These findings served as input for her design: positive emotions pointed to features worth keeping or amplifying; negative ones revealed where the design fell short.

Eva designed a completely new wheelchair from scratch (see image 3.2). Her experimentation with new materials, bold shapes, and creative features resulted in a design that was not only functionally better, but also *a lot* more fun. Children

1. While exact numbers are not available due to gaps in global disability data, the calculation of 25 million children provides a reasonable and evidence-based approximation. It was based on global data from UNICEF (2022) and the World Health Organization (Borg & Khasnabis, 2008).

2. Stichting Bio Kinderrevalidatie.

3.2 The redesigned wheelchair by Eva Dijkhuis

and parents alike were captivated by the prototype—it was unlike anything they'd seen before.

Eva's design process wasn't straightforward at all. Weaving the broad overview of emotional insights into one coherent design proved to be a real challenge. While each emotion posed its own opportunity or constraint, one negative emotion, in particular, stood out: children felt a strong aversion towards wheelchairs with push handles. Most children *hated* these handles, especially the larger ones (see image 3.1). It was puzzling: why such strong feelings about a feature that they never touched? The handles are there for caregivers, after all. But as we explore in this chapter, that single emotion turned out to reflect something much deeper—something essential to how the children saw themselves and their place in the world.

The parents, meanwhile, felt very differently. To them, the handles were indispensable. They relied on them to maneuver the kids' wheelchairs safely and efficiently during everyday outings, such as going to school. In fact, they expressed the strongest, most positive feelings towards wheelchairs that had large, comfortable handles. These opposing emotions put Eva in a bind: the new wheelchair had to include a feature the children despised, but omitting it was simply not an option. And the obvious compromise, to use smaller handles, wouldn't have satisfied either group.

Eva didn't have to settle for a comprise. Once she uncovered the deeper meaning those handles held for the children, an entirely new design space opened up. She found an elegant solution that delighted both children and parents. In doing so, she hit on the central insight of this chapter: when faced with a negative emotion that seems impossible to address through design, the key is to dig deeper—beyond the surface cause—and uncover the underlying needs driving the emotion.

The essence of this approach lies in exploring the space between emotions and fundamental needs: the realm of *need ladders*, the hierarchical structures connecting specific preferences to deeper human needs. These need hierarchies are potent tools for design innovation, offering ways to solve seemingly unsolvable problems.

The Power of Need Laddering

The relationship between emotions and needs has come up throughout the previous chapters, and it's worth reiterating here. In Chapter 1, we introduced the First Law of Emotional Design, which states that every emotion is rooted in a specific need. When one of your needs is satisfied, you feel positive emotions; when a need is compromised, you experience negative ones.

So how do you find out which need lies beneath a specific emotion? The only way is to *ask* the person who experienced it. And the way to ask is deceptively simple. Just ask the right kind of "why" questions.[3]

Always start with the emotion. Ask, "What did you feel?" Next, identify the cause by asking, "What caused the feeling?" And finally, dig deeper. Ask, "Why did [cause] make you feel this way?" With this line of questioning, you begin to uncover the needs hiding behind the emotion.

Figure 3.3 shows an example from a conversation with one of the children from the wheelchair study, "Sam" (not their real name), about their feelings towards a particular model. The figure gives a summary of five consecutive questions (Q1 to Q5).

Let's break down what happened in this conversation. The first question (Q1) uncovered an emotion: frustration. The second (Q2) identified the triggering event: the wheelchair felt heavy and slow. The third (Q3) revealed an initial need: "I want my wheelchair to be fast and easy to maneuver;" this we will call need A.

At first glance, the step from "It was slow and heavy" to "I want it to go faster and be easier to turn" might seem like a small one, almost as if Sam was saying the same thing using different words. But between those statements is an important shift with significant implications for design. Emotions and the events that trigger them are fleeting. They live in specific moments. Needs, by contrast, are continuous. They persist long after the emotion has faded. Sam's need for a maneuverable wheelchair doesn't disappear once recess is over; it continues to be relevant every single day in countless situations.

Even more importantly, people's needs are not random. They are interconnected

3. In qualitative interview research, directly asking "why" is often avoided because it can make participants feel defensive, provoke rationalized (rather than reflective) responses, and limit the depth or nuance of their answers. However, in laddering interviews—where the goal is to uncover the connections between concrete experiences and underlying needs—asking "why" repeatedly is central to the method. Nevertheless, it must be applied with care. It requires that interviewers build trust, vary phrasing, and remain attentive to participant comfort to avoid the common pitfalls associated with asking "why."

Interviewer	Sam	Interpretation
Q1: How did you feel when you first tried the wheelchair?	*It made me feel like* [points at depiction of "frustration"]. *I didn't like it.*	Sam expresses their feeling.
Q2: What about the wheelchair made you feel that way?	*It was really heavy and slow, like I had to push so hard to get it to move.*	Here, Sam shares the cause of their emotion.
Q3: Why did it make you feel that way?	*I wanted it to go faster and be easier to turn. It didn't do what I wanted.*	This is need A (the need underlying Sam's emotion).
Q4: Why do you want it to go faster and be easier to turn?	*My wheelchair needs to be fast so I can move around like the other kids. If it's slow, I can't keep up with everyone during games, like at recess.*	This is need B (the need underlying need A).
Q5: And why is it important to keep up during recess?	*I want to play games with my friends, like tag or races. If I can't move fast enough, I can't really join in, and I just have to watch them play instead of being part of the fun.*	This is need C (the need underlying need B)

3.3 A need ladder from the wheelchair study for "Sam"

within hierarchical structures, from surface preferences to deeper human motives. This becomes clear when you look at how the conversation with Sam continued with questions 4 and 5. The interviewer probed further into Sam's needs. Here are the three need statements distilled from the exchange:

- Need A: I want my wheelchair to be fast and easy to maneuver.
- Need B: I want to participate in physical games during recess.
- Need C: I want to have fun with other kids.

By continuing to ask "why," Eva uncovered not only the immediate need (easy to maneuver) but also the deeper ones (participate and have fun). Together, they form what we call a *need ladder.*[4] A need ladder moves downward from specific to general needs. The more specific a need, the easier it is to pinpoint an immediate cause. The more general, the more broadly the need is felt across different situations. In Sam's case, the need for speed and nimbleness was tied to recess—a

4. Laddering is a one-on-one interviewing technique rooted in Jonathan Gutman's means-end theory (Gutman, 1982; Reynolds & Gutman, 1988). Traditionally, it focuses on how product attributes (means) link to users' personal values (ends). In emotional design, we have adapted laddering to uncover need hierarchies that underly emotional responses to products and services.

specific moment in their day. But the deeper need—to have fun with their peers—applied to many situations. Like all children, Sam wanted to be included, to play, to enjoy time with friends. In the context of wheelchair design, their general need *operationalized* into a preference for speed and maneuverability.

Making Space for Solutions

Eva's seemingly impossible challenge with the wheelchair handles was that the children despised them, but the parents considered them essential. It represented a design deadlock: a situation with no viable *solution space*. The children wanted a wheelchair without handles, while the parents needed them for everyday tasks. These two conflicting needs cannot be satisfied with a single design.

This is precisely where need ladders demonstrate their value. Framing needs at different levels allows you to expand or narrow the solution space of a given design problem. Eva discovered she could break through the design impasse by refocusing on the deeply felt needs that lay beneath the handle-related desires, which, because they were more general, expanded her solution space. This essential insight is expressed by the third law of emotional design:

THE THIRD LAW OF EMOTIONAL DESIGN

Mapping surface needs to deeper motivations reveals breakthrough design possibilities

In design and innovation, the solution space represents all the possible ways to fulfill a given design challenge. This is the territory of potential answers, the landscape of "what could be." Designers navigate this solution space when discovering, exploring, and envisioning creative ideas.

There are obvious benefits to having a larger solution space: it opens the doorway to exploration and discovery, beckons creativity, and makes room for breakthrough ideas. But that vastness is not without its design challenges. Without focus, you risk getting lost in endless possibilities. A narrow space gives you focus and clarity, just as searching for your keys in a small drawer is easier than scouring the entire house. You're more likely to find what you are looking for quickly. A compact solution space can lead to lead to efficient,

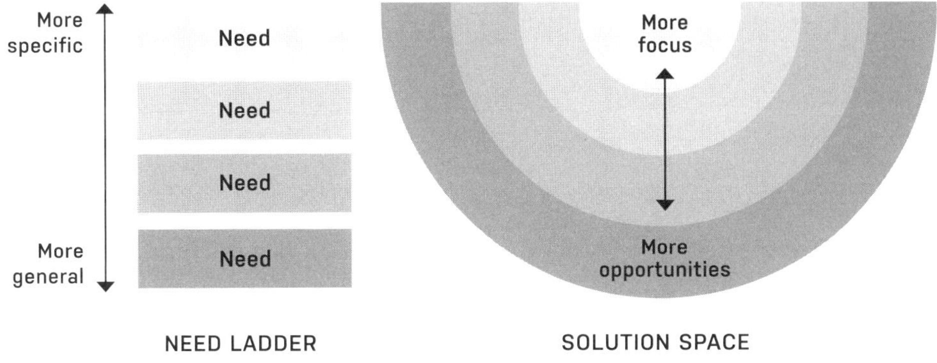

3.4 The relation between a need ladder and the corresponding solution space

targeted design solutions. Be warned, however: efficiency comes at a cost. The most innovative ideas often lie outside the boundaries you initially draw.

The optimal space is wide enough to allow for creativity but not so wide it becomes unmanageable. Need ladders are a powerful tool for exploring this balance: you can narrow the space by focusing on more specific needs and broaden it by focusing on more general needs. Diagram 3.4 illustrates this trade-off.

Jamie's comments	Need statement	Interpretation
I didn't want to use it at all. I really didn't want those big handles on the back.	Need A: I want a wheelchair without handles.	This expresses a concrete preference related to the physical design of the wheelchair.
(Why?) It's nice that people help me get places, and most of them mean well… But you wouldn't like to be grabbed and pulled away when you're walking somewhere, would you?	Need B: I want others to know when they can and cannot push me.	This represents a move away from the product and towards a social implication. The child wants to communicate their personal boundaries.
(Why?) Sometimes, I like having someone push me, like for longer walks. But most of the time I want to decide where I'm going for myself.	Need C: I want to be in control of where I go and when.	This need is even broader and emphasizes the need for control over personal actions and decisions.
	[Need for Autonomy]	Need C points to the fundamental need that drives the entire hierarchy.

3.5 A need ladder from the wheelchair study for "Jamie"

Digging Deeper: The Handle Challenge

To make this idea more tangible, let's look at how Eva tackled the handle challenge. Digging deeper and asking why enabled her to map out the need ladder underlying the simple dislike for handles. Figure 3.5 gives a snapshot of what she uncovered in a conversation with one of the children we call "Jamie".

If Eva had stopped her inquiry at the first level of need (A: *"I want a wheelchair without push handles"*), she would have been left with a narrow solution space. There was virtually no room for creativity, which would have resulted in an unsatisfactory compromise at best.

But once she reached the second level (B: *"I want others to respect my boundaries"*), the solution space widened significantly. The shift from "no handles" to "communication of boundaries" changed everything. Now, instead of just removing the handles, Eva could explore a variety of options. Here are some examples of ideas drawn from this new opportunity space:

- *Advocacy stickers*: Stickers or badges placed on the wheelchair that read "Ask Before You Help," encouraging respectful interaction.
- *Signal handles*: LED lights embedded in the wheelchair handles, controlled by the child. Green means "OK to push," red signals "Not right now."
- *Peer awareness kit*: Posters and leaflets distributed at schools to help classmates understand how and when to offer support.

Eva's final design solution was as simple as it was ingenious: a large handlebar that children can easily adjust while seated in the wheelchair (see image 3.6). In the upper position, it serves as a comfortable handle for caregivers. Tucked into the lower position, it blends seamlessly with the wheelchair frame, making it nearly invisible. This design didn't require new technology or radical changes to how the

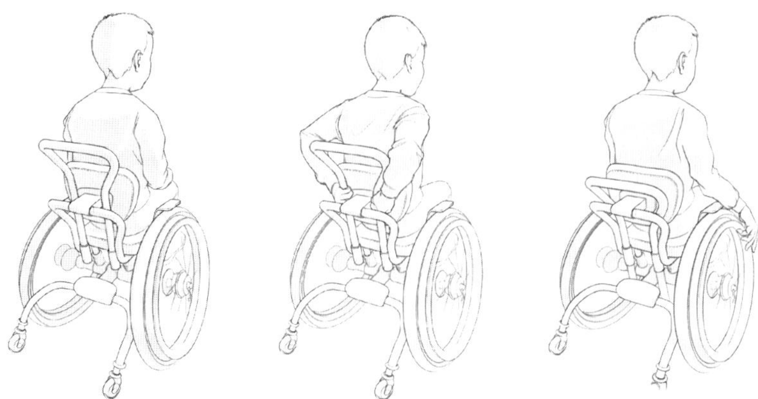

3.6 The wheelchair's retractable handlebar

wheelchair was used. But it did effectively eliminate the negative emotions children felt about the handles while also serving the practical needs of the caretaker.

Stepping Further Down the Ladder

The solution space for the second-level need (B: "*I want others to know when they can and cannot push me*") was already significantly broader than the first. But what happens when you go another step down the ladder?

Consider the deeper need (C: "*I want to be in control of where I go and when*"). At this level, the conversation is no longer about the wheelchair; it's about autonomy, freedom of movement, and independence more broadly. This need opens up a much larger solution space. Here are several potential solutions within this space:

- *Ride link app*: A mobile app that lets children request assistance or schedule rides with a child-friendly network.
- *Mobility circle*: A peer support group where children can exchange practical tips and personal strategies for navigating their worlds.
- *Audit program*: A school-based accessibility program that identifies and resolves common pain points.

These ideas are diverse and potentially impactful. But they also highlight the trade-off: as the solution space grows, so does the risk of losing focus. There are so many ways to address the need for freedom of movement that it will require much more time to explore and validate the possibilities. For example, a peer group might work beautifully for an extroverted child but feel daunting to one who is shy or overwhelmed. An app may excite one family but be impractical for another. In other words, a larger solution space may be beneficial because it contains more "good" solutions, but it also contains more solutions that are ineffective or unfeasible.

Even more importantly, the further down the need ladder you go, the more you run the risk of finding solutions that drift away from the original product. Each level of the ladder pushes you further from the product's immediate scope and into broader territory. You may end up addressing important needs—but no longer through the thing you set out to design!

Which rung of the ladder, which level of need opens up the optimal solution space? There is no general rule. In our experience, flexibility has been the real power granted us by these need ladders. The solution space isn't fixed. Throughout the design process, there may be moments when it is useful to tighten the boundaries and other times when it is better to blow those boundaries wide open. Moving up and down the ladder helps you to balance creativity and feasibility until an optimal solution emerges.

Adding Precision to User Needs

So far, we've have been focusing on one of the most powerful uses of need ladders: resizing the solution space. But they provide additional benefits. In this section and the next, we highlight two benefits that we've found especially useful in our design practice.

The first is that need ladders add a layer of precision and detail to your understanding of what users actually want. This extra clarity gives you more touchpoints to create more refined solutions.

Let's take the needs associated with the wheelchair's sturdiness as an example. Here, the children and the parents shared an experience: they expressed negative emotions toward fragile-looking wheelchairs. On the surface, there is what seems like a straightforward design directive: make it sturdy. But upon examining the need ladders, you may find more nuance. Have a look at the children's and parents' need ladders related to this issue in Figure 3.7.

	Children	**Parents**
Emotion	Feeling contempt	Feeling worried
Cause	Seeing the fragility of the wheelchair	Seeing the fragility of the wheelchair.
Need A	*I want a wheelchair that* looks *robust.*	*I want a wheelchair that* is *robust.*
Need B	*I want other children to know I can take some rough handling.*	*The wheelchair should be able to endure considerable wear and tear.*
Need C	*I want to engage in active play without reservations.*	*I want to buy a wheelchair that will last.*

3.7 Wheelchair study need ladders: children versus parents

The parents' worry about fragility was ultimately related to their need for *durability*. A wheelchair is quite an investment, and so it should stand up to prolonged everyday wear and tear. The children, however, were focused on something else entirely: how other children perceived their wheelchair. More than just *being* tough, it had to *look* tough. Why? Otherwise, the other kids would be too careful around them during playtime. Even though most wheelchairs are sturdy, their fragile appearance discourages kids from initiating rough-and-tumble play when a wheelchair is involved. The children wanted their wheelchair to give a signal, to say to their peers, "No need to be gentle—I can handle it."

Eva took these insights and turned them into something special. She not only made the design strong, she gave it a bold, robust look, with thick metal tubing and a visual stance that feels ready for action. A clever creative touch was a rubber impact bumper with soft "spikes" just above the front wheel (see image 3.2).

The bumper wasn't intended solely for protection—it sent a message to the other kids that bumping into the wheelchair was perfectly fine, even encouraged. The wheelchair became, quite literally, an invitation for rough play. Without laddering, this subtle design opportunity would likely have been missed. The surface-level imperative to "make it sturdy" would have led to a safe structure but probably not to a more inclusive play experience.

Overarching Need Themes

The third advantage emerges when you start collecting a larger number of need ladders. While specific individual needs might seem unique on the surface, as you dig deeper, you will begin to see that some of them are connected. Connected needs may belong to overarching *need themes* that are important to a user group as a whole. Let's take a closer look at some of the emotions that surfaced during the wheelchair project. The children felt:

- *Contempt* for wheelchairs that looked slow or bulky;
- *Boredom* with dull grey designs and uninspiring materials;
- *Desire* for wheelchairs that felt nimble, playful, and trick-capable; and
- *Fascination* with designs that looked unconventional and didn't scream 'wheelchair.'

At first glance, these emotions and the specific needs behind them seemed unrelated. A designer could address each of these needs individually by making the wheelchair maneuverable, colorful, sporty, unconventional, and so forth. But when Eva laddered down to the deeper needs, a larger theme began to surface. The children did not want a wheelchair that was colorful, subtle, or invincible. They wanted their wheelchair to be the coolest thing in the classroom. They weren't looking for something that was "cool—for a wheelchair, they wanted something that was "cool—period."

Eva put herself in the mindset of what children at that age think is "cool." She drew inspiration from BMX bikes and other "cool" vehicles associated with speed, freedom, and flair. She gave the wheelchair slanted wheels, like those used in basketball or tennis wheelchairs, and added treaded tires that suggested adventure. The frame was angled and dynamic, making the whole chair look like it wanted to move. She also ensured the design could handle simple tricks—to give children that sense of control and expression that comes with pushing boundaries.

On the surface, the emotions may appear unrelated, coming as they did from different moments in the children's lives. But the overarching "need for cool" tied a social situation, a practical issue, and an abstract aspiration together. Moreover, the kids' observations encompass both positive and negative emotions, which designers typically approach differently: managing negatives, and keeping or elevating positives. At the deeper needs level, however, such differences don't matter. All emotions point to things that users need. When you compare and cluster these needs, you get a clearer picture of what users might really want, regardless of how well an existing product delivers.

Herein lies the real strength of need themes: they enable you to break free from the limitations imposed by the status quo. Rather than merely patching flaws or amplifying well-loved features, you have the space and freedom to design something that addresses users' core needs without being limited by existing products.

Specific Needs and Fundamental Needs

When you ask people about their needs, you cannot keep asking "why" forever. At some point, you'll hit a wall—not because the person is unwilling to answer, but because there is simply no deeper place to go. They might shrug and say, "I just want it because I want it." That is the moment you know you have reached the bottom rung of the ladder: a need that is no longer in service of some deeper need but one that stands on its own. A need that feels, for that person, fundamental.

This is where the concept of fundamental needs comes back into the picture. As we saw in Chapter 1, fundamental needs are the psychological building blocks of human well-being. They aren't specific to a task, situation, or product—they're what people universally care about and strive for, whether they're conscious of it or not.

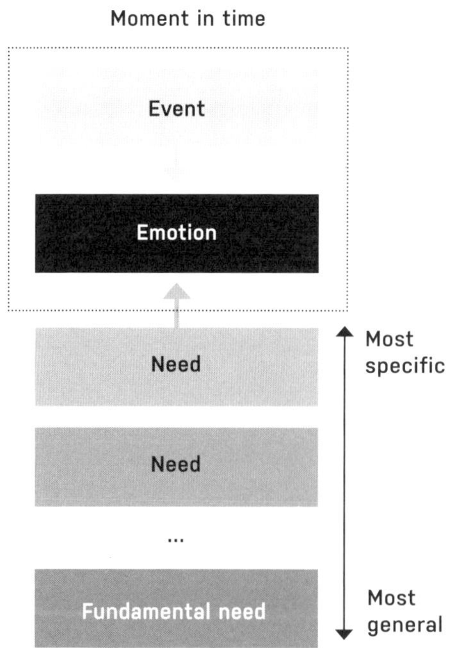

3.8 From surface events to deep needs: the structure behind emotional responses

With this final piece of the puzzle in place, the relationship between events, emotions, specific needs, and fundamental needs is complete. Diagram 3.8 illustrates how they connect, from fleeting experiences at the surface to enduring motives at the core.

Let's review. At the bottom rung of the ladder is some fundamental need. Although the need is shared by all people, the ways it operationalizes or manifests in an individual's everyday activities can differ enormously from one person to the next. Why? That concise set of fundamental needs can give rise to a virtually infinite number of specific needs shaped by differences in upbringing, social context, culture, and life stage, in addition to individual preference (see Chapter 1). Take, for example, the need for Recognition. This fundamental need manifests very differently across life stages. A toddler might seek it through praise for putting on their own jacket. A teenager might crave admiration from classmates for their new sneakers. A professional athlete might chase it by competing in a major tournament. Same fundamental need—three very different, very specific manifestations.

As you travel up the ladder, the various rungs reflect increasingly specific needs. How many rungs does a need ladder have? It depends. Some needs are easily traced up two or three clear steps. Others unfold through a longer series. The number of rungs varies from situation to situation and from person to person.

At the top of the need ladder, you find the emotion and the event that evoked it. This emotion serves as a signpost: it points to a need being fulfilled or compromised. Most of the time, people aren't aware of their needs until an emotion brings those needs into focus. Without emotions, it would be impossible for you to know your needs in the first place. That's why emotions are such powerful entry points and why laddering from emotion to need is more effective than simply asking someone directly what they need. In the deep dive at the end of this chapter, we discuss the relationship between emotions and needs in more detail.

Urges, Goals, Values, Preferences—What's the Difference?

Unlike fundamental needs, it's impossible to make a definitive list of specific needs—there are simply too many. They vary from person to person and from situation to situation. But you can still bring some structure to this complexity by grouping specific needs into four main types: urges, goals, values, and preferences.[5]

To bring these need types to life, we've created four illustrated scenes filled with people caught in the act of being human. Each one offers a window into how specific needs surface in different settings—from spontaneous urges in the park to personal preferences in a café. As you explore these scenes, you'll notice how the same fundamental needs manifest in markedly different forms, each shaped by individual context, personality, and intention.

5. This categorization is based on our research and practice in emotional design over the past two decades, synthesizing frameworks from psychology, design, and user experience research. Three influential sources have been the work of Ortony, Clore, and Collins (1988); Ford (2013); and Rokeach (1973).

1. Urges in action

2. Goals in action

3. Values in action

4. Preferences in action

1. Urges – Sudden Impulses that Push You into Action

The park drawing shows urges at work. In each scene, someone feels a sudden, powerful impulse that demands immediate action—regardless of any plans they might have had. While you might associate urges with children, like the one chasing after the ducks, adults experience them just as often.

Urges originate in our evolutionary psychology, with deep roots in our neurobiology. The brain's reward circuitry—particularly involving neurotransmitters like dopamine—creates these compelling impulses that drive us toward immediate action.[6] These ancient mechanisms long predate our ability to set future goals or live according to values.

Urges can be triggered by basic physical sensations like hunger, thirst, and pain. They are also sparked by fundamental psychological needs that must be fulfilled promptly. When one of your metaphorical need "jars" is running empty, you might experience an overwhelming urge to do something to refill it. For example, if you've been feeling trapped by responsibilities for weeks, you might desperately crave a sense of freedom (Autonomy), even if it means making a rash decision. Or, if you haven't seen a friendly face in days, you might feel an intense urge to meet up with a friend (Relatedness).

Urges often arise from internal triggers, but they can also be sparked by external stimuli. A delicious-looking pastry in a bakery window might tempt you to step inside, while hearing a favorite song might give you the urge to sing or dance.

When an urge is strong enough, it has the power to override goals, values, and preferences, thereby causing a person to act impulsively—like the child in the drawing who is trying to catch ducks. When something happens that satisfies an urge, you might feel pleasure, delight, or even euphoria. Conversely, when you are unable to satisfy an urge, you may experience boredom, dissatisfaction, or distress.

2. Goals – Desired States Requiring Planning and Effort

The drawing of the mall shows people pursuing goals. Each person is thinking several steps ahead, working toward something they want to achieve—whether it's landing a job, growing a business, or hitting their daily step count.

These examples demonstrate how goals stand in contrast to urges. While urges make us react to immediate circumstances, goals allow us to deliberately plan, monitor, and evaluate steps in anticipation of future needs. For example, let's say a person cannot adequately fulfill their need for

6. Dopamine plays a crucial role in creating anticipation and driving reward-seeking behavior, essentially signaling "this will feel good" before a person even experiences pleasure. Serotonin helps regulate impulse control, with lower levels potentially leading to difficulty resisting urges. These neurochemical systems evolved to drive survival behaviors but can sometimes lead to persistent urges that feel compelling and difficult to resist.

Autonomy at their job. Translated into an urge, they might feel like taking a day off to go shopping or hiking. Translated into a goal, they might decide to find a new line of work. Although the latter approach won't immediately change their situation, it might be a better long-term solution.

Goals, therefore, ask that people delay gratification from "right now" to some moment in the future. This might be the distant future, as in "I want to start a successful business," but it could just as well be a few hours from now, as in "I want to exercise today." Goals help you delay gratification because when you form a mental picture of what you want, you immediately derive some pleasure from imagining yourself achieving it. For this approach to work, you must feel the goal is reachable and be willing to put in the necessary effort.

Because goals are consciously formulated with clear reasoning and future orientation, they are typically easier to ladder than urges. Urges emerge as immediate, often unconscious impulses without the deliberate, logical structure that naturally leads to more general needs. Specific goals are in service of more general ones. For example, a long-term goal like "find a new romantic interest" can be broken down into smaller, actionable steps like "shop for new clothes," "join a cooking class," and "practice flirting basics."

When you reach or get closer to your goals, you might feel excitement, determination, or confidence. When your goals are thwarted, or you get further from reaching them, you might experience frustration, disappointment, or regret.

3. Values – Beliefs About What Is Morally or Ethically Just

The museum drawing shows how values shape behavior. Each person is acting according to their principles about how they and others should behave.

Values are not things that people pursue; rather, they provide the ethical boundaries within which behavior should unfold. Values thus shape how people go about reaching their goals and other needs. For example, if a person has the goal of getting a promotion to become a company team leader, their values will influence *how* they approach this challenge. If they hold diligence, integrity, and kindness as core values, they won't resort to deceit or manipulation to get ahead. If they instead prioritize status, competition, and independence, they might be more willing to use aggressive tactics.

As with goals, values range from specific and concrete ("I should call my parents at least once a week") to general and abstract ("I should maintain strong family connections"). Concrete values are sometimes expressed as "norms," which can be personal or social. At their core, values primarily connect to the fundamental need for Morality. They also relate to the specific fundamental needs they address. For example, Autonomy relates to the value of independence, Relatedness can relate to the value of kindness, and Impact might relate to the value of contribution.

Even though values are not typically pursued for their own sake, they are powerful needs. When something happens that directly involves a person's values, it often leads to strong emotional reactions. When you do things that align with your values, you might feel pride or virtuousness. When others do things that align with your values, you might feel admiration or affirmation. When you act counter to your own values, you might experience guilt or regret. And when others violate your values, you might feel indignation or disapproval.

4. Preferences – Personal Tastes or Likings

The drawing of the coffee shop shows preferences in action. Each person has their own version of the ideal coffee shop experience—whether that's seeking solitude, perfect organization of their workspace, or a front-row seat to the barista action.

Preferences are the specific ways people like to fulfill their needs. While everyone has the fundamental needs in common, how people choose to satisfy them varies greatly. One person might seek Stimulation through visiting an art gallery, while another might get their thrills from skydiving.

Preferences can feel random or inexplicable. Why do some people love chocolate while others prefer vanilla? These are deeply personal choices, and even if you could trace them back to previous experiences or cultural influences, understanding the exact reasons behind them isn't always useful. Preferences are simply part of what makes each person unique. This is why preferences both express and shape individuality. The need to choose—to exercise preference—emerges early in human development and remains a powerful force throughout life. When a young child insists on wearing shorts in winter or demands the blue cup instead of the red one, they aren't just being difficult—they're asserting their emerging identity through their choices.

While individual preferences may seem unpredictable, patterns do emerge across groups of people. For example, certain lifestyles or design sensibilities are essentially combinations of shared preferences. Consider minimalism, for example, which combines preferences for clean lines, reduced clutter, neutral colors, and functional simplicity. This kind of shared preference pattern helps us understand how personal tastes can form coherent systems that reflect both individual identity and cultural influences.

When you are able to fulfill a preference, you might feel satisfaction, contentment, or relief. When your preferences are unfeasible, denied, or overlooked, you might experience dissatisfaction, annoyance, or negative surprise.

The Messy Reality of Needs

Despite their tangibility, real life is much messier than the four types of needs would have you believe. These categories aren't separate containers but more like colors on a spectrum. Sometimes, a need clearly falls into a single category, but more often, it combines two or more.

Need types interact and evolve in myriad ways. A need might begin as an urge, develop into a goal, align with personal values, *and* reflect a preference—all at once or in an evolutionary manner. The museum-goer's sense that "Art should be accessible to all," part of their value system, might evolve into a goal to start organizing fundraisers. The impulsive tree-climbing senior in the park might set a goal to take a rock-climbing class. Human needs rarely respect the tidy boundaries we have drawn around them.

Sometimes, need types create tension in everyday life. Imagine that the quiet-loving café visitor from the illustration suddenly spots an old friend in the queue whom he's been meaning to ask for career advice. His preference for solitude now clashes with one of his goals, and a decision becomes necessary. Needs also conflict across domains. Consider the professional buying a sharp suit for a job interview—he might realize that his long-term goal of career advancement pulls him away from the deeply held value of spending more time with his family. In the same way that the formally dressed person in the park spontaneously joins the soccer game, urges sometimes override more deliberate intentions. In Chapter 5, we will extensively discuss clashing needs.

This complex, interconnected network of needs cannot be reached through direct questioning. If you were to ask park visitors about their "outdoor space needs," you probably wouldn't hear respondents say, "I need the opportunity to indulge in my spontaneous ice-cream cravings," or "I need accessible trees suitable for impromptu climbing." But those needs do exist—and are brought to the surface by emotions. This is why emotions are the most reliable gateway to identifying needs. The excitement of the child running toward ducks, the pride of the person returning lost keys at the museum, the contentment of the café patron in their quiet corner—emotional responses are the noticeable manifestations of needs being fulfilled.

For designers, the practical value of the need typology does not lie in its tidy categorizations. Take the statement, "I want to eat a sandwich," for example. Does it express a goal, an urge, or a preference? The answer depends entirely on the context and the speaker's state of mind. What really matters isn't the neat little label, it's the conscious awareness that needs come in various forms. If you focus exclusively on goals, you'll miss crucial urges. If you only look at values, you might overlook defining preferences.

By appreciating the diversity of human needs—purposeful and spontaneous, moral and practical, universal and personal—and by learning to read the emotional signals they generate, we can create designs that resonate with the full spectrum of lived experience, messy as it may be.

RESEARCH OPPORTUNITY: HOW TO CAPTURE USER NEEDS

People have thousands of specific needs influencing their daily lives. How do you identify the ones most relevant for a design? We have developed the User Need Capture (UNC) approach for exactly this purpose.

The UNC approach builds on the Micro-Emotion Scan (MES) introduced in Chapter 2, just with a different focus. While the MES identifies and documents emotional responses, UNC takes the critical next step: uncovering the needs behind those emotions. It is a set of guidelines based on a few key principles, not a rigid protocol. The approach covers both the interview and data analysis stages. You can find the UNC in *Tools & Techniques*, pages 239-242.

DESIGN OPPORTUNITY: TARGET SPECIFIC NEEDS

The approaches in this chapter—capturing genuine user needs and constructing need ladders—offer enormous design potential, as the wheelchair project demonstrates. Both approaches enable you to map what people want in rich detail, resize your solution space strategically, and identify overarching need themes that tie seemingly unrelated observations together. These insights create a foundation for innovation that goes far beyond surface-level improvements.

In reality, of course, the design process is never as straightforward as systematically working through need ladders one by one. Some ladders will prove more actionable than others. Others may only emerge among a single subset of users, requiring you to decide whether they're universally relevant. You may encounter need ladders that seem to conflict with each other (see also Chapter 5). And there may be need ladders that prove difficult to design for within your constraints. The art lies in identifying which needs offer the richest opportunities for your specific design challenge.

A good example of a design that utilized need ladders is *Mindful Bites* (see image 3.9). Domestic cats don't feed themselves—their humans do. And all too often, humans overdo it. In the Netherlands, over half of all cats are overweight. The primary cause is overfeeding, often driven by affection. Our student, Alev, set out to develop a solution. She mapped the needs driving the feeding behavior. The surface need, "I want to give my cat a treat," was evident. And the deeper need behind it—the fundamental need for Relatedness—was also unsurprising. The middle layer, however, opened up her solution space. Four distinct needs emerged through laddering: "I should compensate" (for guilt after being

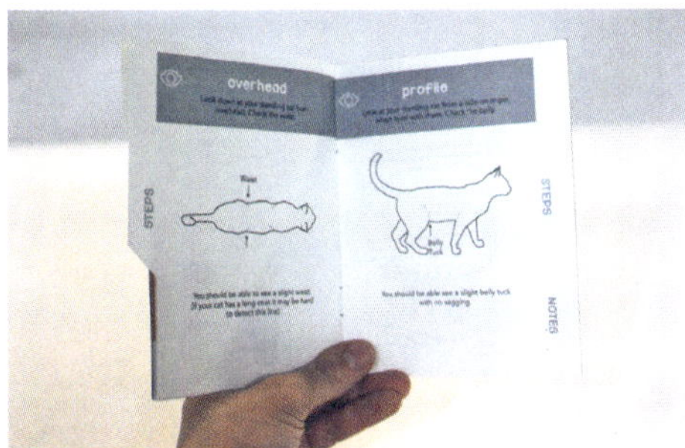

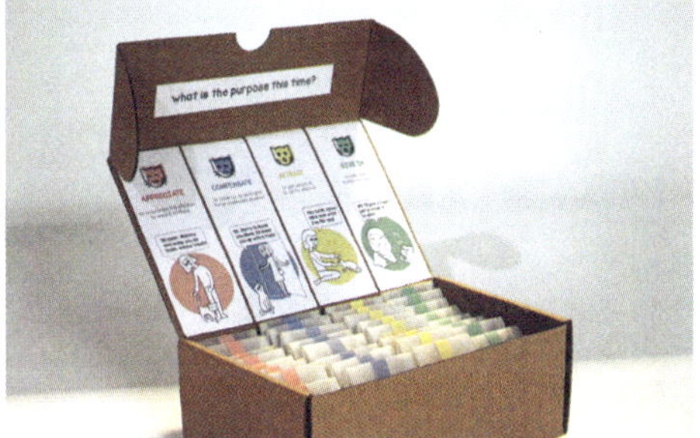

3.9 Mindful Bites by Alev Sönmez

absent), "I want to reward" (for good behavior), "I like to attract attention" (to gain affection), and "I want to avoid conflict" (to preserve good relations). Alev designed *Mindful Bites* to meet those needs. This set of three products reshapes the everyday act of feeding into a more mindful and balanced interaction—one that nurtures both emotional connection and physical well-being by helping cat owners care for their pets in fulfilling yet nutritionally responsible ways. The set includes:

- *Mindful Meals*: A hand-feeding bowl that brings intimacy to everyday feeding, turning meals into moments of connection.
- *Mindful Strokes:* A tactile guidebook that helps owners assess their cat's body condition through gentle touch.
- *Mindful Treats*: A snack box categorized by emotional intent. Owners reflect on their motivation while receiving tips and gentle nudges related to weight management.

THEORETICAL DEEP DIVE

Capturing User Needs

Why should you capture emotions when you are interested in needs?
The approach in this chapter builds on the previous one, which explored how measuring emotions helps you understand how people really experience a product. We have shown you how emotions are linked to needs and how laddering these needs uncovers deeper insights. But why should you take such a roundabout route?

Why not just ask people directly about their needs?
Paradoxically, asking people direct questions about their needs can be one of the least effective ways of revealing them. Inquiring about emotions, on the other hand, usually leads to natural and truthful insights.

Surveys, interviews, and focus groups routinely probe consumers' needs. "What are your most important needs when cooking?" or "How well does [Product] meet your needs?" or even "What is the greatest benefit of using [Product]?" Companies collectively spend billions on this type of market research—and base major innovation decisions on the answers. But there's been a fair amount of criticism directed at this approach, and historically, innovation leaders have been skeptical.

Henry Ford is famously quoted as saying, *"If I had asked people what they wanted, they would have said faster horses."* Whether he actually said it or not, the statement perfectly captures his philosophy. And he wasn't alone. Consider these quotes from contemporary visionaries:

"It's really hard to design products by focus groups. A lot of times, people don't know what they want until you show it to them." – Steve Jobs (Co-founder of Apple)

"Do not spend a lot of time in focus groups because people don't know what they want." – Seth Godin (Marketing guru)

"We don't believe in market research for a new product unknown to the public. So we never do any. We are the experts." – Akio Morita (Co-founder of Sony)

3.10 Designing according to captured user needs

The standard argument is that people either don't know what they want, or at best, they imagine slight improvements on what they already have. That makes direct questioning a poor source of innovation.

So, who's right—the traditionalists or the iconoclasts?

In truth, both have a point. In our experience, there is value in conducting research with users in the early stages of development—not to ask them for solutions but to uncover their needs. In fact, without this type of research, you risk making flawed assumptions or projecting your own needs onto the product. However, we do agree that directly asking people about their needs, especially in "neutral" settings like surveys or focus groups, rarely works. Why?

Because most specific needs are not top of mind. Our thirteen fundamental needs may manifest in thousands, if not millions, of specific needs, but each is only relevant in certain situations and moments. As strange as it might sound, human beings are only consciously aware of a small fraction of their needs at any given time. People simply do not have the cognitive bandwidth to keep all of them in their conscious awareness.

So, how do people become aware of their needs?

There are two main pathways. First, people are usually aware of the goals they are actively pursuing, whether short-term ("I want to exercise today") or longer-term ("I want to graduate this year"). When asked about these goals, most people can readily describe them. Second, people become aware of needs when they have recently been fulfilled or thwarted. New parents, for example, will be acutely aware of their need for eight hours of uninterrupted sleep. And someone starting a new job will suddenly notice their need to know what others expect of them. But the vast majority of needs go unnoticed until they suddenly become relevant—and the way people notice them is through (you guessed it) feeling emotions. An emotion is simply the body's signal that something is affecting a need you weren't consciously considering.[1] That awareness suddenly arises, lingers for a little while after the emotion fades, and eventually slips away from the thinking mind once more.

What happens, then, when a survey or focus group task invites people to speak directly about their needs?

If the product relates to an actively pursued goal or a recently activated need, people will be able to describe needs with relative ease. But even in an ideal world, their responses will only represent a small portion of potentially relevant needs. The needs that immediately spring to mind will dominate the conversation.

Moreover, people tend to mention needs they *think they have* rather than needs they *actually* have, which poses several significant risks. First, there is the trap of aspirational needs—people report what they believe they *ought* to want based on social expectations or idealized self-images. The fitness enthusiast who claims to need detailed performance analytics might rarely check these data in practice, because they actually crave simple encouragement. Second, people often mistake others' needs for their own, particularly when influenced by marketing or peer pressure. A parent might insist they need a particular feature in a baby product because parenting forums emphasize its importance, even if their own parenting style doesn't require it.

This opens the door to idealization and socially desirable responses. People tend to highlight the needs and values that cast them in a favorable light. They're more likely to emphasize needs that suggest they're thoughtful, responsible, or sophisticated rather than those revealing comfort-seeking or status-oriented motivations. A person shopping for a car might emphasize their need for safety features and fuel efficiency while downplaying their desire for a vehicle that impresses neighbors or colleagues. This self-presentation bias is rarely conscious deception—most people genuinely believe their reported needs align with their actual motivations, unaware of how social desirability shapes their responses.

And that's why the approach we advocate takes a different route. Instead of

1. The eminent emotion scholar Nico Frijda (2007, p. 7) wrote, "Emotions arise in response to events that are important to the individual's concerns. Every emotion hides a concern, that is, a motive or need, a major goal or value, a more or less enduring disposition to prefer particular states of the world. A concern is what gives a particular event its emotional meaning."

pointedly asking people to list their needs, you guide them through a natural setting, walking them through all the relevant stages of product use, and measure their emotions. Then, in the follow-up discussion, use the emotions and the event as solid anchors from which to collaboratively explore their true underlying needs. This method allows for a deeper, more transparent look into what people need, cutting through the noise of idealized answers and helping uncover the needs that might not have been apparent through direct questioning alone.

4

EMOTIONS *in Context*

We never imagined we would be mapping emotions at 10,000 meters over the Atlantic. Yet there we were—hunched in the aisle with our PrEmo cartoons, pens, and notebooks, having breakfast conversations with jet-lagged passengers.

When people are asked to name a product that brings them joy, airline food rarely makes the shortlist. None of our students has ever held up an in-flight casserole as their object of joy—and not just due to the logistical challenge of bringing one to class. Economy-class meals have a few jobs: to be shelf stable, cost effective, and nutritionally adequate. Culinary flair is not on the menu.

Like many frequent flyers, we had endured our share of lackluster airline meals, but we had never thought about them from a design perspective. That changed when we received a call from the leader of an international airline's passenger experience team. Her question was both straightforward and intriguing: could we develop an airline breakfast that evokes positive emotions? Their main challenge was the economy-class breakfast service on long-haul flights. This was not their first attempt to improve it. A barrage of negative feedback—bland taste, soggy texture, stale aroma—had already prompted several rounds of revisions. So far, none had taken off. In their most recent effort, a renowned fine-dining chef had redeveloped their recipes. This had produced a more expensive breakfast, but unfortunately, not happier passengers.

Designing airline food is not the easiest of challenges. It comes with a daunting checklist of constraints that work against almost everything people associate with good food. Meals are prepared hours ahead at remote facilities, chilled, and then reheated in bulk inside convection ovens that prioritize efficiency over flavor. Fresh, high-quality ingredients are mostly off-limits due to costs and food safety concerns. Anything too flavorful is shunned to avoid offending passengers with widely varying dietary habits and cultural preferences. And then there's the dining room: a sealed tube of dry air, low pressure, and constant engine noise, all of which dull the senses of taste and smell, making even well-prepared food taste bland.[1]

We were blissfully unaware of these challenges at the time. As always, our first step was to map the emotions evoked by the existing product. Because the meal and the act of eating are both shaped by the physical conditions of air travel, we had to gather our data on board. Our client agreed and booked us return flights from Amsterdam to New York. As the plane taxied for takeoff, the purser gracefully introduced us over the intercom. "Good morning, ladies and gentlemen," they intoned, "today we have two university researchers on board.

1. In a food perception study, Woods et al. (2011) had participants consume various foods while exposed to different noise levels. They found that background noise significantly reduced perceived sweetness and saltiness compared to quiet conditions. This may explain why airplane food tastes bland—the constant engine noise could be literally dulling our taste perception.

They'll be looking for volunteers willing to share their inflight experiences." By the time we landed back in Amsterdam three days later, we had documented the emotional inflight journeys of thirty passengers.

As expected, breakfast was not a highlight of their journeys. The two most commonly reported emotions were disappointment and irritation, and their sources were predictable. First was the meal's taste and smell. The passengers described the food as bland and artificial. For some, just waking up to the smell of airline food was enough to kill their appetite. Second, there was the social discomfort. Not everyone is ready to eat at the same time, yet there everyone is, eating simultaneously, shoulder to shoulder. Some passengers felt uneasy watching their neighbor eat while not feeling hungry themselves. Others felt their personal space shrink as elbows extended and packaging spread out. Third, the timing: some had been woken up just for the meal to be served, but their body still thought it was 3 a.m. Others were still chewing when trays were whisked away. Either way, the meal service rarely aligned with the rhythm of the passengers.

4.1 Enjoy your breakfast

The experience was bad, but it was bad in a useful way. We saw all kinds of design opportunities. What if the tray released a fresh scent when opened, thanks to a built-in aromatherapy pod? What if passengers could customize their meals with sachets of lemon zest or fresh herbs? We even considered a self-serve breakfast station somewhere mid-cabin. We were optimistic about our long list of creative ideas.

But that optimism was short-lived. When presenting the ideas to the client, we got polite smiles and shakes of the head. Every idea would either increase costs, violate the strict onboard safety regulations, increase the workload of the cabin crew, or a combination of those. None of our proposals—not a single one—made it through.

We tried again. What if the serving container could preserve heat longer? Could we simplify preparation routines to create more flexible service? We looked for clever hacks. But in the end, we simply weren't able to establish a feasible solution space to address the negative emotions. Even probing for deeper needs with the laddering technique (see Chapter 3) didn't help us. The need for tasty food or the wish to eat on your own terms aren't proxies for deeper needs—they're already fundamental. No clever reframing could dig us out of the tray-table trench.

The breakthrough came when we shifted our focus away from the meal. To explain how, let's look at how the study was designed. When the purser introduced us, he deliberately didn't mention breakfast. He kept it general, mentioning that we were interested in how the passenger experience evolved over the course of a flight. The idea was that this would avoid priming and maximize the chance of capturing honest, unprompted reactions. Participating passengers reported their emotions at six random points during the flight. We asked them what they felt and why. Naturally, one of these "random" points came just after the breakfast service.

The result was a large collection of contextual emotion data—not about the breakfast, but about the broader experience of being in the air. At first, we ignored most of these data, as they were irrelevant to the design brief. But since our client had also asked if we could summarize the full inflight experience, we dug up the data and ran the analysis—and that's when something shifted. The was not *just* background information. It was the key to an entirely new set of opportunities.

The overview of inflight experiences yielded deep insight into the needs of passengers traveling on an intercontinental flight—those that are fulfilled and those that are not. What if the breakfast could be designed to address these "contextual" needs? Once we asked that question, a new solution space opened up. This resulted in *Morning Tapas*, a reimagination of the airline breakfast. Before we present it, let's take a closer look at the mechanisms that underly the human emotional system.

Your Emotions Know What Matters Most

Emotions serve as a sophisticated detection system, constantly scanning the environment for signs of personal relevance. This happens at an incredible speed and completely outside of our conscious awareness. Our brains rely on emotional detection because our deliberate cognitive resources are severely limited. Consciously, we can only process a small amount of information at once. As noted in Chapter 2, only about one-millionth of a percent of all sensory information reaches our conscious mind: the equivalent of a single drop of water in 100 Olympic swimming pools. While our awareness inspects that lone drop, our emotional system handles the rest, continuously evaluating everything against our spectrum of needs. And that spectrum is vast. As Chapter 4 showed, each person navigates life with an ever-shifting, endless constellation of goals, values, urges, values, and preferences. Our emotional system evaluates *all* incoming information against this *entire* matrix. It's a task no deliberate thought process could hope to manage.

A compelling example comes from Daniel Kahneman's book *Thinking, Fast and Slow.*[2] A team of firefighters entered a house where the kitchen was on fire. Shortly after they began hosing down the fire, the commander suddenly felt a surge of panic, hearing himself shout, "Get out of here!" without knowing why. Moments later, the floor collapsed. Luckily, they had escaped in time. The heart of the fire, it turned out, had been in the basement. Only later did the commander realize that subtle cues—the strange quiet of the fire, the heat in his ears—had triggered his emotional alarm bells before his conscious mind could catch up.

The commander was confronted by information that had enormous personal relevance, and his emotional system had detected the threat before his awareness had caught up. Essentially, we can *feel* before we know *why* we're feeling. This unconscious processing isn't limited to threats. By quickly and efficiently processing sensory input, our emotions also alert us to potential opportunities regarding the fulfillment of any one of our needs, allowing us to react and adapt without overwhelming our conscious awareness.

Psychologists call this process *appraisal*: the rapid assessment of whether something in the environment matters to us personally. The idea was first formalized by Magda Arnold,[3] who proposed that emotions arise from how we evaluate a situation, not just from the situation itself. This insight became the foundation for modern appraisal theories, which view the emotion system as a powerful and sophisticated "meaning-making engine."[4]

What makes the process remarkable isn't just its speed but its holistic nature. Rather than analyzing isolated cues—like a computer scanning individual pixels—our emotional system perceives patterns and relationships all at once. It doesn't simply register a quiet fire; it picks up the incongruity of that quiet within the broader expectations of a kitchen blaze. This holistic intelligence enables us to respond to the messy reality of situations rather than isolated events.

Why Emotions Are Never Just About the Product

The holistic nature of the emotional system means that emotions are rarely isolated reactions. While each emotion may have its own trigger and seem distinct, it's part of a continuous, interconnected experience. The theoretical deep dive at the end of this chapter discusses in detail how emotions influence each other.

Take one passenger from our breakfast study—we'll call him Johan. He reported feeling *anxious* during a bout of mid-flight turbulence. Later, during breakfast, he experienced *gratitude* when a flight attendant offered him a second cup of coffee. At first glance, the two emotions seem unrelated: one was caused

2. Kahneman (2011).

3. Arnold (1960).

4. For a clear overview of appraisal theory, see Moors et al. (2013).

by shaking wings, the other by a kind gesture. But Johan later told us that the attendant's kindness had helped to reassure him. Her gesture made him feel safer and more in professional hands. The gratitude wasn't just about the coffee. It resolved the earlier anxiety.

This example illustrates an insight that is relevant to design. If we were designing an in-flight coffee service in isolation, with no particular context, safety concerns might never enter our considerations. We'd focus on taste, temperature, serving efficiency, maybe the aesthetics of the cup. But in the context of an airplane cabin—especially after turbulence—coffee suddenly gains the potential to fulfill needs that have nothing to do with caffeine or refreshment. It can restore calm.

The flight attendant hadn't served the second cup with therapeutic intent. She did so because it was part of her routine. But what if she had known about Johan's lingering unease? Even better, what if the entire coffee service had been designed with the understanding that passengers can experience anxiety during flights? Perhaps the attendant could reassure passengers with a calm comment about how smooth the flight is expected to be. The cup itself could have a broader base, subtly conveying stability. The coffee might even include soothing aromatics. When designers pay attention to the broader emotional landscape of product use, new opportunities emerge—opportunities to directly support the emotional needs that arise naturally in context. This principle is captured in the fourth law of emotional design.

THE FOURTH LAW OF EMOTIONAL DESIGN

Most user emotions arise from context, not from the product

Before the breakfast project nudged us in a new direction, we had been focused on emotions directly triggered by products in use: the frustration of a slow app, the joy of a well-crafted chair, or, in this case, the disappointment of an airplane breakfast. These product-related emotions matter. But they're only part of the picture.

Once we had broadened our view, a pattern emerged across our projects. We saw that many of the emotions people experience during product use aren't about the product at all. They're related to the context: the environment, the

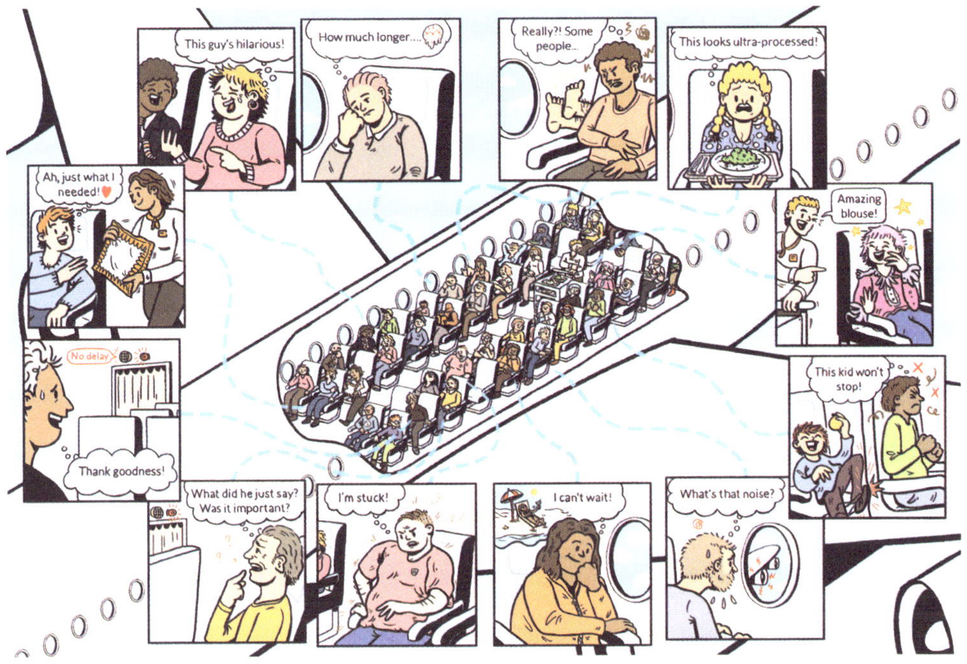

4.2 A shared journey of irritations and delights

moment, and the social dynamics surrounding the user. When you limit your focus to the product itself, you miss these contextual emotions and the needs they reveal. But when you bring those needs into the frame, entirely new design possibilities emerge.

Morning Tapas: Designing for Autonomy and Play at Altitude

We had tried and failed to address breakfast-related emotions. Safety, hygiene, logistics, and cost left us with very little room to make food or service improvements. So, we broadened the scope of our attention. Rather than focusing on the product, we revisited all the emotions we had captured during the flight—including the contextual ones.

When we looked at the emotional landscape of flying, we felt a spark of recognition. Airplanes are strange places. Three hundred people, mostly strangers, sat shoulder to shoulder in a metal tube for nine hours. From takeoff to landing, we share the same air, the same toilets, the same timetable. It's an in-between space: no longer where we came from, not yet where we're going. A pause in life, stretched across time zones. And in that space, people experience a kaleidoscope of emotions.

Image 4.2 provides a glimpse into the onboard emotional landscape. Take a moment to scan the image—you might recognize a few of these feelings yourself. Many feelings, from gratitude to frustration to anxiety, are experienced. Emotions had arisen from social interactions, environmental factors, the passengers' thoughts about their destination, and, yes, from the food service.

Now that we had this broader view, the next question was: which emotions could we work with? Two stood out as promising: frustration and boredom. You can find them in the image: the person thinking, "I'm stuck!" and the one thinking, "How much longer..." We were drawn to them for several reasons. First, they were common. Emotions are personal, but when several people report the same feelings, it suggests a pattern. Then there was the timing. Both emotions occurred toward the end of the flight, during the same window of time when the breakfast was being served. And finally, they pointed to needs we believed a redesigned breakfast could realistically support.

Frustration came from feeling physically confined in a seat with little room to move. Laddering down, this pointed to the need for Autonomy. Even when passengers rationally accept the limitations of long-haul travel, the emotional system still registers the deprivation. It doesn't ask whether the constraint is reasonable—it simply signals that something is missing. Boredom was also especially prevalent toward the end of the flight. After hours of sitting, reading, watching films, or simply waiting, passengers began to crave mental engagement—pointing to the need for Stimulation.

A Metaphor to Guide the Experience

We took Autonomy and Stimulation as the starting points for the design process. In collaboration with Reframing Studio, we developed a new breakfast concept aimed at supporting both.

We used an *experience metaphor* (a technique we explore in Chapter 8) to guide our design process: "A morning stroll in the park." It helped us imagine how the new breakfast experience should unfold. A morning walk in the park is refreshing but unhurried. You choose your own path and pace, pausing whenever something catches your attention or sparks your curiosity. For us, this image captured both the needs we were working with: Autonomy (exercising control over pace and sequence) and Stimulation (encountering variety and sensory change).

We translated the metaphor into three design principles. First: offer a sense of choice and exploration, so passengers shape the sequence and combination of what they eat. Second: create visual clarity and immediate legibility: passengers should be able to see their options at a glance. Third: include subtle sensory cues to create gentle moments of stimulation and refreshment. Together, these principles supported both needs while preserving the light, self-paced quality of the metaphor. It set the stage for what would become a rather different kind of airline breakfast—one we called *Morning Tapas* (see image 4.3).[5]

5. See Desmet and Schifferstein (2012) for additional information on the breakfast project.

4.3 Morning Tapas by Rick Porcelijn (Reframing Studio) and Pieter Desmet

The Morning Tapas breakfast offers a composed selection of options, balancing hearty and light, warm and cool, sweet and savory. The tray itself is something between a tray and a box. Made from recycled paper and covered with a clear plastic lid, it holds each bowl in place, preventing mid-flight drift and creating a clear, inviting layout. The effect is orderly but informal, structured to reassure, and open to explore.

Inside are four bowls arranged like tapas. The top left bowl contains warm, savory food, such as an omelet. The top right offers cool, savory items, such as cheeses. The bottom left contains warm, sweet food, such as lightly spiced rice pudding. The bottom right holds cold, sweet foods, such as fruit yogurt. The two small cups in the center offer optional toppings, perhaps nuts and honey, to personalize each bite.

To the side, passengers find two drinks: one warm (a choice of coffee, tea, or hot chocolate) and one lightly chilled herbal tea. The herbal tea helps passengers to gently awaken the senses and signal the beginning of the meal.

The design doesn't favor savory over sweet or warm over cold. Each bowl is the same size, leaving passengers free to shape the meal as they see fit. They choose what to eat, in what order, and whether to combine elements or keep them separate. The small cups in the center offer optional extras—nuts, honey, and so on—letting passengers add their personal touch to a meal that's usually decided for them.

The interplay of warm, cold, savory, and sweet items along with the interactive aspect of mixing and matching the meal components managed to introduce a hint of playfulness. With four bowls and two optional toppings, the breakfast offers eight distinct flavor combinations. Enough to keep the experience engaging.

Once the design was complete, it needed to be tested. Our client wasn't going to roll out a new breakfast service across continents without some evidence passengers would actually enjoy it. They invested in real-life prototypes and served them on a commercial flight, which turned our test into a genuine moment of truth. So we found ourselves on another flight to New York, this time to map emotions in response to *Morning Tapas*.

The results were clear: passengers reported significantly more positive emotions and fewer negative ones. As we had seen in the original study, the traditional breakfast typically elicited irritation and disappointment. With *Morning Tapas*, the picture reversed: fascination and joy took the top spots, while irritation and disappointment barely registered on our scale. We were pleased—and yes, a little relieved.

But the positive impact wasn't limited to the breakfast experience. About two weeks after the test flight, our client called. With some excitement, she shared something that had come up in a meeting with the marketing team, reviewing their routine post-flight overall satisfaction data. Someone had flagged a curious spike in the post-flight satisfaction scale for one flight. The difference was moderate but noticeable. They wondered what could have caused it. A quick check revealed it had been the flight with our breakfast!

Those findings illustrated once more that experience is a holistic system. As you may have noticed, emotions rarely stay in their lane. A moment of delight, one that arrived late in the journey no less, was able to shift how passengers felt about the experience as a whole. The breakfast may not have widened the cramped seats or shortened the long flight, but it left people with a better taste in their mouths—emotionally as well as literally. The concept was rolled out on all intercontinental flights between Europe and Asia. It remained in service for two years, much longer than the typical lifespan of an airplane meal.

RESEARCH OPPORTUNITY: MAPPING CONTEXTUAL EMOTIONS

The case of *Morning Tapas* shows how understanding contextual emotions can reframe a design challenge. The research opportunity is a straightforward one: map all the emotions present in a chosen situation, not just those that are evoked by a product or service. Those emotions point to underlying contextual needs, which are valuable design inputs, even if they weren't originally part of the product brief.

If you've read Chapters 2 and 3, you already know the foundations of contextual emotion mapping. Chapter 2 introduced the Micro-Emotion Scan, a method for capturing emotions as they arise in real time. Chapter 3 showed you how to link

4.4 Forest by Shion Ito

those emotions to underlying needs. Here, we build on the method by including feelings that aren't elicited by the product directly but still emerge naturally in the situation where it is being used.

This approach seeks to answer two fundamental questions. Prior to data collection: where does a "context of use" begin and end? And after data collection: which contextual emotions should you focus on? For the complete methodology, including practical guidelines for defining context boundaries and prioritizing contextual emotions, see *Tools & Techniques*, pages 243-245.

DESIGN OPPORTUNITIES: WORKING WITH CONTEXTUAL EMOTIONS

Once you recognize that you can work with emotions from the wider context, not just those elicited by the product itself, new design possibilities naturally open up. The following two opportunities show how you can use contextual emotions as a source of design inspiration.

Design Opportunity 1. Redesign an Existing Product: The intention of a redesign is to improve the product. Similar to the process we followed to redesign the airline breakfast, you map the emotions experienced in the context of use and use those as a source of inspiration.

An inspiring example is *Forest* (see image 4.4), a creative reinvention of traditional desk dividers used in classrooms to support children with ADHD. Think of it as a tiny study booth, about 35 cm high—a minimalist cubicle with three neutral grey panes (two at the sides, one at the front) that block out the visual bustle of the classroom. It is placed on a desk when focus is needed.

Shion noticed that the existing barriers served their function well: they reduced distractions. But when observing the classroom dynamics, he saw something else. The children were at their happiest when they felt connected to their peers, even during individual work. The joy of being part of a group stood out in every classroom interaction. This contextual emotion sparked a new direction. With *Forest*, he transformed a standard desk partition into an interactive, customizable landscape of wooden trees, animals, and plants. Students create their own miniature "forests" to manage visual distractions without losing their sense of being part of a community. By enabling children to personalize their workspace and collaborate in shaping these micro-landscapes, Forest turns a solitary experience into a shared, joyful interaction. The pieces vary in size and shape, allowing children to adjust their forest to match their momentary needs for focus or connection. Rather than simply shielding children from their environment, Forest provides subtle seclusion while also reinforcing a sense of inclusion, community, and shared enjoyment.

Design Opportunity 2. Start From the Situation: The second design opportunity resembles the first, but with one key difference: you use a situation, not a product, as your starting point. The goal is to design something meaningful for that situation, something that introduces positive emotions or helps reduce negative ones. Since the starting point is the lived context, contextual emotions are your most natural guide.

4.5 Street Debater by Tomo Kihara

This approach is vividly illustrated by two student projects. The first is the *Street Debater* (see image 4.5). While walking through Paris, Tomo noticed the strained interactions between people asking for money and those passing by. These exchanges were often awkward and dehumanizing. Determined to improve the emotional quality of these encounters, he immersed himself in the setting, spending time on the streets of several European cities and speaking with people who relied on donations to get by. Together, they explored interactions that are more positive and human. This resulted in the *Street Debater*, which turns a stigmatized situation into something public, participatory, and even joyful.

Street Debater is a portable wooden scale with two trays, each representing a different opinion. It comes with a board upon which the host/user writes a "question of the day." People walking by are invited to vote by placing coins in one of the trays, tipping the scale, and showing which opinion is in the lead. The person hosting the setup earns money not by appealing to pity but by sparking curiosity, debate, and small moments of engagement.

4.6 Bond by Mirjam de Korte

The second example is *Bond* (see image 4.6). For children visiting a hospital emergency room, the experience can feel like a frightening whirlwind of unfamiliar faces and flickering machines. Seeking to ease their anxiety, Mirjam found inspiration in an overlooked object: the hospital wristband. Every patient gets one of these purely functional objects upon arrival. But what if it could become the starting point of an adventure? Her design transforms the wristband into a passport to a miniature safari, where every hospital interaction becomes a moment of discovery. Each medical professional becomes a friendly exotic animal, a Nurse Elephant or a Doctor Tiger, wearing colorful badges to signal their new wild identities. The child receives a safari booklet and sets off on a mini-adventure through the hospital. Every time a nurse or doctor completes their examination, the child earns an animal sticker for their wristband. Gradually, the band fills with a cheerful menagerie. Back home, the wristband can be slipped into the booklet and become a souvenir. What begins as a coldly clinical, often distressing environment is transformed into a lighthearted place of discovery—one filled with clear roles, playful rituals, and small, shared triumphs.

What's particularly insightful about this case is that it demonstrates a key insight: even when you start from a situation and not an existing product, you may still end up redesigning a product used in that context. But the path you take and the needs you address will be shaped by the emotional contours of the context.

THEORETICAL DEEP DIVE

Interacting Emotions

In this book, we describe emotions as discrete responses, each linked to a triggering event and an underlying need. That framing is helpful, but it doesn't capture the dynamic interplay of emotional experience. Emotions don't operate in isolation. They influence one another. The following two questions allow for a deeper dive into the interactive nature of human emotions.

How do emotions influence each other?
Psychologists have described several ways in which emotions interact over time. These patterns show how emotions influence not only what you feel, but also how you make sense of what you feel. While there is no single theory that explains every dynamic, most patterns fall into four recurring types.

1. *Resolution: when one emotion replaces another:* Elena sits in a hospital corridor, anxiety tightening her chest as she waits for news about her daughter's surgery. When the doctor appears and says, "Everything went perfectly," her relief doesn't add to her anxiety—it replaces it. The worry that had consumed her just moments earlier now feels distant. This is *resolution*: a new emotion provides information that directly counters the basis of a prior emotion.[1] Resolution can work both positively and negatively. Mei, thrilled by the prospect of a long-awaited concert, receives news that it's been canceled. Her excitement cannot linger. It vanishes. Disappointment is the only emotion that makes sense now. As the situation changed, the appraisal changed, and with it, the emotional response.

2. *Spillover: when past emotions color the present:* Marcus receives harsh criticism during a morning meeting. Hours later, at dinner in his favorite restaurant, he finds himself irritated for no clear reason. The music, the waiter's small talk, even the taste of his usual dish seems off. Nothing about the restaurant has changed. However, his appraisal of it has been colored by the residue of his earlier emotions: this is *spillover*.[2] Emotional responses bleed from one situation into our experience of unrelated events. Lingering emotions don't respect boundaries; they seep into new situations, shifting how we interpret what would otherwise feel neutral. Spillover also works for positive emotions. After getting a promotion, Isaac notices that his commute feels more pleasant. The sunset seems richer, the city more alive. The commute hasn't changed—his emotional outlook has.

3. Amplification: when one emotion heightens the next: Carlos, a graduate student, feels a flicker of nervousness before his presentation. As he steps to the podium, he drops his notes. A small embarrassment, but it causes his emotions to spiral. His anxiety deepens. His voice starts to shake. His mind goes blank at a transition he knew perfectly an hour ago. Each stumble hits harder. A minor emotional state has turned into a self-reinforcing loop. This is *amplification.*[3] One emotion increases your reactivity to new emotional input, making you susceptible to emotional escalation. You become primed to interpret events in line with the dominant emotion. Even mild tension can make you more reactive, priming you to interpret new events as threatening. Positive spirals work the same way. Jamal is mildly pleased to get a coffee discount. A kind word from the barista lifts him further. A good-news text from a friend tips him into full-blown joy. Each small moment builds on the last. It's not the size of each event—it's how the first one sets the tone.

4. Transformation: when new information reshapes a feeling: Ahmed feels anger when another driver cuts him off in traffic. At the next light, he sees that the other driver is an elderly woman, clearly confused and distressed. His pounding heart remains, but his anger changes into concern. The situation hasn't changed, but his understanding of it has. This is *transformation.*[4] It happens when new information leads us to reappraise a situation. It's not just that a new emotion replaces the old; the new emotions are qualitatively different. The original one becomes inappropriate in light of a new interpretation. Transformations can change an emotion from negative to positive and vice versa. The joy of receiving a gift might shift to guilt upon learning the giver is in financial trouble. Disappointment over a canceled outing might become relief after learning about the severe weather warnings that would have made travel dangerous.

What is the purpose of emotions influencing one another?

Emotions help you respond to what matters in the moment, pointing your attention toward your most pressing needs. Emotions influencing one another might seem counterproductive. Why muddy the signal? Shouldn't each emotion stand alone, clearly tied to its trigger, so you can act on it without confusion?

This kind of emotional interplay isn't a bug in the system—it's a feature.[5] As discussed earlier, emotions arise from appraisals: moment-to-moment evaluations of what a situation means for our needs. The power of appraisals is that they aren't set in stone. They're fluid and revisable as new information comes in. Studies show that appraisals update in real time as new information becomes available.[6] The system seeks coherence. Rather than holding two conflicting appraisals in parallel, it revises earlier ones in light of the latest input.

The iterative reprocessing model explains how this works.[7] Emotional appraisals cycle through fast, automatic loops and slower, more reflective ones. Each round refines the previous one by integrating new information—context, memory, social cues. In other words, your emotional processing system operates on a temporal continuum, with evaluations becoming increasingly refined as it integrates more information from diverse sources through multiple processing cycles.

This capacity for revision is essential: it allows the system to adapt to evolving situations. It's efficient: rather than generate a new response from scratch, it updates what is already in play. It's socially adept: it absorbs subtle cues that help shift how you interpret your environment. Most importantly, it keeps emotional life coherent. You're not reacting to isolated incidents; you're building a story. Without this system, you'd be emotionally fragmented, reacting to each moment separately, unable to adjust. A stressful encounter earlier in the day would cling to you unprocessed, unaffected by later reassurance or context. Every emotion would remain as it first appeared—regardless of what followed.

1. Gross (1998); Miller, Kiverstein, and Rietveld (2022); Ochsner and Gross (2005).
2. Lapate et al. (2017); Pakman (2006).
3. Goldenberg et al. (2020).
4. Hoemann et al. (2021).
5. Cunningham and Zelazo (2007); Kuppens and Verduyn (2017).
6. Barrett and Satpute (2019); Ellsworth and Scherer (2003).
7. Cunningham et al. (2007).

5

Clashing NEEDS

5.1 What we were watching in 1965 and 2010

First: the familiar gong. Then: "Good evening. This is the eight o'clock news."

This simple greeting has opened the Netherlands' most-watched news broadcast for decades. The Dutch National News Broadcast (NOS) has been an institution since 1964, consistently drawing the country's highest television ratings since its inception. Like many in the Netherlands, we grew up with it. For generations, it has been the trusted source of news for millions of viewers who tune in every evening at eight o'clock.

While the NOS's credibility as a news source had remained unquestioned, by the early 2010s, its broadcast format was beginning to feel dated: a news anchor methodically reading items from a teleprompter while footage played on a screen behind them. The coverage was reliable and authoritative, but also rigid and austere. Meanwhile, the media landscape was shifting, with commercial news channels gaining ground. While some news programs emulated the public broadcaster's timeworn approach, others opted for snappier, more entertainment-focused formats.

The NOS approached us with an intriguing proposal: could we help shape a new vision for its future by analyzing the emotions the daily news program evoked? It was a challenge that seemed well suited to the methods we've been exploring in the book. At first glance, the brief appeared straightforward: identify the emotions viewers experienced, ladder to their underlying needs, and recommend changes that would better fulfill these needs. One strict condition raised the bar: our recommendations could only impact the presentation—the studio, the anchor's delivery, and the audiovisual element—not the journalistic content of the news. The editorial team operated entirely independently and was responsible for maintaining the stellar journalistic standards that had made the broadcast a trusted source of information for decades.

As we began interviewing viewers, something fascinating emerged. Their responses revealed seemingly contradictory needs about their evening news experience. They wanted their news to be detailed yet broad in scope, authoritative yet entertaining, and nuanced yet clear. And this wasn't merely a case of different viewers wanting different things; we found that individual viewers held contradictory desires all at once.

Here was a situation we had not explicitly encountered before: people holding two or more competing needs that seemed to pull them in opposite directions. When we first noticed this pattern, which we now call a *clash in needs*, we assumed it might be unique to certain domains, as in the news industry. But as our research expanded across products, services, and contexts —from workplace design to healthcare to personal relationships—the same pattern kept appearing.

Needs clash everywhere. What's more, when they clash, there is a golden opportunity for innovation. A clash in needs signifies two ideal conditions for creative breakthroughs: a clear problem and unexplored territory for new solutions. This principle is expressed by the fifth law of emotional design.

THE FIFTH LAW OF EMOTIONAL DESIGN

Clashing user needs present both design tensions and innovation opportunities

Stay tuned for a closer look at how we helped reshape the evening news. Right now, we take a closer look at how needs clash and how clashes can be transformed from frustrating dilemmas into exciting design opportunities.

The Hidden Tensions in Everyday Choices

Picture yourself shopping for a new phone: you want the largest screen possible so you can watch videos and browse photos, but you also want the phone to fit comfortably in your pocket. Or imagine planning dinner: you want to cook a healthy, homemade meal, but you also want to spend the evening relaxing with your family instead of rushing around the kitchen. Both are everyday examples of clashing needs.

In previous chapters, we've explored how products and services can be improved by identifying unfulfilled needs and designing with those needs in mind. For clarity, we've treated needs as if they were independent islands, each one calling for its own solution. But in reality, needs don't exist in isolation; they are multiple and interconnected. Since these needs arise together in product and service use, they can come into tension with one another. People often need multiple things simultaneously—but in practice, they may only satisfy one, partially meet a few others, and leave some unfulfilled.

The essence of clashing needs can be expressed in a simple structure: *"I want X, but I also want Y."* This might remind you of the need statements we explored in Chapter 4, but with a crucial difference: now there are two needs—separated by a "but"—and they pull in different directions.

Design that Creates Clashing Needs

Needs don't just clash due to life's complexity or a person's internal contradictions. The clash can also come from the very products and services designed to make our lives better. Sometimes, a design solves one problem but creates another by unintentionally sparking new tensions within. This dynamic is easiest to see in products that take the fulfillment of a single need to the extreme. In Chapter 1, we explored thirteen chairs (pages 33-35), each designed to excel at fulfilling one particular fundamental need. But looking at them through the lens of clashing needs reveals something interesting: most of the chairs end up compromising other needs in the process.

Take the *Body* chair. The long, rice-filled cushion offers ultimate Autonomy—you can shape it to support any position you like. But that same flexibility clashes with the need for Ease: you have to work up a sweat just to cajole it into a shape you can actually sit on. Or consider the Vismara Luxor Tech, engineered for maximum Ease with its cooled cup holder, charging station, and backrest that leans back at the push of a button. While it excels at convenience and comfort, it may compromise the needs for Fitness (by promoting inactivity) and Recognition (by projecting utter couch-potato energy). Then there's the *Hush* pod. Designed to shield you from the outside world, it delivers a strong sense of Security, but at the cost of Relatedness—try striking up a conversation with someone who is literally cocooned.

These unintended frictions are more common than we often realize. When you start looking through the lens of clashing needs, you'll spot them everywhere.

Take the standing desk. It has a surprisingly long history—Leonardo da Vinci reportedly used one while sketching his inventions. The modern comeback was driven by a new mantra, "Sitting is the new smoking." Standing desks deliver real benefits: better posture, more energy, and a healthier lifestyle. But after the initial standing ovations accompanying their launch, fatigue set in—literally. Users reported sore feet and aching legs. A classic clash in needs: the long-term desire for health colliding with the short-term need for comfort.

This dynamic isn't limited to physical products. Many digital and consumer electronics products reveal similar tensions in their users. In 2015, Apple set out to make its MacBook thinner and more elegant than ever before. The result was a complete keyboard redesign featuring a "butterfly" mechanism—a new type of key shape that hardly moved when pressed. The result looked elegant and helped slim down the laptop, but it came at a cost. Many users found the typing experience stiff and unsatisfying. A design that excelled at fulfilling the need for sophisticated aesthetics ended up compromising the need for comfort.[1]

Some of the most striking examples of clashing needs show up in digital products, where the consequences of optimization can be far-reaching. YouTube's "Up Next" recommendation algorithm, introduced in 2012, was designed to maximize user engagement by suggesting personalized content after each video. It worked remarkably well—too well. Users found themselves watching longer than intended, sometimes for hours, their need for entertainment fulfilled at the expense of their need for Autonomy and Competence. There were other consequences, too. The algorithm's relentless pursuit of engagement could amplify sensational or misleading content, clashing with users' needs for reliable information and meaningful experiences. What began as a tool for discovery gradually evolved into a system capable of eroding attention, distorting trust, and reshaping how people relate to the world around them.[2]

Once you notice the pattern, it's hard to unsee: multi-factor authentication provides online security but disrupts workflow; endless photo libraries preserve memories while diluting their meaning; fitness trackers boost motivation yet undermine a sense of agency. These aren't fringe cases; they're part of how design works.

Design that Resolves Clashing Needs

The good news is products don't just create clashes in needs. They can also resolve them. When carefully designed with a deep understanding of usage situations, products can help users navigate trade-offs that once seemed impossible to reconcile. In fact, many of the products and services we now take for granted began as clever solutions to exactly this kind of tension.

Consider a simple flowerpot. It might seem unremarkable, but it elegantly resolves a clash of two needs: "I want to bring nature into my home, but I also want to keep my home clean and tidy." The pot contains the soil while

1. The poor typing experience wasn't the only issue. The butterfly mechanism proved to be extremely sensitive to dust and debris, leading to widespread reliability issues. In hindsight, introducing the butterfly keyboard became one of Apple's most controversial design decisions. The mechanism was phased out between 2019 and 2020.

2. Digital platforms—especially those designed to maximize "engagement"—create a clash in needs that has been studied extensively. These platforms offer people immediate pleasures (entertainment, novelty, a quick dopamine hit) while often undermining fundamental needs such as Autonomy, Competence, and Purpose. For an analysis, see Sahebi and Formosa (2022).

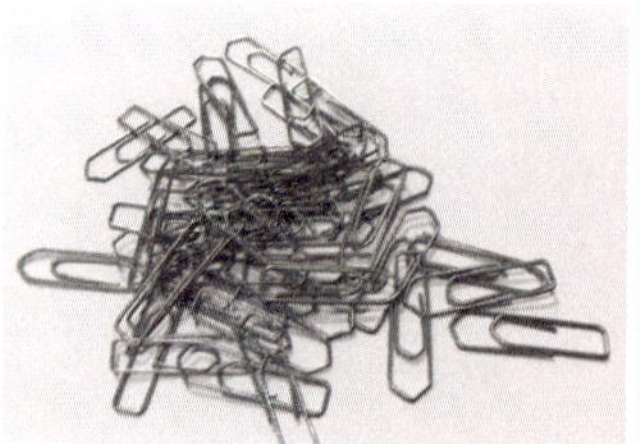

5.2 Resolving everyday clashes in needs

complementing the plant's aesthetic appeal. Or take something even more modest: the paperclip. Its design is so understated that it's easy to overlook the ingenuity behind it. The most familiar version is the Gem clip, which was first introduced in the 1870s. It addresses a subtle clash in needs: "I want to keep papers together, but I also want to keep them intact and be able to separate them easily." It's a solution without glue, staples, or damage—just tension and clever bending.

These are two product examples, but many services are specifically designed to address clashing needs. Take library click-and-collect systems. Public libraries have long offered open access to rich collections of books. Traditionally, borrowing books requires visiting in person during limited opening hours. As daily life became more digital and time-constrained, that model began to clash with new expectations: "I want the depth and serendipity of a library, but I also want the speed and convenience of online ordering." Click-and-collect services emerged as a practical solution: you browse the catalog online, reserve titles, and pick them up at a time that suits you.

Just as these products and services were once clever innovations that solved previously unresolved clashes, today's world is full of clashing needs still waiting for creative solutions. This chapter offers a systematic approach to identifying and resolving them. But first, let's explore the different types of clashes we might encounter.

The Anatomy of Clashes in Needs

A clash in needs can take many forms. While all clashes share the same basic structure—"I want X, but I also want Y"—they differ in important ways. To understand and address them effectively, we'll look at two factors that shape the character of a clash in needs: the *nature* of the clash and the *kinds of needs* involved.

The Nature of a Clash

Why are the needs in clash mutually exclusive? Either because the situation in which they come up puts them in opposition (situational clashes) or because they both require the same, limited resource (resource-based clashes). Let's explore these in turn.

In *situational clashes*, fulfilling one need means shutting the door for the other need because of the particulars of the situation. For example, imagine a colleague, someone you get along with well, asking for feedback on their performance in a project, which you happen to think was poor. This could spark a clash: "I want to be honest with my colleague about her performance, but I also want to maintain our friendly working relationship." There is no inherent conflict between being honest and being on good terms with someone, but this particular situation brings those two needs into conflict. Or consider another clash: "I want to protect the environment, but I also want to travel to other countries." Again, these needs aren't fundamentally opposing—the tension arises from the practical reality that most forms of travel, whether by air, rail, or car, have an environmental cost.

The second type is the *resource-based clash*. These occur when both needs draw from the same limited resource. Resources can be all sorts of things, but they are typically time, money, attention, or effort. "I want to relax after this long day, but I should also finish the chores piling up at home," is a good example. Here, time is the limited resource being contested. Another example is, "I want to save for my vacation, but I also want to enjoy a night out with my friends." In this case, money is the resource. "I want to have a good talk with my brother, but I should also keep an eye on my children." Here, attention is the limited resource that cannot simultaneously serve both needs. In each case, the needs are not really in opposition—there is simply not enough time, money, or attention to fulfill both.

The Battle Between Goals, Values, Urges, and Preferences

It is also insightful to look at the individual needs in a clash. In Chapter 4, we explored four types of specific human needs: goals, urges, values, and preferences. When these different need types come into conflict with one another, they create distinctive patterns. Let's explore the six most common combinations that produce clashes we encounter in design challenges.

1. *When good competes with good*

2. *Two rights make one wrong*

3. *Personal gain at moral cost*

4. *Willpower in the moment*

1. Aspiration Clash: Goal vs. Goal

You're working at home, and it's getting late. You want to finish a project because it could really help your career. But you also promised your kids you'd play a game with them tonight. There's only so much time in a day, and both goals matter to you.

Aspiration clashes occur when two goals a person genuinely cares about compete for the same resource. These clashes can also be situational. For example, you want your children to eat healthy food, but you also want dinner to be a pleasant family moment. When your Brussels sprouts are met with loud groans, you're forced to negotiate between providing good nutrition and enjoying dinnertime harmony.

What makes these clashes difficult is that neither goal is wrong—letting go of either can feel like failure or even betrayal.

2. Ethics Clash: Value vs. Value

Your close colleague calls in sick, but you happen to know he's actually partying at a festival. You also know that his team will have to work overtime to cover for his absence. You feel his action is deeply unfair, but you also value loyalty. Do you report your colleague or keep silent? This is a clash between the values of justice and loyalty, each pointing toward a different course of action.

Other examples of values that are likely to come into conflict are courage versus prudence (opting for bold action or for careful consideration of risk), acceptance versus ambition (being content with what you have or striving for more), and spontaneity versus discipline (living in the moment or honoring long-term commitments)

But in practice, any two values can come into conflict, depending on the situation. Imagine that your parents' political views diverge sharply from yours. When the conversation turns to politics during a family gathering, you may experience a dilemma between voicing your unfiltered opinion (authenticity) and respecting your parents' perspective (harmony and respect).

Ethics clashes can create genuine inner conflict because they force you to choose a course of action that violates at least one of your deeply held values.

3. Integrity Clash: Goal vs. Value

A new opportunity arises for a promotion—one that only you and one of your colleagues are eligible for. The deadline is today. Do you keep silent and submit your application, or do you inform your colleague and risk your chances? This exemplifies an integrity clash—when a personal goal comes in conflict with a moral value.

Many integrity clashes play out in social settings, like wanting to skip to the front of a checkout line but choosing not to out of a belief in fairness. Others occur privately, like wanting to work on a personal project instead of studying, despite valuing academic responsibility.

5. Impulse challenges the inner compass

6. Best intentions or sweet comfort

What makes these clashes distinctive is the internal conversation they trigger between what we want to achieve and what we believe is the right thing to do. That is why these are called integrity clashes—they test whether a person's actions align with their principles.

4. Temptation Clash: Urge vs. Goal

Let's say someone in your department is celebrating their birthday and brings cake for everyone.[3] It's a red velvet cake–your favorite. But only two days ago, you decided to go on a diet. Can you resist the temptation?

Or, imagine it's nearly midnight, and you're curled up on the couch. You've been trying to get more sleep, but the next episode starts in five seconds. Just one more? These are temptation clashes—when immediate impulses conflict with longer-term objectives.

What makes temptation clashes so universal is their connection to human evolutionary history.[4] The human brain is wired to prioritize immediate rewards over distant benefits, which is why the immediate pleasure of cake

3. In the Netherlands (and some other Northern European countries), the birthday person brings the treats. It keeps us humble.

4. This tendency is well documented in research on "temporal discounting"—our inclination to devalue future rewards in favor of immediate ones. For a recent discussion, see Villmoare et al. (2024).

today so often wins out over the abstract benefit of health tomorrow. Most people rationally favor their goals when discussing temptation clashes. But in a heated moment, it is usually people's urges pulling the strings because satisfying an urge offers immediate gratification while fulfilling a goal requires patience and persistence.[5]

5. Decency Clash: Urge vs. Value

You're alone on an open highway. The road curves gently ahead, not a car in sight. You feel the pull to floor the accelerator, to let the engine roar, and find out what your car can really do. However, something holds you back: your commitment to driving safely and your principles about adhering to the law.

Or perhaps you're hanging out with friends, and one of them says something that begs for a perfectly timed, cutting joke. You've got it locked and loaded, but your deeper value of kindness makes you swallow the quip.

Such clashes reveal the tension between spontaneous desires and internal rules and principles: your sense of decency is at stake. Similar to clashes that call your integrity into question, they test your adherence to your values, but with the added challenge that urges are often more powerful and less rational than goals. The momentary thrill of speeding or the emotional release of a sharp comment can feel irresistible, even when you know these actions contradict your values.

6. Convenience Clash: Goal vs. Preference

You want to do some arts and crafts with your kids to stimulate their creative skills, which you genuinely value. You're thinking something along the lines of tidy and civilized, like drawing. But they're set on clay modeling, which you inwardly loathe because of the mess it spreads all over the house.

Or perhaps you want to exercise regularly for your health, but you hate waking up early and can't stand getting sweaty before breakfast. Both are examples of convenience clashes—when meaningful objectives conflict with personal preferences you're reluctant to negotiate with.

What distinguishes convenience clashes is the way they set future-oriented wishes against an appetite for immediate comfort. Unlike temptation clashes, which involve strong urges, convenience clashes hinge on milder preferences yet still create friction with a person's goals. They don't typically lead to outright abandonment of the goal, but they do invite delay, resistance, or endless procrastination, making them subtle but persistent obstacles in people's daily lives.

5. Özkaramanlı, Özcan, and Desmet (2017) explored these self-control dilemmas in depth, proposing that designers can facilitate long-term goal pursuit by making potential losses of temptations tangible, creating barriers to temptation, or adding new sources of displeasure to temptations. Alternatively, they can motivate long-term goals by making their potential gains tangible, creating enablers, or adding other sources of pleasure to them.

When You Know You're Torn—And When You Don't

When the Clash Is Felt

When people consciously experience a clash in needs and must choose between different courses of action, we call this a *dilemma*. Consider this morning quandary: do I get up now and arrive at work in time to calmly prepare for the morning meeting, or do I steal another half hour of much-needed sleep and show up just in time, unprepared and counting on my improvisation skills?

A dilemma involves two needs and a clear, decisive moment when you must prioritize one at the expense of the other. Dilemmas are always accompanied by emotions because choosing to fulfill one need (triggering a positive emotion) inevitably means sacrificing another need (triggering a negative emotion). Schematically, dilemmas can be visualized as in image 5.3.

There's a special relationship between the positive emotion from one need and the negative emotion from the other: they are counterparts. If you get out of bed exhausted, you feel discomfort. If you stay in bed, you feel comfort. If you arrive well-prepared for the meeting (having foregone extra sleep), you feel pleased with yourself. If you show up unprepared (having chosen sleep), you feel embarrassed. This is what makes it a dilemma—each option implies a reward *and* a consequence, both of which are represented by different emotions.

Dilemmas are an excellent starting point for design.[6] A powerful example is the birth control pill, introduced in the early 1960s. It addressed a deeply felt tension: "I want to practice my sexuality freely, but I also want to avoid unintended pregnancy." Before the pill, this was a key dilemma—especially for women—forcing couples to choose between intimacy and control, desire and risk. The pill resolved this conflict by giving users reliable reproductive control without limiting their sexual freedom. It redefined the relationship between sexuality, responsibility, and independence. More than sixty years later, it remains one of the most transformative design interventions in everyday life.[7]

When the Clash Is Hidden

The format of need clash statements ("I want X, but I also want Y") might suggest that every clash is experienced as a dilemma—that users always feel tension between competing needs and must consciously choose between them at specific moments. But most clashes in needs are not consciously experienced and

6. The concept of designing for dilemmas has been developed in the doctoral research of Deger Özkaramanlı (2017). Özkaramanlı, Desmet, and Özcan (2016) give a good introduction into the theoretical foundation and methodological approaches to dilemmas.

7. The psychological, cultural, and societal impact of the birth control pill has been widely documented. See Marks (2001) and Watkins (1998).

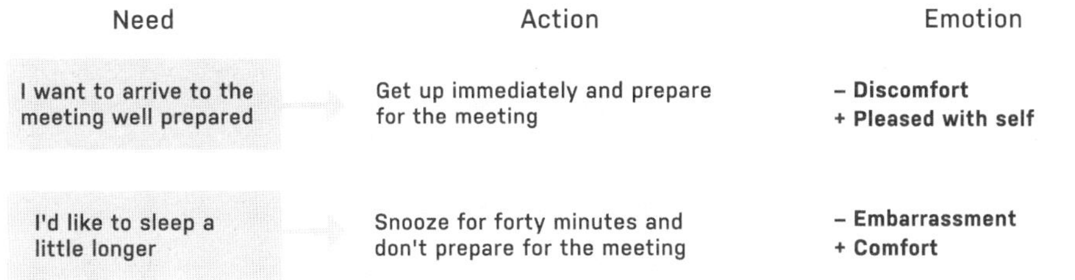

5.3 Dilemma: to hit or not to hit the snooze button?

therefore cannot be directly asked about in user interviews. Later in this chapter, we'll show you how you can detect these hidden tensions.

Design history is full of examples where a hidden clash in needs sparked a breakthrough. Take the iPad: think back to 2010, right before it was introduced. People had smartphones with small screens and laptops that were heavier and had shorter battery life than what we are used to today. Smartphones were used for messaging and quick browsing; laptops were the go-to for work and more elaborate tasks.

Apple had identified an unrecognized clash: people wanted a simple, lightweight device they could use to conduct personal matters and light work tasks while relaxing on the couch—yet they also wanted a larger screen and expanded capabilities. The first set of needs was met by existing smartphones, and the second by laptops. No single product satisfied both. However, few people had experienced these competing needs as a dilemma. If asked, they likely wouldn't have framed it in that way. Users simply alternated between devices—not because it was ideal, but because they accepted it as the natural order of things. This helps explain the initial skepticism about the iPad's value. Many dismissed it as "just a big iPod Touch" and questioned whether anyone actually needed it.[8] But Steve Jobs' vision proved accurate. The iPad gave users the experience of a truly "home" computer: it could be used from the couch and easily carried around for impromptu information checks and longer browsing sessions. It resolved a clash in needs many users didn't even know they had.

The iPad story is well known, but good examples of hidden clashes can also be found in far simpler inventions. Take Breaker, a portable yogurt on the Dutch market designed for people on the move. When it was introduced, it addressed a common but rarely articulated tension: "I want to eat a proper breakfast, but I also want to do it while walking, biking, or standing in a crowded train." Before Breaker, most people didn't experience this as a clash in needs. They

8. The initial skepticism surrounding the iPad is nicely captured in a 2010 Wired magazine poll of over 1,100 readers. Alongside widespread critique of the name—sounding more pharmaceutical than digital—71% of the respondents reported being perfectly content with their existing devices and saw no need for a tablet (Ganapati, 2010).

5.4 When visionaries spot the clashing needs that users haven't articulated

simply skipped breakfast or reached for convenience foods. But the design team spotted the latent clash and responded with a small but clever intervention. In the early 2000s, they launched the country's first yogurt in a squeeze pouch: a full breakfast you could eat with one hand: no spoon, no spill. By resolving the clashing needs that few users would have been able to articulate, Breaker carved out a new product category and has remained the market leader in the Netherlands for nearly 25 years.

These examples show that new products can resolve clashes even when users don't consciously experience them as dilemmas. Even if people are aware of some of their needs, often thanks to their emotions, they don't necessarily make the connection between various needs or recognize when their needs conflict.

You can identify these hidden clashes by carefully observing how people use products and noting where their needs seem constrained (see Chapter 3). While they take more effort to spot, non-conscious clashes typically offer greater innovation potential than visible dilemmas precisely because they're less present in the users' minds. There's a greater chance that no one has previously noticed these hidden tensions, let alone addressed them.

Putting Clashes on the Map

You can visualize how products handle clashing needs using a 2-dimensional plot (see image 5.5). The axes represent the fulfillment of Need X and Need Y, ranging from completely unsatisfied to completely satisfied. Points on the plot correspond to available solutions, with their positions indicating how well they fulfill each of the two needs.

To interpret a plot like this, it helps to look at the quadrants. The upper right, shaded in light green, is the domain of the most promising solutions: designs that successfully support both needs. The solutions in the top-right corner are rare but ideal: they avoid trade-offs and, instead, resolve the tension at the heart of the clash. In contrast, the bottom left quadrant (shaded in

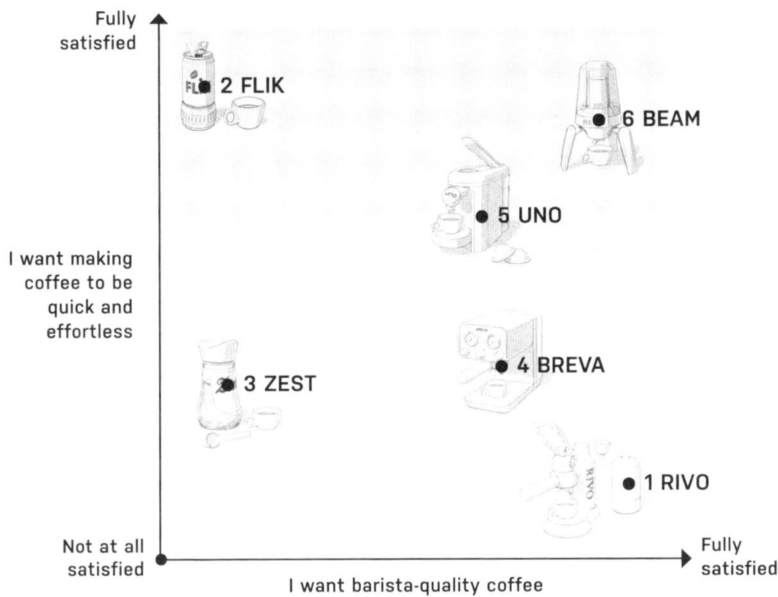

5.5 A need clash plot with six coffee solutions

red) contains the weakest options: those that fall short on both needs.[9] The remaining quadrants, shaded in grey, represent one-sided solutions: they do well on one need but compromise the other.

Let's illustrate this with an example. You've been loyal to your local barista for years. The espresso is spot-on, and the small talk reliably tolerable. But lately, you've started wondering if you're a little too dependent on your daily routine. The queue and high price grate on you. A plan emerges: the time has come for good coffee options at home, at least some of the time. But what would that look like? What product should you choose? You have two primal needs as your guides: "I want barista-level quality" and "I want making coffee to be quick and effortless."

There are plenty of options out there—machines, gadgets, powders, pods, cans—each offering a different balance of quality and convenience. Some lean hard into simplicity. Others demand more effort in return for better results. The question is: which option fits your needs best? Let's have a closer look at six possible solutions in the inset. The numbers correspond to points on the need clash plot.

If coffee quality and convenience were truly the only needs that mattered (beyond practical concerns related to cost and counter space), then BEAM (6) would be the ideal solution. It sits alone in the upper right corner: ultra-high-quality,

9. This doesn't necessarily mean they're poorly designed; they might still be strong from a technical, aesthetic, or commercial perspective. It simply means they don't address this particular clash in needs effectively.

ultra-convenient. The worst solution would be ZEST (3), the instant option. It's neither satisfying nor seamless: it's a hassle to make, and the result tastes like liquid cardboard.

The plot shows two other solutions that are less than ideal for different reasons. RIVO (1) makes near-perfect coffee but demands time, technique, a dedicated workflow, plus a whole lot of cleaning. FLIK (2) is the opposite: minimal effort but also minimal flavor. Both represent classic trade-offs—winning on one front, losing on the other.

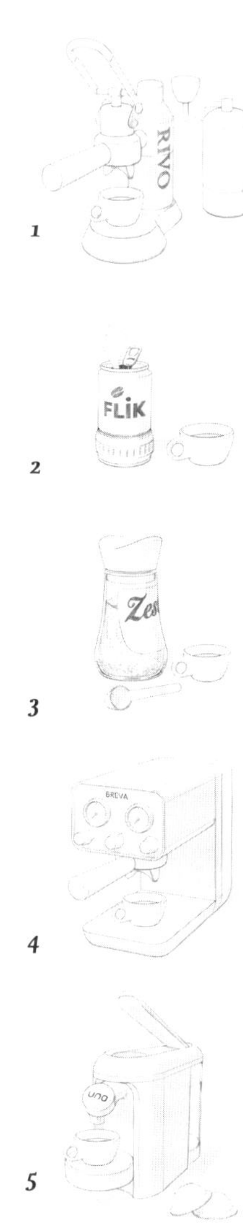

1) RIVO – A set of professional espresso tools that includes a manual grinder, tamper, and lever-based machine, designed for hands-on preparation with full control over every brewing variable.

2) FLIK – A sealed can of ready-to-drink coffee with built-in self-heating technology, activated by twisting the base to trigger a thermal reaction that warms the beverage within minutes.

3) ZEST – A dehydrated coffee product in powdered form, packaged in a jar and prepared by manually spooning it into hot water, requiring users to measure, mix, and adjust to taste.

4) BREVA – A compact home espresso machine that automates temperature and pressure but requires manual input for grinding and tamping, blending control with programmable features.

5) UNO – A countertop coffee system that brews using single-serve pods, activated by one-touch operation and designed to produce consistent espresso shots with little effort.

6) BEAM – A fully automatic, AI-powered device that uses micro-batch coffee cartridges and ultrasonic brewing to extract flavor from freshly ground beans, offering café-quality results with zero effort.

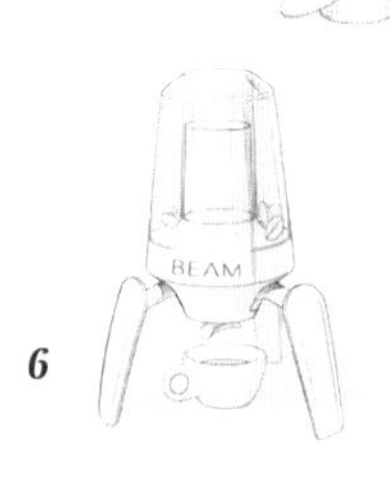

BREVA (4) and UNO (5) land somewhere in the middle. They offer different strengths: one leans towards higher quality, the other towards greater ease, but their overall balance is similar. They offer similar levels of combined need fulfillment, meaning that the sum of X and Y is roughly the same. From a purely quantitative perspective, UNO offers a slightly better trade-off, assuming that both needs carry equal weight.[10] But preferences aren't always evenly split. If quality outweighs ease for you, you might favor BREVA over UNO.

10. You could quantify need fulfillment to make such calculations, but this is not something we do or recommend. It would require you to reduce emotions and needs to numbers in a way that conflicts with their holistic and qualitative nature, as we discussed in Chapters 2 and 3. The need clash plot is meant as a conceptual tool to illustrate trade-offs in need fulfillment. The placement of the solutions is based on qualitative judgment.

Of course, this is a simplified case. In real-life decisions, many other needs (sustainability, maintenance, aesthetics, price) will also come into play. These cannot be captured in a two-dimensional plot, but the principle holds: when you isolate two conflicting needs, visualizing the trade-offs can help clarify where design can make a real difference.

Designing a Newsroom That Feels Like a Story

The Eight 'O Clock News presented a clear tension: how do we design a news broadcast that feels both trustworthy and engaging, both serious enough to inform and compelling enough to hold attention? After talking to news viewers, we summarized their core clashing needs as follows:

"I want the TV news to be a complete and nuanced account of today's important events, delivered objectively by trusted anchors, but I also want the news program to be captivating and entertaining enough for me to sit through the full broadcast."

This was a situational clash between two goals. There's nothing inherently contradictory about news being both nuanced and objective while also being captivating and entertaining. The clash arose because viewers were used to choosing between public-service broadcasts, which focused on the first set of needs, and commercial broadcasts, which prioritized the second. Because topic selection and segment length and sequence remained under the control of the editorial team, our design freedom was limited to the presentation and framing of the news.

Here is what we proposed: one of the most fascinating aspects of news is its tremendous variety. Within a 20-minute broadcast, viewers might encounter a natural disaster in a distant country, a domestic political crisis, a literary award ceremony, a scientific breakthrough, and a sporting event. Each of these topics carries its own emotional tone, or "vibe." Each might be considered important, concerning, inspiring, or fascinating for a variety of reasons.

Rather than keeping these distinct emotional qualities at arm's length, we suggested "inviting them into the studio"—and, by extension, into the viewer's living room. Each item's distinctive quality would be reflected in the set design, the anchor's tone, and the presentation style. We also wanted to transform the role of the anchor from a neutral "teacher" distantly reporting on current events to a "travel guide" drawing the viewer into the story and enticing them to experience what has happened.

NOS embraced this vision enthusiastically. Editors, directors, and set designers worked together to create a revolutionary new format. The studio underwent a complete transformation. Instead of a single backdrop screen, multiple displays of various sizes were installed that were able to operate independently or combine into one large canvas (see image 5.6).

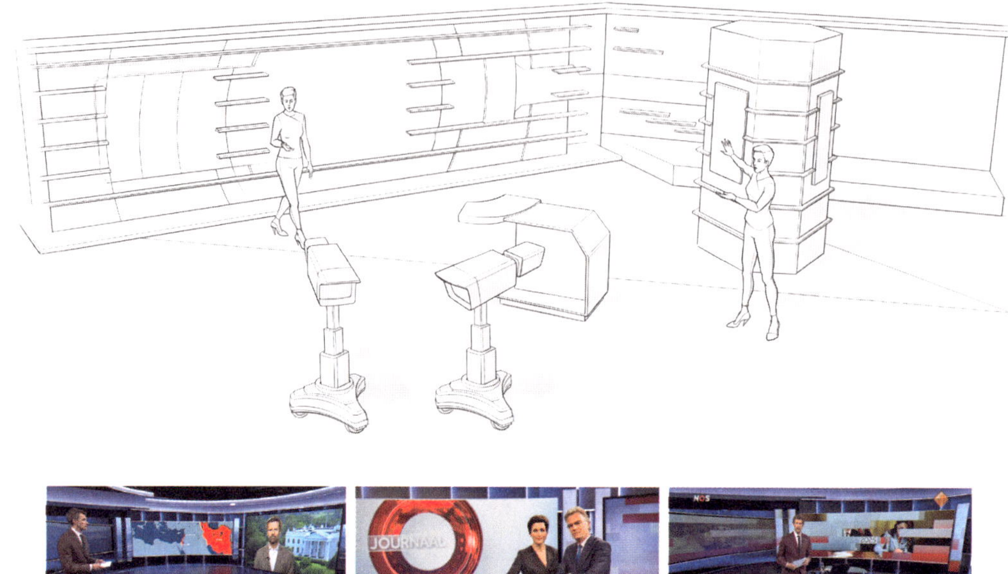

5.7 Presenting the news after the redesign

The most striking change: the news anchors no longer sat behind desks. They stood and moved through the space, the cameras moving with them. The anchors could reveal different parts of the display during a news item, quite literally unfolding the story across the visual space. For major news items, the full display system was used to convey scope and gravity. Lighter items used just a single screen, creating a visual rhythm and hierarchy that helped viewers intuitively grasp each story's relative weight.

When the new format debuted in 2012, it was shocking to many. The news program that had had the same look and feel for the past fifty years suddenly looked completely different. Viewers were stunned. "The anchor has legs!" Yet within months, both fans and critics agreed: this was the future of news presentation. Within a year, several commercial news programs had followed suit.

RESEARCH OPPORTUNITY: IDENTIFYING CLASHES IN NEEDS

Clashing needs represent some of the most promising opportunities for design innovation, but they require a systematic approach if you wish to uncover them effectively. To identify clashes, you need to start a comprehensive understanding of user needs within your specific design context. The User Need Capture (UNC) approach (Chapter 3) provides an excellent starting point. When you capture emotions during concrete user experiences and ladder to their underlying needs, you create the rich dataset necessary to spot clashing needs. The detailed guidelines for systematically identifying and documenting clashes in needs can be found in *Tools & Techniques*, pages 246-249.

DESIGN OPPORTUNITIES: TURNING TENSION INTO INNOVATION

Once you've identified a clash in needs, you can pursue several strategies to resolve it or, at the very least, improve the situation for users. The need clash plot in image 5.8 visualizes two different design directions.[11]

Design Opportunity 1. Resolve or Ease the Clash: The Holy Grail of need clash resolution is to create something that fully satisfies both needs, effectively eliminating the clash altogether. This places you in the upper-right corner of image 5.8 (marked "1A"). Even if that ideal is out of reach, there may still be a lot of room for innovation. A new product or service can introduce a better set of trade-offs than the existing solutions (marked "1B" in image 5.8). A good starting point is to place the existing products on the need clash plot to spot where better trade-offs are still waiting to be designed.

When you consider the four examples on page 138, you can see some clever trade-offs. Barefoot shoes offer a grounded, natural running sensation while still protecting your feet from sharp objects and hard surfaces. However, they neither provide the total freedom of going barefoot nor the full protection of traditional running shoes. Meal kits bring back the hands-on satisfaction of home cooking without the hassle of planning or grocery shopping. But they don't offer the complete convenience of takeout, nor the full creative freedom of designing your own meals from scratch.

The two other examples may exemplify what hitting the sweet spot looks like. A virtual coworking platform doesn't ask you to compromise. You have the full benefits of working at home and of social presence. The same may be true for non-alcoholic beer if the flavor is truly on par with the real thing.

The distinction between "sweet spot" and "trade-off" is fluid and can shift over time. If you remember the early non-alcoholic beer varieties, you'll probably agree that there were clear trade-offs involved in consuming them. However, as

11. These strategies build on the work of Özkaramanlı, Desmet, and Özcan (2016).

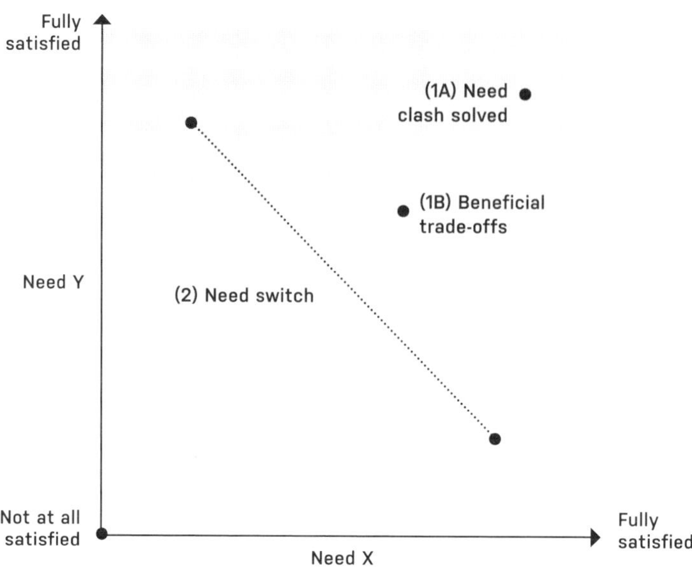

5.8 Two design opportunities to address clashing needs

their flavor has improved, they have moved closer to the upper right corner of the plot. The same could happen for other trade-off products, too. New materials might one day recreate the full sensation of running barefoot while providing complete protection, and AI could enable meal kits that adapt flexibly to your preferences and schedule.

How do you design to resolve a clash in needs? Start by exploring how you might fulfill need X and need Y individually, and then look for overlap between the two sets of solutions. We recommend to ladder both needs to uncover their deeper motivations (see Chapter 3). If Need X is framed as "I want a small car," and Need Y as "I want a big car," you'll never find overlap. But if you uncover the underlying reasons (maneuverability versus family comfort, for example) opportunities for reconciliation begin to emerge. In many cases, what first appeared to be mutually exclusive needs turn out to be compatible once their underlying drivers are better understood.

This approach can lead to surprisingly elegant solutions, even in cases where the conflict initially seems impossible to reconcile. Consider a resource-based clash such as "I want to spend quality time with my young children at the end of a workday, but I also want to prepare a healthy and delicious dinner for my family." The deeper needs here are connection versus nourishment—but limited time seems to pit them against each other. How might one activity support both needs at once? Design student Lotte took up this challenge and created *Kookid*, a playful set of cooking tools that turns meal preparation into shared parent-child time (see image 5.9).

5.9 Kookid by Lotte Jacobse

Kookid is a set of playful kitchen tools that allow toddlers to safely cut, mash, and break ingredients alongside their parents. Designed around natural toddler movements, the tools invite sensory exploration and active participation. By involving children in meal preparation, *Kookid* helps parents and toddlers share meaningful time together and supports a smoother transition from cooking to eating, helping toddlers build a positive connection with food.

Design Opportunity 2. Support Alternating User Needs: Even when resolution isn't feasible, and no better trade-off can be found, there is still a powerful design move left on the table: create solutions that help users switch *between* their needs. Instead of trying to fulfill both needs at once, you design a solution that allows users to fulfill them at different times. Think of this as a temporal trade-off: not "either/or" but "now this, then that."

On the need clash plot, these solutions don't sit at a single point. Instead, they allow users to toggle between two distinct positions—one high on Need X, the other high on Need Y (marked "2" in image 5.8).

All four examples on page 139 show how products and services can support this kind of switching. Instead of forcing a compromise, they let users fulfill one need at the moment and the other later on. This strategy may seem like a compromise, but it can lead to remarkably successful innovations. The Nintendo Switch is a good example. For years, gamers had to choose between the power and immersion of a home console and the portability of a handheld device. The Switch changed that. It lets players shift seamlessly between the two by docking the console for living-room play or taking it on the go. As its name demonstrates, the Switch was designed to address a long-standing tension that had once seemed like an unavoidable part of gaming life.

The effectiveness of this design strategy hinges on how smoothly the change can be made. Ideally, the transition happens with minimal effort and at a moment that fits naturally into the user's routine. The car-sharing platform lets users select different car types for different journeys. The detachable heel shoes let users effortlessly slip off their heels when the dancing begins. Of course, friction can still occur: a colleague might be taking a taking a power nap in the privacy booth just when you need to make a call. Nonetheless, these designs succeed not by erasing the tension between needs but by giving users control over when and how they meet each one.

DESIGN CONSIDERATION: DON'T CREATE SOLUTIONS THAT TRIGGER CLASHES

The design strategies we've explored so far focus on resolving existing clashes in needs. But as we saw earlier in this chapter, new products and services can inadvertently create clashes as well. This highlights an equally important aspect of need-clash thinking: when developing ideas for new products or features, you must carefully consider whether you are unintentionally introducing new tensions. Even the most elegant solution to one problem can create unexpected complications elsewhere in the user experience journey.

Take wireless earbuds, introduced to solve the frustrations of wired headphones: tangled cables, cords getting caught on objects, and the awkwardness of threading wires through clothing. The solution seemed elegant: cut the cord entirely. Wireless earbuds delivered on their promise, freeing users from cable wrestling. But removing the physical connection created an unexpected clash: "I want tangle-free listening, but I also want earbuds that stay securely with me and remain easily accessible." Users traded cable tangles for the anxiety of losing tiny, expensive devices. Once this issue emerged, manufacturers responded with incremental improvements like find-my-earbud features and neckband styles that kept the buds tethered together. The original problem was solved, but it took additional innovation cycles to resolve the new tensions that had been inadvertently introduced.

Therefore, it's important to be aware of *potential* clashes even when you're not actively solving them. Preventing clashes requires the same skills as identifying them: a deep understanding of users' needs across contexts, sensitivity to potential tensions, and a willingness to consider long-term impacts. By anticipating possible clashes during the design process rather than discovering them after launch, you can create balanced, thoughtful products and services without introducing new frustrations. We always begin by considering the full range of emotional responses a product might evoke—the constellation of underlying needs. Even when our client suggests that they "know what the problem is," we step back and take a broader view. The tools introduced in this book, such as emotion mapping and laddering, can be used not just to diagnose existing tensions, but also to explore potential and unintended consequences early in the design process.

DESIGNED TO RESOLVE OR EASE THE CLASH

Non-alcoholic beer gives you the ritual, taste, and social inclusion of drinking beer while keeping you clear-headed and in control.

Clashing needs: *I want to savor the flavor of beer in good company, but I also want to stay clear-headed and in control.*

"Barefoot" running shoes offer the natural running sensation while protecting your feet from pavement, gravel, and the occasional sharp twig.

Clashing needs: *I want the freedom and sensation of running barefoot, but I also want to protect my feet from rough terrain.*

Meal kit delivery services eliminate the burden of meal planning while preserving the experience of cooking and the connection to fresh ingredients.

Clashing needs: *I want the satisfaction of preparing my own meals, but I also want meal planning and shopping to be quick and effortless.*

Virtual coworking platforms let you work alongside a stranger via video, which creates the gentle social pressure you need to stay focused without having to leave your home or change your routine.

Clashing needs: *I want the flexibility and comfort of working from home, but I also want the social accountability benefits of a shared workspace.*

DESIGNED TO SUPPORT ALTERNATING USER NEEDS

Car-sharing platforms let users select different vehicles for different situations. A compact car is ideal for city errands, while a spacious one suits weekend trips with luggage or bikes.

Clashing needs: *I want a roomy car for weekend trips, but I also want a compact car for city parking.*

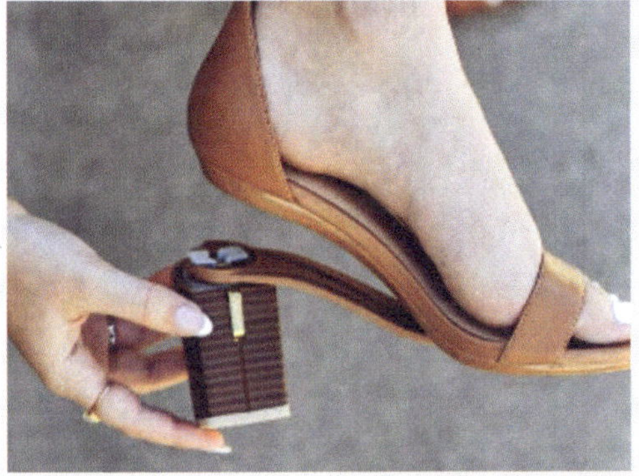

Detachable-heel shoes allow users to wear heels when style matters, then switch to flats for comfort. One pair of shoes adjusts to different settings throughout the day.

Clashing needs: *I want to wear elegant heels at formal events, but I also want to feel comfortable when I move or dance.*

Office pods Open office environments with privacy pods offer social spaces and private areas. Users can chat and collaborate, then step away for quiet calls or focused work without leaving the office.

Clashing needs: *I want to interact with colleagues during the day, but I also want to work in silence when I need to concentrate.*

Nintendo Switch is a hybrid gaming console that works in both TV and handheld modes. Players can enjoy immersive games at home then continue playing on the go.

Clashing needs: *I want a high-quality gaming experience at home, but I also want to play the same games while traveling.*

6

SHADES OF

Joy

6.1 Ready for boarding

What do flight attendants do before they board your flight? This is an aspect of air travel that few ever pause to consider. The truth is that your cabin crew has not just come straight from home. Their workday begins elsewhere, in a building dedicated to them: the crew center.

One of our clients invited us to visit theirs, and the experience was an eye-opening peek behind the curtain. We had stepped into a hive of activity. Hundreds of crew members were getting ready for takeoff: reviewing flight schedules and safety procedures, meeting teammates—often for the first time—and shifting into their professional roles. The building itself was impressive and well equipped. It had dedicated spaces for briefings, training sessions, and all kinds of professional services. And the atmosphere? It was efficient but also formal and strangely flat. It lacked the kind of energy you'd hope the crew would carry on board.

That exact same feeling had struck our client—a forward-thinking manager with a clear vision. She'd recently returned from a visit to a world-famous family theme park that included a tour of its backstage crew facilities. The entire experience was radically different from the airline's crew center: the space had been intentionally designed to spark joy and anticipation. The atmosphere was vibrant and energizing, lifting performers into their roles before they ever stepped "on stage" and into the park. Inspired by this approach, she imagined doing the same for the airline crew: transforming the pre-flight experience into something uplifting, something that would ripple into every passenger interaction.

To realize this ambition, we launched a project in which twenty students would design a series of interventions to be staged inside the crew center, each one evoking a positive emotion. We began with a kick-off meeting on site that brought the key stakeholders together: brand managers, building managers, and crew representatives. Everyone agreed that the goal was to create a more positive atmosphere. However, when it came to writing the design brief, the conversation stalled because the people gathered around the table did not share a common vocabulary to describe positive feelings.

Luckily, we had encountered this situation before and had a ready solution to hand. We placed a deck of cards on the meeting table, each representing a distinct positive emotion with a corresponding image and short description. People began flipping through the cards, pointing to the ones that matched their vision, including pride, excitement, and inspiration. By the end of the session, the group had collaboratively selected a shortlist of emotions that defined their ideal positive atmosphere.

Armed with these specific positive emotions, the students set to work. They developed more than 300 ideas, of which thirty were selected and implemented. Each idea was a tangible step toward a more emotionally attuned crew experience. Here are four examples, which are illustrated in image 6.2:[1]

- *Whispering Trees* (emotion: serenity) offers a serene retreat from the crew center's activity: a circular bench beneath cascading, tree-like structures, with soft light filtering through the branches: a quiet place for reflection and inspiration before takeoff.
- *Big Button* (emotion: determination) builds team spirit through ritual. Before a flight, crew members place their hands on a large button. As more join in, the light grows brighter. When all hands are in, the button prints a keepsake, symbolizing shared determination.
- *Showtime* (emotion: excitement) transforms the gateway to the airport into a theatrical moment. A curtain separates the crew center from the terminal. As crew members approach, lights brighten, and the curtain opens slowly—inviting them to step onto their metaphorical stage.
- *Crew Garden* (emotion: affection) brings people together around care. Each plant is co-parented by two crew members, who leave notes on the pots when they water them. It's a small but powerful act of connection and mutual attention.

The crew center project highlights a key challenge for designers seeking to evoke positive emotions: there are many shades of joy. In psychological terms, humans experience a wide spectrum of positive emotions, each distinct in character. While they all share the common ground of *feeling good,* they are far from identical. Beyond feeling good, emotions like gratitude, inspiration, and hope are also

1. *Showtime* and *Crew Garden* by Inge van der Lee, Amanda Lee Jakobsen, Suwen Shen, and Maik de Rooij. *Whispering Trees* and *Big Button* by Noortje Habets, Lorenzo Romagnoli, Manon Kühne, and Mitra Malkamy.

6.2 Pre-flight lift: four positive emotions, four interventions

fundamentally different from one another. This raises important questions. Are there certain emotions you should design for, or are all positive emotions equally desirable? Do different positive emotions call for different design approaches? To answer these questions, let's first take a step back and consider something more fundamental. Why do humans experience positive emotions in the first place? What purpose do they serve?

More Than a Feeling: What Joy Actually Does

Two decades ago, a team of researchers set out to answer a deceptively simple question: what role do positive emotions play in life successes? To find out, they conducted an impressive meta-analysis of more than 300 studies, spanning decades of research.[2] Their first finding was hardly surprising. Whether it is found at work, in a relationship, or in another area of life, success tends to generate positive emotions. Of course it does. We feel joy when we reach a goal and pride when we overcome a challenge.

But their second finding made the study famous. The link between success and positive emotions, it turned out, runs *both ways*: past and future. Success leads to joy now, and that joy leads to more success. Positive emotions don't simply reflect how well life is going; they actively shape it. They strengthen

2. Lyubomirsky, King, and Diener (2005).

friendships, deepen relationships, and improve teamwork. They even contribute to better health, a higher income, and even a longer life.[3] In short, joy isn't just the icing on the cake of life. It's an essential ingredient.

How is this possible? As we've seen throughout the book, emotions aren't random. They signal when something matters to our needs, and they push us to respond. Every emotion comes with an *action tendency*: the built-in urge towards a certain type of response. You can think of action tendencies like an emotion's behavioral nudge. With negative emotions, that push is obvious: fear urges avoidance, anger urges confrontation, sadness urges comfort. These impulses help us cope with threats and challenges. What's less visible—but equally important—is that positive emotions come with their own behavioral nudges. Their signals may be gentler, but they shape our actions all the same. Joy draws us into connection. Gratitude nudges us to strengthen relationships. Fascination invites exploration. These tendencies, in turn, help us grow. They support the development of personal resources like knowledge, resilience, and communication skills. To see these links in action, consider a small moment from everyday life.

Nina and Omar had been working late on a project with a tight deadline. When it was finally delivered successfully, both felt uplifted—but in different ways.

Nina felt gratitude. *She appreciated how Omar had supported her during a stressful week. Offering help, checking in, and even picking up some of her tasks. It made her feel seen and valued, and it deepened her trust in their working relationship. That evening, she sent Omar a heartfelt message, thanking him for his support and suggesting they grab coffee later that week to discuss future collaborations.*

Omar, meanwhile, experienced admiration. *Watching Nina stay calm under pressure, lead the team, and solve problems with clarity had impressed him deeply. He found himself thinking about his own approach to work; he often rushed to fix things, whereas Nina took a step back and asked the right questions. That night, he made a note to be more deliberate in team discussions and to speak up only after truly listening.*

Same moment, different emotions—and different outcomes. This is the hidden power of positive emotions: they guide action that supports personal growth. Their impact is not always dramatic or even visible. It may only lead to small shifts that shape the ways a person thinks, relates, and acts.

3. This idea has been expressed most explicitly in Barbara Fredrickson's broaden-and-build theory; see Fredrickson (1998), and Fredrickson and Branigan (2005). The theory posits that positive emotions expand individuals' momentary thought-action repertoires, encouraging exploration, creativity, and social connection. Over time, these broadened behaviors help build enduring personal resources, such as resilience, knowledge, and social bonds, which can be drawn upon when seeking to overcome future challenges. This theory highlights how positive emotions contribute not only to immediate well-being, but also to long-term growth and flourishing.

Similar examples exist for other emotions. Pride might lead you to aim higher. Amusement keeps your mind playful and open. Hope helps you persist when the path ahead is uncertain. Each emotion encourages a different kind of response, and each response may help you grow. Such growth is meaningful because it outlasts the emotional moment. The resources you build—stronger bonds, new skills, a better sense of purpose—stick with you. They help you navigate future challenges and opportunities. A more resilient friendship, for example, can provide comfort when the going gets rough, and newly developed problem-solving skills can help you tackle future interpersonal challenges. And, over time, these resources and emotions start to feed each other. Joy leads to growth. Growth leads to more joy. Researchers call this an "upward spiral"—a virtuous cycle of emotional and personal flourishing.[4]

The role that positive emotions play in building lasting resources perhaps explains why we are equipped with an entire repertoire of joy rather than one or two types. Life presents us with varied opportunities, and no single emotion can capture them all. You don't need playful amusement in every situation; sometimes, you need the calmness of serenity, the optimism of hope, or the focus of fascination. Humans have evolved a whole inventory of positive emotions, each serving a distinct purpose.

Positive Emotions in Design

Which positive emotions do people experience in response to products and services? When we set out to answer this question, we expected to find only a handful of familiar feelings: satisfaction when a product works well, fascination when exploring a product's capabilities, and perhaps surprise at discovering an unexpected feature. But the reality was far more nuanced. In practice, designed things can evoke the full spectrum of positive emotions.[5] The way a product looks, works, or fits into a person's life can become the source of every human emotion imaginable, from the subtle glow of admiration to the thrill of euphoria to the spark of inspiration.

4. We do not subscribe to the notion that people can manifest their dreams or desires solely through positive thinking. This idea, often referred to as "manifesting" or "the power of attraction," suggests that visualizing success can attract wealth, relationships, or other goals. Despite its popularity, this idea lacks any scientific support. In fact, this notion of self-help can be harmful, leading to victim blaming, disappointment, and diminished self-esteem when aspirations are unmet (D'Olimpio, 2024; Ehrenreich, 2009). Research does show that optimistic thinking has basic benefits, such as improving psychological resilience (Emmons & McCullough, 2003). However, unlike manifesting, which overestimates human control over external circumstances, evidence-based research supports the idea that positive emotions influence behaviors and decisions, which in turn contribute to positive outcomes over time.

5. See Desmet (2012) for an overview.

We've collected thousands of real-life examples of products and services and the positive emotions they inspire. A running app that fuels determination. A music app feature that sparks fascination. A meal kit that becomes the object of affection. Again and again, we see how products, when designed thoughtfully, can reach people in unexpected ways. This is true even of emotions you might not associate with products, such as elevation or gratitude. The process has been illuminating, revealing just how versatile emotion by design can be. This brings us to the sixth law of emotional design.

THE SIXTH LAW OF EMOTIONAL DESIGN

Every positive emotion is a potential design goal, because each drives behavior in a unique way

Each emotion offers something distinct: a differently-colored experience, a different behavioral nudge, a different kind of long-term benefit. That's why good emotional design isn't about trying to hit the same emotional note every single time. It's about finding the right emotion for the right moment, guided by the needs and context of your users, the behaviors you hope to inspire, and the lasting impact you want to create.

The Joy Spectrum

The idea that each positive emotion is a worthy design goal is inspiring; it's also a bit overwhelming. Where do you start? To help bring focus, we've chosen a set of ten emotions that strike a useful balance between focus and diversity. These ten cover a wide span of the emotional landscape and have consistently proven themselves meaningful and actionable in design contexts.[6]

Chapter 1 imagined what it would be like to live on a deserted island—a place stripped of distractions, where fundamental needs clearly reveal themselves. Let's return to that island and consider the positive emotions the islanders experience. The inset on the next pages shows ten of their stories.

6. Of course, they are not the only emotions that matter. For a broader view of positive and negative emotions, we've developed an extensive online resource: https://emotiontypology.com. This open-access typology offers a structured overview of the full emotional spectrum.

Fascination

You're wandering through the jungle when something makes you stop: a cluster of bird nests hanging from the trees. Delicately woven, complex, interconnected, almost architectural. You've never seen anything like it. You tilt your head, eyes tracing the patterns. How did they build this? And why? You don't have the answers, but you can't look away.

Fascination strikes when something is new and intriguing but gives the sense that if only you looked a little closer, you might understand it. The object draws you in and invites a sharper focus. It compels you to investigate and connect what you see to what you know. In doing so, it helps build a curious mind, one more observant and able to make surprising connections.

Amusement

The trap you spent hours building, meticulously designed to catch crabs, has been claimed by the island monkey now parading around camp wearing it on its head. You and your fellow castaways erupt with laughter. The tension of the day lifts. For a moment, you're not survivors—you're kids again.

Amusement bubbles up in moments of lightness, surprise, and shared absurdity. It helps us reframe the serious. It releases stress and creates bonds between people. Over time, these small moments build something deeper: a sense of playfulness, emotional flexibility, and the kind of social glue that makes groups more resilient.

Gratitude

You wake up to find a small pile of fruit and freshly boiled water beside your shelter, along with a note saying, "Thought you might need a little extra today – J." You smile. Yesterday, you helped another survivor fix a leaky roof. You didn't expect anything in return, but here it is.

Gratitude arises when someone takes care of something you find onerous or goes out of their way to help you or give you something. It's not about getting what you deserve—it's about receiving the unexpected. Gratitude builds trust, deepens bonds, and often makes you want to give something back. It helps you see the good in others and often sparks a chain reaction of kindness.

Affection

After dinner, you sit side by side with your favorite islander, watching the fire crackle. No words are exchanged, just warmth—from the flames, the shared silence, the knowing you're not alone. One of you gently leans your head on the other's shoulder. It's a small gesture, but it's enough.

Affection lives in quiet moments of closeness. It is expressed in presence, softness, and mutual regard. It enhances relationships, making us more open, more trusting, more inclined to care. And in doing so, it helps build the kind of bonds that can weather even the harshest of seasons.

Pride

Your raft floats steadily in the shallows: bamboo lashed together with vines and sheer tenacity. This is your third attempt, and it holds! On the beach, the others cheer. You wade back towards the shore and feel a rising in your chest: you did it.

Pride swells when you overcome a challenge or realize accomplishments that reflect your values. It transcends external validation; it's about knowing something meaningful has occurred and feeling genuinely connected to that achievement. Pride fuels confidence. It drives you to aim higher, try harder, take on more challenges. And when pride is shared, it can lift a whole group, building mutual respect, energy, and momentum.

Determination

The others gave up an hour ago. But you're still here, kneeling in the sand, focused on a pile of twigs and dry leaves. Your fingers move with quiet intent, rubbing, striking, adjusting, not out of hope—out of resolve. You've forgotten the time. You're making it happen.

Determination doesn't sparkle. It smolders—slow and steady, like an ember. It arises when you face obstacles that matter and believe that your effort can make a difference. Determination sharpens focus, fueling grit and persistence. It helps you keep going. Over time, it shapes something more durable than momentary success: confidence in yourself.

Admiration

You watch quietly as one of your fellow castaways constructs a fishing net from vines and driftwood. Their fingers move with calm precision, tying knots you couldn't dream of mastering. They don't boast; in fact, they aren't aware you are watching. Something inside you shifts—not envy, more an aspiration.

Admiration comes from witnessing excellence: when someone does something with grace or skill that feels just out of your own reach. It makes you want to grow—to become better, wiser, more skilled. Admiration invites reflection, modeling, and ambition. It helps you stretch, and over time, it builds your capacity for self-improvement and meaningful aspiration.

Hope

The storm hit harder than expected. Supplies were damaged. The raft—your lifeline—drifted out to sea. But this morning, the sky is clear. A soft breeze brushes your skin. Then you spot a ship on the horizon. It's not close. Its crew might not even see you. Even so, your heart lifts. "Maybe... just maybe," you think.

Hope rises when something desirable seems possible but uncertain. The outcome is not assured but the door is open, inviting you to persist. Hope urges you to take one more step, make one more signal fire, try again. And in heeding its call, you build resilience: the strength to persevere in hard times and believe in the value of your effort.

Serenity

At dusk, everything settles. The waves hush. The air stills. You lie in a hammock, belly full, limbs warm from the sun. Nothing calls for your attention. No tasks. No noise. There is only breath, light, and the gentle hum of life around you.

Serenity is the quiet relation of joy—gentle, still, and deeply nourishing. It emerges when life feels in balance, and nothing urgent presses in. It invites

you to pause, to notice, to simply be. In this calm, your mind opens. You reflect and replenish. Serenity supports well-being by giving you space to rest and gather strength.

Elevation

You're heading back to camp when you spot something in the distance. Someone crouches at the forest edge, coaxing a wounded bird into a nest of leaves. She moves gently and speaks in whispers. She thinks she's alone.

Elevation transpires when you witness acts of virtue—kindness, courage, generosity—especially when they come without ego or reward. It creates a warm, swelling feeling in the chest and a subtle urge to be your best. This emotion makes us want to do good. And when it stays with us, it strengthens our moral compass, building a sense of purpose, compassion, and belief in shared humanity.

The island stories illustrate that these ten emotions span a wide range of action tendencies, from slowing down and reflecting to striving, exploring, and resolving to do better. This variety opens up exciting possibilities for design. Designers can choose the emotions that align with the experiences they want to evoke and the behavior they want to encourage. To stimulate a particular tendency, such as compassion, stamina, or focus, you can work backwards from the emotion that brings it about. Target the right emotion, and you can nudge people toward trying something new (fascination), connecting more openly (affection), or pushing through difficulty with confidence (determination).

While this approach may sound abstract, in practice, it arises intuitively. When the crew center stakeholders were pointing at emotion cards that resonated with their vision, they weren't picking emotions at random—they were thinking about the behaviors they hoped to support. They chose *determination* to foster a sense of readiness, *affection* to nurture interpersonal bonds, *excitement* to energize the transition to the flight, and *serenity* to encourage calm reflection.

The Mechanics of Emotion

Chapter 1 introduced the First Law of Emotional Design: a product sparks a positive emotion when it fulfills a genuine user need. A crucial question remains, however: how do *different* positive emotions arise? What makes one design evoke pride, another relief, and yet another fascination?

Emotions arise from appraisals, the mental evaluations of what a situation means for our needs, goals, or values. These evaluations happen quickly, often without a person's conscious awareness, and guide emotional responses in remarkably consistent ways. Moreover, they do more than check whether a need is fulfilled or compromised; they shape the character of what people feel. You can think of them as a set of silent evaluative questions. Is this new? Is it relevant? Is it safe, comprehensible, challenging? The answers to these questions determine which specific emotion arises, even though you answer them without thinking, in the blink of an eye.

The good news for design is that while emotional triggers may differ from person to person, the underlying appraisals are surprisingly *universal*. Each specific emotion arises from a distinct appraisal pattern. Gratitude, for example, emerges when someone performs an intended act of kindness. Admiration is sparked by witnessing excellence that is seen as well-earned and meaningful. These patterns offer designers a practical tool. They act as schemas that can be used to evoke desired emotions.

There are two complementary ways of describing what evokes an emotion. The first way is via an *appraisal theme*, which is a holistic account of how an emotion is triggered and explains the kind of meaning a person makes of a situation. For instance, serenity arises when you are "feeling at peace when needs are met, and nothing demands immediate action." *Appraisal components* break the way the emotion is triggered down into a list of verifiable items such as "fulfillment," "absence of urgency," and "stability." Designers can actively use appraisal components to inform or guide their work. Both emotional perspectives offer distinct value: appraisal themes explain what kind of story the emotion is telling, while appraisal components translate that story into designable ingredients.

A full overview of these appraisals can be found in *Tools & Techniques,* pages 250-251, which includes the appraisal themes and appraisal components for each of the ten positive emotions.

Understanding appraisals allows designers to take a systematic approach to emotional design. Rather than guessing how a new feature will make users feel, we can work backward from the appraisal. Say you're designing a museum audio guide and want to evoke fascination. You might ask: which elements of the narration should feel novel or unexpected? How can the interface encourage exploration without overwhelming first-time visitors? Or, if you're optimizing a hospital discharge process and want to evoke gratitude, you might ask: where in the patient journey can we build in small, intentional gestures of care—a warm handover, a thank-you note from the staff, or a follow-up message that shows continued attention?

Appraisals offer a way to move from the subjectivity of emotion to a clearer understanding of what to design for. They don't prescribe solutions; they help define the solution space, turning felt experience into something we can approach with focus and intent.

The Emotion Blueprint: Turning Emotions into Design Directions

Appraisals are a good first step toward designing for emotion, but on their own, they can be too abstract to guide design decisions. Appraisals tell us what conditions trigger emotions—novelty, challenge, intentionality—but not how to translate these into design features or user interactions. An appraisal is like a recipe that lists the ingredients but skips the instructions: you know what goes in but not how to bring everything together.

Take fascination, for example. It requires something that feels *new and intriguing*. But what counts as "new and intriguing" depends heavily on your users' abilities, preferences, and prior experiences. Overlooking these differences risks misinterpretation: designs that are meant to spark fascination might end up feeling confusing, overwhelming, or simply irrelevant.

To bridge this gap, we created the *emotion blueprint*: a practical translation of emotional theory into concrete inspiration. It links universal

6.3 An example "affection" emotion blueprint for the crew center project

patterns—appraisals and action tendencies—to real-world user perspectives and contextual details. Think of it as a map of the connections between psychological ingredients and design possibilities. Throughout a project, it works as a shared emotional lens that keeps teams aligned and focused on achieving the emotional goal.

Image 6.3 shows an example of an emotion blueprint from the crew center project. One student team set out to design for affection. They began by exploring the theory behind this emotion. On the action tendency side, affection involves nurturing, expressing warmth, and giving undivided attention. The appraisal side involves positive regard, closeness, and reciprocity.

But what would those qualities actually look like in the crew's pre-flight environment? To find out, the students conducted focus groups and creative workshops with crew members. They gathered short stories and everyday gestures of affection the crewmembers fondly recounted. These ranged from subtle gestures ("a hand on the shoulder, a cup of tea") to lasting tokens of support ("a handwritten note kept in a wallet"). One participant pointed at a bench by the window, saying, "That's where people go to take a breath; and sometimes, that's where someone joins you." As the students collected these details, a metaphor emerged: "Affection is like watering a plant." That metaphor became the seed for their final concept, the *Crew Garden* (see image 6.2).

The blueprint brought together theory, observation, and small design triggers. It helped the team stay emotionally focused while working toward a concept that felt both relevant and quietly meaningful. *Tools & Techniques*, page 252, lays out the steps to create your own emotion blueprint.

DESIGN OPPORTUNITIES: PUTTING EMOTION BLUEPRINTS TO WORK

Most products and services are not designed with the intent of evoking specific positive emotions. They don't involve affection gardens or theatrical curtains. But even when evoking emotions via products and services isn't the conscious objective, an emotion blueprint can still help bring strategic goals to life.

Most companies and organizations we've worked with have a vision of the experience they want to provide their customers. That vision is often captured within brand guidelines or customer experience strategies, which describe the ideal experience across touchpoints on a timeline. This kind of documentation is valuable when setting a strategic direction, but the actual means of eliciting the desired experiences are often unclear. Guidelines and strategies might describe what an outcome should feel like without establishing *how* to bring that feeling to life through design.

This is where the overview of positive emotions becomes especially useful. It can help bridge the gap between strategic vision and design outcomes. By identifying which specific emotions to evoke, design teams establish a shared vocabulary that facilitates discussion about user experience—a topic that's often ignored at the strategic level. It also offers a reference point from which to evaluate success. Does the design achieve the intended emotional effect? In the following sections, we introduce three design opportunities that are based on emotion blueprints.[7]

Design Opportunity 1. Use Emotions to Guide User Behavior: If you know what kind of action or mindset you want to encourage, you can identify the emotion that naturally brings it about and design to evoke that emotion. Say you want people to focus their attention: design for determination. Say you want them to stay optimistic: design for hope. Or, say you want people to act more playfully: design for amusement.

An illustrative example is *Explore More*, a conceptual feature for the music app Spotify (see image 6.4). Student designer Daniëlle Klomp created it with the intent of helping users break out of their routine listening patterns, explore new genres, and experience the joy of discovery. Instead of merely letting the platform push additional recommendations, she started working backward from the behavior she wanted to achieve: playful exploration. The emotion that naturally supports that behavior is *fascination*.

Explore More is an interface that turns music discovery into a visual, curiosity-driven adventure. It maps out your musical preferences as colorful genre bubbles, gently nudging you into nearby styles. A jazz listener might find a new doorway

7. These three design opportunities are partly based on previous work by Yoon, Pohlmeyer, and Desmet (2016).

6.4 Explore More by Daniëlle Klomp

into Latin Jazz or Bebop simply by exploring the colorful patchwork. Designed to evoke fascination, this feature encourages curiosity, making exploration feel effortless, relevant, and fun.

Design Opportunity 2. Curate the Arc—Design for Emotional Flow: One insight you might recall from Chapter 2 is that products and services rarely evoke a single emotion. Instead, they evoke a stream of micro emotions across user journey touchpoints. The second opportunity is to deliberately craft that journey. Which emotions do you want consumers to experience first? Which should follow? What should the closing emotion be?

This approach is useful for experiences that unfold across multiple stages. A museum visit might begin with curiosity, move through awe, and end in reflection. An exercise app might start with determination and end with pride. We explored this approach during a project for a fine fragrance brand (see image 6.5).[8] The marketing team had a clear emotional arc in mind: hope for the advertisement, admiration for the packaging, and pride for the fragrance itself. That combination of emotions is not unique to this brand: it's a pattern we often see in beauty and fashion products, where the journey typically moves from aspiration to self-expression.

8. To ensure confidentiality, certain details of the brand, product, and advertisement design have been subtly altered.

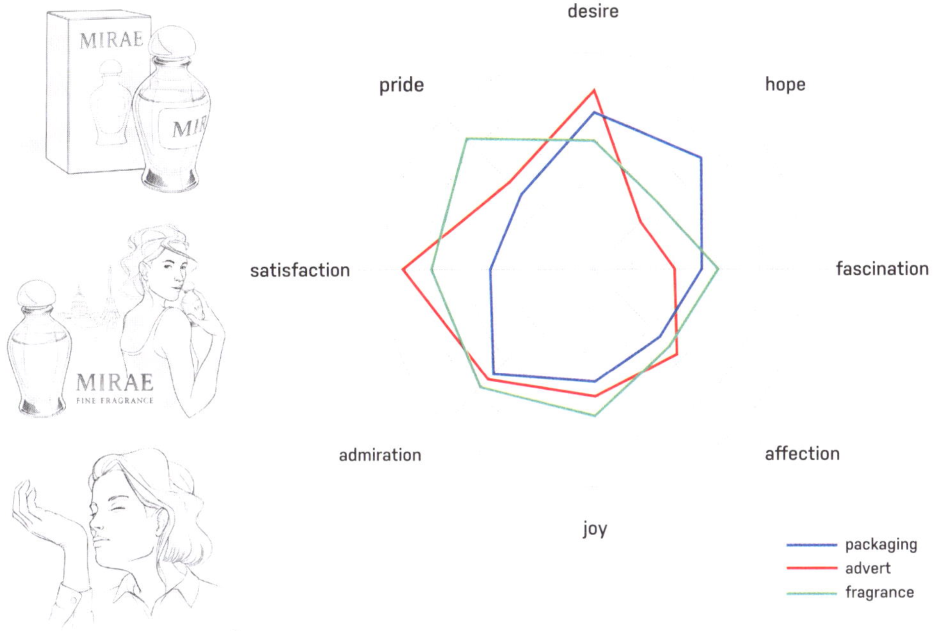

6.5 Fine fragrance: an experience in three acts

We tested whether the target audience actually felt this intended arc and found that the fragrance delivered on pride and the packaging on admiration. But the advertisement revealed that something was missing: it evoked some desire and satisfaction but not much hope (see the radar chart in image 6.5). The ad was revised, placing more emphasis on transformation: "stepping into confidence" and "becoming the best version of yourself." It added a sense of direction; something to move toward. A second test showed that this redesign achieved the feeling of hope the team had aimed for.

Design Opportunity 3. Break the Mold—Design for the Unexpected: The fragrance example illustrates how certain emotions tend to dominate specific domains and industries. Financial services lean on hope. Wellness aims for serenity. Insurance provides relief. These defaults make sense but also flatten the landscape. When every single wellness product evokes serenity, another emotion will make yours stand out. Designing for atypical emotions, which still suit the context and users, can make an experience feel fresh, distinctive, and emotionally memorable. This is the third opportunity: choose a nonobvious emotion; one that provides a refreshing contrast or an exciting twist is likely to please. On pages 160-161, we've added examples, such as the toilet paper that evokes amusement or the travel agency that inspires elevation.

6.6 Light & Shadow by Wim aan de Stegge

An illuminating example is *Light & Shadow*, an extraordinary chandelier (see image 6.6). Suspended in a spacious national park visitor pavilion—a multifunctional hub serving as reception, restaurant, learning space, and gift shop—it offers a counterpoint to the usual cafeteria clatter. While chandeliers often aim to impress via scale, sparkle, or spectacle, student designer Wim chose to anchor his design in serenity: a quiet, contemplative emotion that rarely leads the way in chandelier design. To evoke serenity, Wim translated the dappled light of the forest canopy into a rhythm of shadow and glow, using translucent materials and slow-moving patterns. The result was a chandelier that doesn't dazzle, but calms. It invites you to pause, playing with soft shadows and shifting light that echo the feeling of sunlight filtered through the leaves of a tree.

Design for affection: *AV1 Avatar Robot* evokes affection by helping children with long-term illnesses stay connected to their classmates. The robot sits in the classroom while the child joins remotely—speaking, listening, and staying present. It keeps friendships alive, even at a distance.

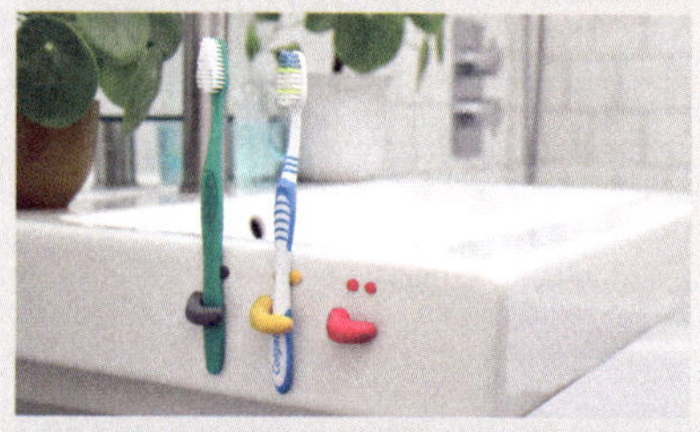

Design for inspiration: *Sugru* evokes inspiration by reframing repair as creative possibility. The colorful, silicone-based glue can be shaped by hand and sticks to almost any surface, allowing people to reimagine broken objects. Whether fixing a cable or creating a custom hook, the process opens new ways for seeing everyday problems.

Design for fascination: The quintessential *lava lamp* evokes fascination through continuous, unpredictable motion. Wax blobs rise and fall in slow, fluid shapes that hold the gaze without offering a clear pattern. It serves no functional purpose, yet people keep watching—pulled in by the pleasure of seeing something they can't quite explain.

Design for elevation: In an outdoor gear market where most brands highlight adventure and performance, *Patagonia* evokes elevation by focusing on environmental activism. Its campaigns urge consumers to take ethical stands, positioning responsibility, not just recreation, at the heart of the message.

Design for amusement: Toilet paper is usually associated with hygiene and necessity; *Who Gives A Crap* evokes amusement by combining eco-friendliness with humor. The brand's cheeky tone and bold messaging turn a mundane product into something unexpectedly delightful.

Design for admiration: Unlike traditional LEGO sets that focus on creativity and play, *LEGO Architecture* evokes admiration through faithful replication of iconic buildings with meticulous detail. This creates a dual admiration: for the brilliance of the original architectural masterpieces and for the skill required to recreate them in LEGO form.

Design for affection: *Tonies* is an audio storytelling toy that evokes affection through a shared ritual. Stories are activated by placing small animal figurines on the speaker—no screens, no buttons. The gentle, unhurried interaction invites care and encourages moments of shared attention, fostering closeness between child and caretaker.

Design for elevation: While most travel services emphasize luxury or excitement, *G Adventures* evokes elevation by fostering genuine connections with local communities. The tours showcase local people's generosity, wisdom, and resilience, creating encounters with human goodness that inspire travelers to reflect on their own values and capacity for positive impact.

Design for gratitude: *Be My Eyes* evokes gratitude by enabling short, practical exchanges between blind users and sighted volunteers. Through the app, users can ask for help with everyday tasks like reading a label or checking colors. These small acts of help are met with sincere appreciation—turning a few seconds of someone's time into something meaningful.

Design for affection: The *CuteCircuit Hug Shirt* allows people to send and receive hugs across distances. Embedded sensors and actuators recreate the sensation of touch, providing comfort to those separated from loved ones.

THEORETICAL DEEP DIVE

Modeling Positive Emotions

This section explores the assumptions underpinning the typology of positive emotions.

How many positive emotions are there?

Counting positive emotions is a bit like counting the colors of a rainbow. Some see seven, others see an infinite spectrum. Emotion researchers are similarly divided. On one side are those who argue for a small, universal set of core emotions; on the other, those who claim there are hundreds, even thousands of them. This divide reflects two dominant paradigms: the *biological* and the *cultural*.

The biological view argues for a compact set of "basic emotions." Emotions are hardwired reactions like fear, anger, sadness, and joy that evolved to help us navigate important survival challenges. These emotions are thought to be universal. For decades, this line of research gave little attention to positive emotions, typically listing only one (joy) or two (joy and interest).[1] In more recent years, the lists have grown.[2] Some researchers now distinguish eight[3] to thirteen[4] basic positive emotions, including pride, amusement, awe, and hope.

In contrast, the cultural view suggests that the number of positive emotions is essentially *infinite*. This view emphasizes that emotions are not biologically fixed but shaped by context, language, and social practice.[5] Each specific emotional experience is deeply personal and context bound, shaped by the unique combination of moment, individual, and environment. In fact, no two emotional experiences are exactly alike, resulting in an infinite array of emotional variations that reflect the diversity of human life.

1. Examples of such pioneering researchers are Izard (1977), whose list of 10 basic emotions included interest and joy, and Ekman (1999), whose set of 6 basic emotions included happiness to represent the positive spectrum.

2. Fredrickson and Cohn (2008); Sauter (2010).

3. From Shiota et al. (2014): pride, amusement, nurturant love, attachment love, contentment, enthusiasm, awe, and sexual desire.

4. Yih et al. (2020) distinguish twelve positive emotions: amusement, awe, determination, compassion, gratitude, hope, interest, joy, pride, relief, affection, and serenity. Tong (2015) recognizes thirteen; the same twelve emotions plus contentment.

5. Key authors in this perspective are Barrett (2017) and Mesquita (2022).

6.7 Faces of joy

Despite these contrasting views—and the heated debates they spark—many contemporary researchers agree that emotions are shaped by both innate factors *and* social influences. One way to visualize this interplay is as a tree-like structure.[6] The trunk represents joy, our most fundamental positive emotion. The main branches represent our basic positive emotions, such as love and interest. These core emotions then split into increasingly nuanced variations, much like branches subdividing into finer limbs. Ultimately, the countless leaves symbolize the highly personal, ever-changing emotional experiences that are uniquely molded by our personal lives and contexts.

Let's take the basic emotion of love as an example. From the trunk of joy, love emerges as a main branch. This branch splits into finer branches, representing distinct types of love: affection, tenderness, and lust. From these finer branches grow leaves, representing specific emotional experiences. For instance, the branch of affection might sprout leaves so unique they can't be described in a single term, like the warmth of reminiscing with a childhood friend or the quiet comfort of sitting with a loved one. On the branch of tenderness, leaves could include an experience of soothing a baby to sleep or the experience of gently caring for a sick partner.

Why does our list include ten positive emotions?

The tree metaphor demonstrates that there is no single "correct" number of emotions in a typology.[7] Typologies are tools, with their level of granularity serving their intended purpose. You can focus on the main branches, the leaves,

6. For examples, see Shaver et al. (1987) and Shiota et al. (2017).

7. Desmet, Sauter, and Shiota (2021).

or anything in between. For our purpose, we chose the level in between. Our goal was to inform and inspire design activities, so we needed a typology that would capture the diversity of positive emotions without overwhelming with excessive nuance.

The set of ten emotions introduced in this chapter strikes a balance: diverse enough to be useful and focused enough to remain workable. Behind this shortlist lies a broader set of 60 emotions that includes 24 positive ones.[8] That extended version is especially useful when you want to explore an emotional landscape in more detail or customize an emotional palette. The entire list is meant as a practical, customizable tool. If you find it more useful to work with broader emotions (like love) or more fine-grained ones (like the specific experience of feeling happy for a close friend when they start a family), you should absolutely do so. The specific typology of 24 positive emotions exists to inspire you. Don't hesitate to curate, refine, or tailor it to meet the needs of your project.

Some readers may wonder: where is "love?" Why isn't "happiness" included? What about feeling "relaxed?" There are several reasons why certain emotions do not appear in the list. First, the emotion may actually be on the list, just under a different name. For example, while "thankfulness" is not listed, it closely aligns with "gratitude," which is. Similarly, some missing emotions are finer offshoots of the emotion tree. "Patriotism" and "triumph," for instance, are finer branches that grow from the pride branch, which is included. The reverse also applies: some emotion words that might appear to be absent, like "love," are larger branches than the ones in the typology. Instead of "love," the typology includes finer offshoots, like "affection" and "tenderness,"[9] each with its own distinct appraisal structure. Finally, some words you might think are missing simply aren't emotions at all—at least not in the way psychologists define them.[10] Terms like "cheerful" or "relaxed," for instance, refer to moods rather than emotions. While emotions are typically tied to specific events, moods are more diffuse, and longer lasting. They also lack clear appraisal patterns and action tendencies, which are key features of emotions.[11]

8. The typology is available at: https://emotiontypology.com

9. Sternberg and Grajek (1984).

10. See Ortony, Clore, and Foss (1987) for a clear overview of distinctions between emotions, behaviors, dispositions, and bodily states.

11. Frijda (1994).

7

WHEN *Bad* FEELS *Good*

For years, we have given our students the same creative brief: design something that evokes a specific positive emotion—which invariably produces results like the ones featured in the previous chapter. The results have always been delightful: hundreds of designs that were amusing, inspiring, or just plain heartwarming. Until one day, we'd had enough. Much like that post-holiday feeling when you can't bear another feel-good movie, saccharine carol, or sugary cookie, we found ourselves saturated with positive emotions.

While brainstorming alternative exercises, one of us suggested, half-jokingly, "Why not have them design for *negative* emotions?" Although completely counterintuitive, we saw the idea's potential as a thought-provoking challenge: choose a specific negative emotion and design a consumer product or service that deliberately evokes it.

The students loved it. They dove into the task with enthusiasm, returning the next week with offensive, melancholic, disturbing, and even frightening designs. There was a clock that scrambled the positions of the hours and minutes on its face; it made telling time an infuriating puzzle. There was a chair that collapsed after an hour, right at the moment you were starting to get comfy. One team created a restaurant table where the diners' cutlery was connected by cables under the table, turning dinner into a constant negotiation—or a tug of war.

When we reviewed these designs in class, everyone agreed that none were likely to hit store shelves; not now, not ever. Each project represented a kind of anti-design, taking universal design values like utility, user-friendliness, and pleasant user experience and turning them upside down.

But there were also designs that took a different turn, transforming negative emotions into something that was somehow enjoyable. The discomfort, frustration, or awkwardness they evoked became the very thing that made the product more interesting or engaging. In fact, some of these ideas struck us as more compelling than many earlier designs based on positive emotions.

What began as a didactic exercise got us thinking. Could negative emotions be utilized deliberately? Could they be a real-life design approach? What powers do the feelings that people usually avoid really harness? And how can designers ensure that negative product experiences are *actually* enjoyable?

Sad Songs, Scary Movies, and Real-Life Melancholy

At first glance, the idea of designing for negative emotions seems absurd. Isn't the ultimate purpose of our method to avoid negative emotions? After all, negative emotions indicate "pain points" that designers strive to eliminate (Chapter 2). They indicate that people's needs have been compromised or unmet (Chapter 3). Products and services evoke negative emotions when they underperform, malfunction, or are incomprehensible—who would deliberately aim for that?

NIGHT EDITION
The World.
BASEBALL & RACING
WOMAN JUMPS FROM BROOKLYN BRIDGE
SURVIVES MAD LEAP!
MONEY GONE AND ALONE, SHE DETERMINED TO DIE.
BASEBALL
BROOKLYN.
NEW YORK.
ROBERTS FIGHTING
GIANTS AND GROOMS IN ANOTHER BATTLE

7.1 The delights of distress

Yet, there are many instances in life when people not only tolerate negative emotions—they actively pursue them. Consider cinema. Of course, many genres are anchored in positive emotions. There are feel-good films (contentment), romantic comedies (love and hope), and lighthearted comedies (amusement). But there are at least as many horror films (fear and disgust), revenge movies (anger), tragedies (despair), thrillers (anxiety), tearjerkers (sadness), and cringe comedies (embarrassment). These "negative" genres are just as popular as their positive counterparts. In fact, negative emotions aren't limited to specific genres at all. Plots almost always revolve around *something* amiss: there's a mystery to solve, a person to rescue, or a conflict to settle. Regardless of whether the ending is happy or tragic, the journey is typically saturated with negative emotions.

Enjoyable negative emotions extend far beyond fiction. People willingly queue for roller coasters and haunted houses. They listen for hours to music that brings a lump to their throats. They click on social media posts that outrage them or spend hours wrestling with frustrating crossword puzzles and games. Crucially, these experiences aren't enjoyable *despite* the negative emotions but *because* of them. Imagine a haunted house without fear, a tearjerker devoid of sadness, or a puzzle that offers no challenge. Remove the negative emotion and you remove the pleasure.[1]

Films, novels, amusement parks, and puzzles are all things people seek out in their leisure time. The experiences they offer exist outside "real life" and offer a temporary escape. But can negative emotions also be pleasurable or worthwhile as part of daily life? Consider these examples.

1. Of course, not everyone enjoys all the examples mentioned. Some people wouldn't board a roller coaster for any amount of money. But that same person might be captivated by the bizarre plot twists of a soap opera or be moved to tears by Bach's *St. Matthew Passion.* In other words, while the enjoyment of specific negative stimuli differs from person to person, the enjoyment of negative emotions in art and entertainment is surprisingly universal.

- *For the first time in your life, you're moving to a new city. The prospect sparks a mix of emotions. You feel sad about leaving behind family and friends, excited about exploring the new city and meeting new people, and anxious about not yet knowing anyone.*
- *While cleaning your attic, you discover a box filled with old photographs and childhood objects. The contents give you a bittersweet feeling as you reflect on beautiful memories and the times and people from your past.*

If you stripped away the sadness and anxiety from these episodes, they would become more enjoyable in the strictest sense of the word. But a crucial element of the experience would also be lost. What meaning does a farewell hold if there is no tinge of sadness? What about an important performance without stage fright? Or a protest without shared outrage?[2]

In short, the enjoyment and meaning of experiences is as complex and layered as people themselves. Emotions—positive and negative alike—bring color and depth to our lives. If you focus exclusively on the positive, you miss out on a wealth of powerful design opportunities.

The Power of Using Negative Emotions

Most consumer products and services aren't designed primarily for emotional impact. Unlike works of art or entertainment, people don't typically buy them when seeking an emotionally powerful experience. But then again, most people aren't pursuing specific positive emotions when they buy a product, either. As we explored in the previous chapter, effective emotional design embeds moments of delight and meaning within a broader experience rather than making any emotion the central focus of the entire product. Negative emotions are an extra set of ingredients that can be included—with moderation and consideration.

Take Spotify, the world's largest music streaming service. Its users appreciate it primarily because of its vast music library, excellent recommendation algorithms, and intuitive interface. Yet, alongside these straightforward features, Spotify experiments with niche features that create unique user experiences, such as *Playlist in a Bottle* (see page 188).

But the question remains: why target negative emotions at all? Why not simply stick to the safe and predictable territory of positive feelings? Can negative emotions deliver something that positive emotions cannot?

2. The value people place on such experiences varies between individuals. Some people dislike nostalgia or tense periods in their lives and prefer to experience exclusively positive emotions. Others consider such experiences part of life or even something to actively seek out as opportunities for personal growth. Cultural and age differences exist too: consumer behavior researchers found that older people and people with an Asian-American background are more likely to accept and embrace mixed emotional experiences than younger people and people with an Anglo-American background (Williams & Aaker, 2002). And Barbara Ehrenreich wrote a book on what she frames as the United States' preoccupation with positive emotions (Ehrenreich, 2009).

Fortunately, emotion psychology offers some answers. Negative emotions are interesting for design because they come with specific action tendencies and because they evoke unique and powerful experiences.

Fear, Guilt, Disgust: Forces, Not Just Feelings

An emotion produces a distinct action tendency: a built-in motivational response that changes how people act and react to their surroundings. In the last chapter, we looked at the action tendencies related to ten positive emotions. Now, we will expand the emotional palette to include negative emotions and action tendencies, opening new opportunities for designers to nudge users in particular directions.

Take *disgust*, for example, which taps into an ancient survival mechanism. Disgust protects us from potentially harmful substances such as rotting food, bodily fluids, or unsanitary conditions. It commands a person's full attention and compels them to stop whatever they're doing until they've distanced themselves or otherwise removed the offending stimulus from the immediate vicinity. Disgust can also be triggered by immaterial or conceptual phenomena, such as deeply immoral acts. Yet, these phenomena often have a certain attraction that runs counter to our tendency to avoid them. Humans are secretly fascinated by these things. Think of rubbernecking at the scene of a serious accident, the appeal of slasher films, or the popularity of reality shows focusing on disgusting or disreputable practices. In other words, a stimulus that evokes disgust is exceptionally good at grabbing attention, which can be useful if you want users to notice something or to make otherwise mundane information compelling.

Another pertinent example is *guilt*. People experience guilt when they believe they've caused harm or discomfort to someone else, be it emotional distress or material damage. Perhaps you forgot a loved one's birthday, accidentally killed your neighbor's plants by neglecting to water them, or told a white lie to skip out on a friend's party. Guilt evolved because humans are inherently social creatures whose survival historically depended on maintaining strong communal ties. Its primary action tendency is to make amends for the harm caused, by confessing wrongdoing, apologizing, compensating victims, or otherwise restoring damaged relationships. Interestingly, resolving these guilt-induced conflicts can sometimes strengthen bonds more than if nothing negative had occurred to begin with.[3]

There is compelling evidence that people intuitively recognize the usefulness of these emotional effects and actively seek out negative emotions whose action tendencies help achieve their goals. In a series of clever experiments, psychologists investigated this idea with video games.[4]

3. Tangney, Stuewig, and Mashek (2007).

4. The video game studies described here combine insights reported by Tamir (2009), Tamir, Mitchell, and Gross (2008), and Tamir and Ford (2009).

Participants imagined playing different types of games—confrontation-based (shooting enemies), avoidance-based (escaping threats), or construction-based (building an empire). They were asked to rate how much they would like to listen to different kinds of music before playing the game. The music had been selected to evoke either anger, fear, positive excitement, or no emotion, but participants weren't told about this connection. The results lined up with common sense: people preparing for combat games unwittingly preferred anger-inducing music, those facing escape scenarios chose fear-inducing tracks, and those preparing for peaceful games preferred positive tracks. Even more remarkably, a follow-up experiment showed that players performed better when their emotional state matched the game's demands: for example, when playing a shooter game, the players who had listened to the angry soundtrack racked up more kills than those who listened to the happy tunes.

Why Negative Emotions Stick With Us

Negative emotions have another intriguing advantage: they deliver incredibly potent experiences, which can be memorable and personally meaningful. Such levels of power are difficult to match using positive emotions alone.

Why is that? People experience positive emotions when something fortunate happens and negative emotions when something unfortunate happens. But there's an asymmetry in how easily these emotions are triggered. Research psychologists Daniel Kahneman and Amos Tversky demonstrated this through their groundbreaking work on loss aversion. They found that people react much more strongly to losses than to gains of identical proportions. Specifically, the prospect of losing a substantial amount of money brings up considerably stronger negative emotions than winning the same amount generates in positive emotions.[5] This principle extends far beyond money. Research has consistently found that people have stronger reactions to hardship or mishap than to similar degrees of favor or luck.

Moreover, negative emotions tend to be more intense and urgent than positive ones. This reflects our evolutionary past: detecting threats required immediate, powerful responses to ensure survival. A rustling bush might be a predator—better to overreact and live than to underreact and become prey. Although positive emotions can certainly be intense, such peak moments are less common in daily life than the immediate, urgent responses that negative emotions demand.

Fear provides an illuminating example. A roller coaster ride produces intense physiological arousal because humans have primal fear responses to rapid movement, loss of balance, and violent shaking. To achieve an equivalent level

5. This research was replicated across numerous studies and contexts and earned Daniel Kahneman a Nobel Prize.

of physiological excitement purely through positive emotions, one would likely need to win the lottery or witness a favorite sports team clinch a championship.[6]

Certain negative emotions also lead to distinct experiences that positive emotions cannot provide. Sadness, for example, has a particular gravity and meaning that is unparalleled among positive emotions. Its action tendency involves withdrawing into your personal bubble and reflecting on your life and choices, which creates a uniquely contemplative experience. This may explain why people sometimes prefer sad music over happy music—it speaks to deeper life experiences in ways that upbeat tunes rarely can.

Turning Distress into Delight

Positive emotions are inherently enjoyable and therefore "safe" to design for. But as we have shown in several examples, negative emotions work in two ways: sometimes they are the drivers of rich, memorable experiences, while other times they are simply unpleasant.

How can you distinguish between rich and unpleasant? And how can you incorporate this rich type of experience into your designs?

Imagine yourself in the following three scenarios:

1. *You're camping deep in a remote forest. While preparing your meal, you spot a grizzly bear slowly approaching. Your heart leaps, panic sets in, and your eyes frantically search for a way to escape. The bear sees you and moves closer, faster now.*
2. *You're visiting a wildlife park where animals roam freely in enclosed areas. As you walk along the fence, you suddenly come face-to-face with a bear standing less than a meter away on the other side. You can count the hairs on its coat, smell its musky odor, and feel the ground vibrate as it moves. Your heart skips a beat. Fortunately, the fence is sturdy and tall enough to keep you safe.*
3. *You're at the wildlife park on a different day. You approach the fence but there's no animal in sight—not even in the distance. After waiting for some time, you head home feeling disappointed.*

The bear without a fence is genuinely terrifying. The bear behind the fence is thrilling. The fence and no bear is dull.

The fence represents a straightforward example of a "protective frame," something that allows you to experience the negative emotion (in this case, fear) while knowing you're protected from its source (the bear). Psychologist Michael Apter introduced this concept as part of his reversal theory, which

6. Note that this comparison doesn't imply that a roller coaster ride is as *pleasurable* as winning the lottery; rather, we're comparing the intensity of physical arousal they generate—the surge of adrenaline, racing heartbeat, and heightened senses that make you vividly aware you're alive.

explains how negative emotions can become enjoyable.[7] A protective frame doesn't remove the negative emotion; instead, it transforms how people experience it. The fear is still present but has become essential to the pleasure of the experience. This insight leads us to a fundamental principle of designing with negative emotions.

THE SEVENTH LAW OF EMOTIONAL DESIGN

Negative emotions within safe boundaries enrich user experience

A protective frame is a psychological phenomenon and not a material object. You can't design it directly—but you can induce it. The design can create the conditions that enable people to experience emotions behind a protective frame of their own making. The wildlife park's fence only functions as a protective frame if visitors believe it will protect them. If someone doubts its strength or isn't sure it extends all the way around the enclosure, they might experience terror rather than thrilling excitement. Personal beliefs, past experiences, and cultural background all influence how effectively a protective frame operates.

Four Ways to Make Negative Emotions Feel Safe

For design purposes, we distinguish four types of protective frames, each offering different opportunities to transform negative emotions into enjoyable experiences.[8]

The Safety-Zone Frame: Close, But Not Too Close: The fence at the wildlife center exemplifies a safety-zone frame. This frame allows a person to experience the source of the negative emotion directly but at a safe physical distance, such as from behind a barrier or mitigated by a specific protective measure.

Designers can amplify or reduce the effectiveness of a safety-zone frame by adjusting the psychological or physical distance. For example, a barely visible glass barrier between a person and a bear makes for a more intense experience than a large fence and a moat.

7. Apter (2007).

8. Michael Apter initially identified three protective frames: detachment, safety zone, and confidence. We've renamed "confidence" as "control" to highlight aspects relevant to design and added a fourth, the "perspective frame," to broaden the range of design opportunities; see Fokkinga and Desmet (2013).

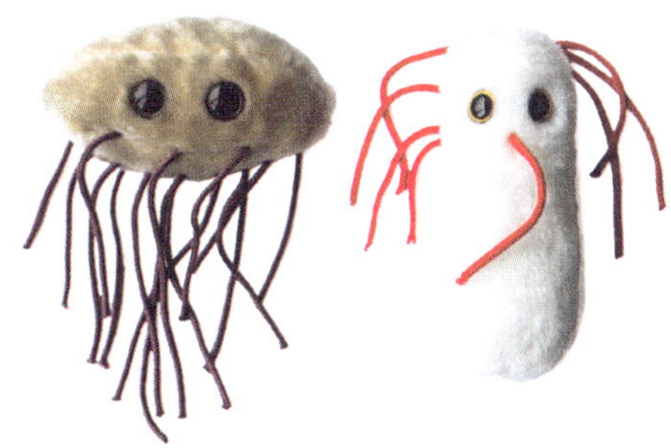

7.2 Aquarium tunnel / 7.3 Stuffed toys of E. coli and Salmonella

Examples: • Seats just beyond the splash zone at a dolphin show: close enough to stir excitement, far enough away to avoid getting soaked • The Ledge at Skydeck in Chicago—a series of glass observation boxes on the Willis Tower's 103rd floor—eliciting fear and exhilaration simultaneously • A glass tunnel through an aquarium: surrounded by awe-inspiring or predatory sea life, feeling immersed yet protected.

The Detachment Frame: Through the Looking Glass: The detachment frame creates an even greater distance than the safety frame. The user no longer interacts directly with the source of the negative emotion but instead encounters a representation of it. A common example is an aggressive person or animal depicted in a photograph, video, or painting, heard in an audio clip, described in a book, or portrayed by an actor. In all these cases, the user isn't actually exposed to the threat but can still experience the fear the attacker would normally provoke.

Designers control the strength of detachment by adjusting how abstract or stylized the representation is. Seeing an artistically refined, black-and-white photograph of a collapsed building gives a different experience than a shaky, low-resolution video does. Reading about a natural disaster feels very different from seeing graphic images of it. Directors of television shows have long known that a close-up of a situation will produce drama, while the same situation filmed with a wider lens can create comedy.

Examples: • Watching a couple having a heated argument in a film scene: uncomfortable in real life but engrossing onscreen • An abstract sculpture representing environmental destruction, using plastic waste to symbolize ocean pollution • "Giant Microbes"—cute stuffed representations of deadly diseases and microbes, eliciting playful disgust.

The Control Frame: Getting a Grip on the Negative: A control frame is present when people feel they can manage a situation that triggers a negative emotion.

7.4 Bulls and runners, Pamplona / 7.5 Ice Bucket Challenge

They are confident that they have the skills, knowledge, or preparation to handle something despite a feeling of danger—or any other negative emotion.

A rock climber scaling a steep cliff without ropes illustrates this perfectly. There are no anchors, harnesses, or safety nets; the only things keeping the climber from certain death are their wits, skill, and physical strength. If they trust in their abilities rather than becoming paralyzed by fear, they will enjoy an extremely heightened sense of focused excitement.

Designers can strengthen a control frame by granting the user more control over a situation or by amplifying users' ability to manage it. Amplification can be physical, making users (feel) strong, fast, or agile enough to handle a challenge, or it can be cognitive, making them (feel) smart, well-informed, skilled, or resourceful enough to accomplish something.

Examples: • An amateur cook attempting a flambé dessert, guided by clear instructions and practiced safety measures. This knowledge helps them remain calm while igniting the pan for the first time • Runners participating in the traditional Pamplona bull race rely on their route knowledge and fitness to experience exhilaration rather than pure terror • A driving school offers an advanced winter driving course in which drivers can practice braking and drifting on slippery surfaces. The course doesn't remove fear from the equation—it teaches people how to navigate it.

The Perspective Frame: Looking Beyond and Feeling Better: The perspective frame doesn't shield people from the negative emotion itself. Instead, it redefines meaning by framing negative emotions in a broader context. For example, waking up at 5:30 a.m. might feel awful if there's no compelling reason to do so. But if you're waking up to get work done before your inbox starts buzzing or to squeeze in a run before the rest of the city wakes up, that same unpleasant moment becomes synonymous with diligence, self-mastery, or care. The discomfort is the same but the perspective from which one views it changes the whole experience.

One helpful way to think about perspective frames is through the lens of virtues: qualities that are morally admirable and socially valued. Each unpleasant experience can be tied to a virtue that gives it meaning. The reluctance which might accompany taking on extra work for the team can trigger feelings of loyalty. Standing up to a bully (fear) expresses courage. Being honest when it's awkward (shame) is a mark of sincerity. By drawing on virtues, designers can reframe displeasure as proof of strength or integrity.

Examples: • Friends standing in a long line for concert tickets. Though boring and physically uncomfortable, they're securing seats to see their favorite artist together—a meaningful shared experience worth the discomfort • A day of spring cleaning—hauling boxes, scrubbing floors, airing out rooms. It's physically tiring and not particularly fun but it's satisfying. The effort becomes a seasonal ritual of renewal, a fresh start after a long, stagnant winter • The Ice Bucket Challenge, an activity that involves pouring a bucket of ice water over a person's head, promotes awareness and encourages donations to research on the disease amyotrophic lateral sclerosis (ALS).

Layering Protection

Protective frames don't exist in isolation. In many rich experiences, several frames operate simultaneously, reinforcing and complementing one another. Consider these two examples:

Worm farm starter kit: A home compost kit with aeration, bedding materials, live worms, and detailed maintenance instructions. The kit's transparent container exposes the interior. The natural revulsion of handling squirmy creatures becomes strangely compelling as users find themselves observing the decomposition process.

- ***Safety-zone frame:*** *The gloves, sealed container, and window let users interact and observe closely without direct contact.*
- ***Control frame:*** *Clear, visual instructions help users confidently care for their worms while preventing mess and odor.*
- ***Perspective frame:*** *Users feel proud to reduce waste and engage in an eco-conscious practice.*

Online investment platform in "practice mode": A digital investment platform with a "practice mode" in which users invest virtual rather than actual money. The genuine stress and fear of financial loss, safely contained within the practice environment, allows users to experience the thrill of investment decisions without real consequences.

- ***Detachment frame:*** *There's no actual money at stake, so losses (and gains) can be experienced without consequences.*
- ***Control frame:*** *Users make their own decisions about where and how much to invest.*

It's important to note that adding and combining protective frames isn't always better. Some experiences become more interesting precisely because a particular frame is absent. For instance, roller coasters and suspenseful films viewed in the theater deliberately lack a control frame—and adding one wouldn't necessarily improve the experience. Sports and other physical games specifically lack a detachment frame—otherwise, they would become video games. The partial absence of protection is often precisely what makes these experiences so compelling.

Rich Experiences in Design

We now have the complete picture. People enjoy negative emotions not in spite of themselves but because the unpleasantness offers something valuable: an action tendency that helps fulfill a need or an experience that is unusually powerful and memorable. That enjoyment depends on an additional condition, however: the person must somehow feel protected or insulated from negative consequences. When all these ingredients are present, the result is a composite emotion that blends negative and positive feelings into one compelling whole. We call these composite states *emotionally rich experiences* or simply *rich experiences.*[9]

In principle, any negative emotion paired with the right protective frame can form the basis for a rich experience and thus become valuable for design. To support this, we have researched and compiled a set of 36 negative emotions, each with their action tendencies and appraisal structures. The full set, available at https://emotiontypology.com, provides a broad palette for you to draw from when designing rich experiences.

Over the years, among our students and in design practice, we've observed that there are nine rich experiences that tend to produce especially intriguing and promising results. We have collected them into a set of named archetypes, each with a distinct emotional tone and dynamic (see pages 180-181).

If you'd like to explore the rich experiences in greater depth, you'll find a table in *Tools & Techniques*, pages 253-256, detailing the appraisal, possible protective frames, and the resulting experience and action tendency for each rich experience.

9. The concept of designing for emotionally rich experiences was introduced in the doctoral research of one of the authors (Fokkinga, 2015).

Rich Experience Blueprints

The previous chapter introduced you to emotion blueprints: a practical approach to translating emotional theory into actionable design insights. These blueprints help bridge the gap between universal psychological principles and real-world design possibilities, providing inspiration without locking you into specific solutions.

The same approach works beautifully for rich experiences—with a few important adaptations.

When creating a *rich experience blueprint,* you start by selecting the *negative emotion* you want to design for. The overview of rich experiences in this chapter, along with the detailed information about action tendencies, appraisals, and protective frames in *Tools & Techniques,* pages 253-256, can guide your choice. Are you aiming for the heightened alertness of the Thrilling? The contemplative weight of the Wistful? The playful tension of the Teasing?

Next, you explore how that emotion might logically and meaningfully emerge within your specific context. What would trigger fear, frustration, or sadness in your users?

The crucial difference from a positive emotion blueprint lies in considering whether users will feel genuinely safe from harm while experiencing the negative emotion. Your blueprint must thoughtfully address which protective frames will transform potential distress into an engaging experience. Will users have control over the intensity? Is there enough psychological distance? Does the broader context give the emotion a meaningful purpose?

The process for creating your own rich experience blueprint, including detailed steps and considerations, can be found in *Tools & Techniques,* pages 257-258. Like its positive counterpart, it's supposed to be a living document that evolves with your insights and keeps your team aligned around the emotional experience you're crafting.

Rich experience	Examples
The Thrilling *Fear* meets with *exhilaration* when you feel danger but are safe from real harm at the same time. Your nervous system floods with adrenaline, heightening every sensation and slowing your perception of time. In this state of intense arousal, you experience life with the kind of remarkable clarity and vividness that ordinary moments rarely provide.	• Watching the final minutes of a tied championship game • Asking someone out on a date for the first time • Handling a snake at a wildlife exhibit • Driving through a severe thunderstorm in a reliable car
The Challenging *Frustration* combines with *determination* when facing obstacles that test your limits without breaking them. This creates a compelling state where struggle becomes satisfying rather than discouraging. People in this experience have a tendency to keep going until the obstacle is overcome.	• Completing the Sunday crossword puzzle • Growing plants from seeds for the first time • Preparing a complex recipe for dinner guests • Attempting to repair household electronics
The Grotesque *Disgust* combines with *fascination* when encountering something that is both repulsive and intriguing. While your instincts tell you to look away, curiosity draws you closer. The initial revulsion quickly transforms into captivation that commands attention and creates memorable, shareable moments.	• Watching pimple-popping videos online • Tasting extremely fermented foods from other cultures • Examining insects under a microscope • Exploring abandoned, decaying buildings
The Scandalous *Indignation* meets *fascination* when a person encounters violations of social norms from a safe distance and without being personally implicated. The initial shock of transgression mingles with an irresistible urge to know more about what's typically forbidden or hidden—and to share it with others.	• Attending a controversial art exhibit • Seeing a documentary about a morally bankrupt public figure • Reading whistleblower revelations about a familiar company • Enjoying reality TV shows about dysfunctional relationships
The Mysterious *Confusion* blends with *enchantment* when a person faces something that defies easy explanation. The disorientation of not knowing mingles with a magical sense of wonder. This combination creates engagement that invites deeper exploration and curiosity.	• Exploring caves or underwater environments where visibility is low • Reading books with deliberately ambiguous endings • Using tarot cards or other divination methods • Hearing stories about local legends that cannot be verified

Rich experience	Examples
The Wistful *Sadness* combines with *desire* in a bittersweet experience that is sometimes called nostalgia, homesickness, or melancholy. This experience deepens emotional connection by highlighting life's impermanence. The feeling acknowledges what's absent or unattainable while finding beauty in that very absence.	• Watching an "In memoriam" segment about an artist who passed away this year • Scrolling through photos of luxury real estate you cannot afford • Visiting your hometown and finding it has changed significantly over the years • Saving voice messages from loved ones who are no longer in our lives
The Absolving When *guilt* is transformed through *determination* with the aim of making amends. This powerful cycle starts by acknowledging the harm caused by your actions, then channels that negativity into taking responsibility, meaningful repair, and ultimately, stronger relationships and commitments.	• Donating to environmental causes after recognizing your carbon footprint • Writing letters to people you've wronged but never directly apologized to • Admitting professional mistakes that affected others • Offering reparations to communities your ancestors harmed
The Self-Sacrificing *Reluctance* meets *pride* during voluntary hardship undertaken for a higher or longer-term purpose. Unlike challenges pursued for personal achievement, this experience finds meaning in the effort and hardship itself, especially when in service of a deeply held value or principle.	• Taking a cold shower each morning as a form of discipline • Adhering to a restrictive diet for ethical reasons • Making an arduous pilgrimage to a sacred or meaningful site • Living with fewer amenities to reduce environmental impact
The Teasing *Annoyance* blends with *amusement* through lighthearted mockery or gentle pranks. Distinguished from bullying by underlying affection, the initial irritation quickly transforms into appreciation for the creativity and attention invested. This creates a special bond where mild transgression strengthens relationships.	• Being the subject of a customized "roast" at a birthday celebration • Having colleagues decorate your workspace with embarrassing childhood photos • Finding your car wrapped in plastic wrap on April Fool's Day • Receiving a custom shirt quoting something embarrassing you once said

DESIGN OPPORTUNITIES: THE PLEASURE OF NEGATIVE EMOTIONS

Rich experiences aren't meant to replace positive emotions or the need-based design approaches we described earlier in this book. Instead, they add new colors to the palette, offering an additional set of tools that can make products and services more engaging, more worthwhile, or more memorable. When orchestrating different aspects of a product experience, you now have access to the full spectrum of human emotion, allowing you to choose the most appropriate shade for each element.

The following three design opportunities show different ways to incorporate rich experiences into your design practice.

Design Opportunity 1. Creatively Add Rich Experiences: This first design opportunity is about exploring what happens when you take an existing product, service, or context and add a rich experience to it. The purpose is to let the different rich experiences inspire you creatively. You explore how they can enhance your product or service.

Review the descriptions, examples, and characteristics of each rich experience. Use these to spark creative possibilities. Don't over-analyze them, however; the goal of this exercise is to generate a multitude of ideas and explore different directions. Consider the tone of various rich experiences. The Wistful evokes an entirely different experience than the Grotesque. Which tone suits your design context? Which would create a striking contrast? Try both!

As in any creative exploration, don't be too quick to judge or discard your ideas. Let them emerge, unfold, and collide. Try to build on them. Some may be strange or silly; others may feel too ambitious or too small. That's fine. An idea that feels absurd may open the door to something subtle and refined.

Remember that adding a rich experience doesn't mean transforming the entire product into an emotional roller coaster. Sometimes, a single feature or interaction that delivers a rich experience can significantly enhance the overall user experience.

To illustrate this design opportunity, let's look at a design challenge we gave to a group of design students. The task was to create interventions for their university library. It was a context they knew well and had easy access to—but it also posed a challenge. Libraries are places of quiet concentration and study, not the first setting you might associate with the Thrilling, the Teasing, or the Grotesque. Illustration 7.6 shows the following selection of their ideas:

- *Pump-a-Doro Chair:* An inflatable chair that slowly deflates when study time is up. Students must manually re-inflate it, building movement breaks into their study sessions (the Teasing).

7.6 Shaking up the university library with five rich experiences

- *Scream Room*: A soundproof space with privacy curtains and volume-responsive lights. It allows safe stress release in an academic environment (the Cathartic).
- *Toilet Detour*: Signage that leads people on an intentionally longer route to the toilets. A quote at the end explains how walks during study breaks enhance creativity (the Self-Sacrificing).
- *Restricted Section*: A bookcase with black covers where touching the spine reveals the title. The additional effort to find specific books metaphorically addresses censorship (the Challenging).
- *Confession Booth*: Students and university staff anonymously share academic struggles and hear redemptions stories left by others. The booth transforms individual guilt into collective determination, creating an emotional archive of academic resilience (the Absolving).

Design Opportunity 2. Harness Beneficial Action Tendencies: This design opportunity starts with the question: what behavior would help your users achieve something, including a certain state of mind? As we've seen, each emotion comes with its own action tendency: a built-in behavioral nudge that can be incredibly useful. When channeled thoughtfully, negative emotions' action tendencies can be just as useful.

Consider the heightened attention that comes with fear, the determination that emerges from frustration, or the reflection sparked by sadness. These behavioral tendencies can benefit users, depending on context. Perhaps you want people to slow down and reflect in a fast-paced environment. Maybe you need users to pay closer attention to important information. Or you might want to encourage people to persist through a challenging but worthwhile learning process.

To explore this systematically, create a rich experience blueprint that starts with the action tendency as your goal for Step 1 (see pages 257-258). Work backward from the beneficial behavior to identify which negative emotion naturally produces it, then explore how to evoke that emotion safely and meaningfully within your context. The key is ensuring the negative emotion serves the user's interests. The rich experience should lead to something valuable—greater safety, deeper learning, stronger relationships, or personal growth.

Design Opportunity 3. Create Your Own Rich Experiences: The nine rich experiences we've described in this chapter offer a reliable foundation for designing emotionally layered experiences. But it's also a valuable and enjoyable exercise to build your own rich experiences from different combinations of negative and positive emotions. There are two starting points:

1. Your own experiences. Think back to moments in your life—big or small—that made a lasting impression. What were the emotional dynamics? What negative emotions were present, and how did they become meaningful? You can also draw from art, books, music, and film. What emotional combinations have moved you in those realms?

2. Emotion typologies and theory. At https://emotiontypology.com, you'll find detailed descriptions of 36 negative and 24 positive emotions, including their appraisals and action tendencies. And there are many other resources online and in the academic literature to help you understand the nuances of different emotional states.

Once you've found an emotion or a combination of emotions that intrigues you, craft a vivid description of the experience you want to create. Include the specific emotions involved and examples of what this would look like in actual products or services. You can use metaphors or personal memories to help bring the idea to life. You can also dive deeper into psychological theory or cultural perspectives on the emotion to give your design more grounding.

In our workshops, students and designers have used this approach to craft dozens of novel rich experiences. Here are a few examples:

- *The Coveting (Envy)*: The experience of wanting to improve yourself when seeing someone who is better off. Unlike pure envy, which is just painful, this experience channels the energy of envy into productive motivation.
- *The Languishing (Boredom)*: The experience of deliberately doing nothing with your time. Protected by the knowledge that the time-wasting is voluntary, it transforms boredom into a form of indulgence and luxury.
- *The Cringe (Embarrassment)*: The experience of discomfort and delight when witnessing harmless social mishaps—feeling awkward on someone's behalf while secretly enjoying the spectacle.
- *The Self-Pitying (Pity)*: The partly painful, partly soothing experience of feeling sorry for oneself. While prolonged self-pity can be unhealthy, brief moments of emotional surrender can be cathartic.

THE ETHICS OF EMOTIONAL DESIGN

Throughout this book, we've explored how design shapes emotional experiences, both positive and negative, subtle and profound. One question we are regularly asked is if this approach isn't inherently manipulative. It's a fair concern. Emotional design doesn't just influence user experience; it can steer behavior, shift decisions, and affect overall well-being. For us, the heart of the matter is *intention*. When we design to enhance someone's experience with the genuine intention to fulfill their fundamental needs, it is not manipulation. Manipulation begins when emotions are used to serve external goals—like commercial profit or behavioral control—at the expense of the user's well-being.

Ethical reflections are paramount when working with negative emotions. These emotions can enrich an experience, give it depth, and make it more memorable. But they also introduce risk and, with it, a responsibility. The designer's first priority must be to ensure that people are never exposed to actual harm, be it physical, psychological, or social.

What follows are seven reflections on ethical emotional design. The first four focus on designing for rich experiences; the remaining three broaden to emotional design in general. We offer these reflections not as rules but as thoughtful provocations—questions we return to often in our practice. Our aim is not to tell you what to do but to invite you to participate in the ongoing conversation about responsibility in emotional design.

Ethical Considerations for Rich Experiences

- ***Ensure Protective Frames Genuinely Protect***: Every rich experience relies on a protective frame. That frame needs to do more than just make the emotion enjoyable. It should also shield the user from unintended harm. A detachment frame, for instance, ensures there is no physical danger. But what about psychological safety? Could the experience reignite painful memories or create emotional distress? Always check what kind of protection your frame offers—and what it might be missing.
- ***Provide a Clear Opt-Out Mechanism***: Users must have the ability to step away from the experience. If that's not feasible—as when on a roller coaster—then the experience must come with clear and transparent information. Let users know exactly what they're getting into, and give them a real chance to say no.
- ***Protect Vulnerable Populations:*** This includes not only your intended users but anyone who might be affected by your design. Avoid reinforcing harmful stereotypes or turning marginalized groups into the emotional punchline.

Evoking indignation (the Scandalous), for example, can be powerful—but be thoughtful about who or what becomes the object of that indignation.

- ***Design for Purpose, Not Mere Discomfort:*** Negative emotions should serve a clear purpose in the experience, be it creating fun, building meaningful tension, fostering connection, or enhancing engagement. If your design evokes negative emotions gratuitously without adding genuine value to the user's experience, reconsider your approach.

Ethical Considerations for Emotional Design in General

- ***Design for Genuine Need Fulfillment, Not Exploitation:*** Emotions are powerful levers. They should not be pulled to trick people into engagement. Emotional design becomes exploitative when it uses joy, desire, fear, or shame to manipulate behavior for some calculated end: to increase clicks, compel compliance, or generate virality, for instance. There are serious risks to creating artificial dependencies or "emotional addictions," which undermine long-term well-being. Ask yourself: does this design help users to flourish, or does it serve a purpose at their expense?
- ***Respect User Agency Through Transparency:*** People have the right to understand how and why products are designed to influence their emotions. Transparency enables them to make informed choices. Design with transparency rather than trickery: let people know what emotional journey they're signing up for and ensure they can genuinely consent to it.
- ***Be Mindful of Cultural Differences:*** Emotions are shaped by culture. What delights in one context may offend in another. Some societies place greater value on emotional restraint, while others celebrate emotional expression. This is especially important when working with negative emotions, where cultural boundaries around acceptable emotional expression can vary dramatically. Approach cultural differences with humility, especially when working across regions or with diverse audiences. While emotional frameworks are universal, resist the temptation to project your own feelings, interpretations, or needs into them by assuming they hold true for everyone.

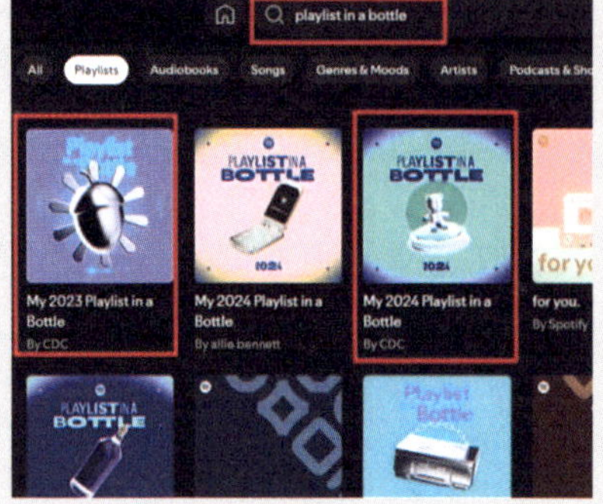

The Wistful (sadness): *Playlist in a Bottle* invites users to create a musical time capsule by selecting songs that capture their current moment, then "sealing" them away for one year. When they reopen it, users experience a bittersweet reunion with their past selves through music tied to specific memories. The passage of time turns what was once immediate into something gone forever, blending gentle nostalgia with appreciation for how far they've come.

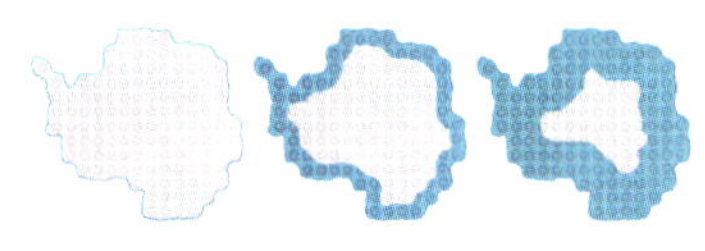

The Absolving (guilt): *Antarctica Shower Mat* project initially shows the continent of Antarctica, but its outlines slowly contract as it comes into contact with water. After fifteen minutes, the continent has disappeared. The product intends to make people aware—and feel a bit guilty—about their water use.

The Teasing (annoyance): *Alla Goccia* (Italian for: "Bottoms up") is a set of shot glasses that cannot be set down until they are empty. They deliberately introduce a problem for the user by taking away a key function that glasses possess. The purpose is to create a humorous atmosphere that also promotes sharing a drink with friends. When empty and set down, the glasses look like different tower bells.

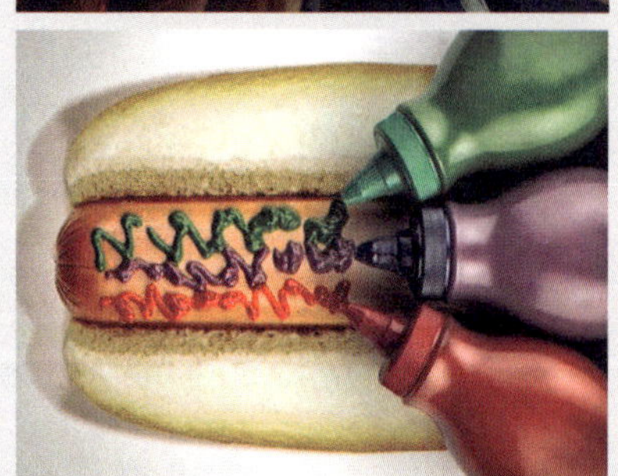

The Grotesque (disgust): *EZ Squirt* was a ketchup line in unnaturally vibrant colors like electric blue, purple, and green that simultaneously disgusted and amused consumers. The product deliberately challenged food color expectations, creating a visceral response of revulsion mixed with curiosity. Children were particularly drawn to its bizarre appeal, delighting in the transgressive experience of squirting alien-colored condiments onto their hotdogs.

The Self-Sacrificing (discomfort): *Moving Lives Platform* is a digital community platform where participants take sports challenges to raise money for charity. Participants willingly subject themselves to an early wake-up, blisters, and muscle fatigue—experiences they would normally avoid—yet feel proud of their hardships. The knowledge that participants support medical research or disaster relief establishes a perspective frame. The app's mapped routes and fundraising tools become tangible symbols of this worthwhile sacrifice.

The Thrilling (fear): *Doritos Roulette* transform snacking into a game of chance. Most chips offer a familiar cheesy flavor, but one in seven delivers an unexpected, blazing-hot spice bomb. The thrill comes from never knowing when you'll bite into fiery pain, creating tension with each chip. Friends gather to watch reactions, turning ordinary snacking into a suspenseful social experience of anticipation and occasional shock.

The Thrilling (fear): *Zombies, Run!* is a fitness app that transforms ordinary jogging into a thrilling survival adventure. As you run, the app immerses you in a post-apocalyptic storyline where you're a crucial runner collecting supplies while evading zombies. When zombie hordes approach, you must physically sprint faster to escape, turning exercise into a gripping mission.

The Scandalous (indignation): Oatly, a Swedish producer of plant-based milk, ran a provocative campaign called *"Ditch Milk,"* which challenged millennia-old thinking about the nutritional benefits of milk. By using bold and provocative messages, they outraged consumers and the media but also managed to attract a lot of attention and fans.

THEORETICAL DEEP DIVE:

The Paradox of Painful Joy – A Brief History

How did people come to enjoy negative emotions?

The idea that humans can derive pleasure from negative emotions dates back at least to ancient Greece. Aristotle (384–322 BCE) was the first known thinker to systematically explore this paradox. His analysis remains relevant and insightful to this day.

Aristotle's *Poetics*[1] focuses particularly on tragedy: theatrical performances centered around catastrophic events and cruel twists of fate. Why, he wonders, would people willingly subject themselves to stories designed to evoke sadness and despair? His explanation introduces *catharsis*: the idea that experiencing powerful emotions in a controlled, aesthetic context allows people to "purge" these feelings. Catharsis doesn't eliminate the emotions; their release transforms them into something simultaneously intense and insightful.

He also touches on the detachment frame as it works in art and entertainment. He argues that *mimesis*, or artistic imitation, allows people to enjoy the representation of reality, even if it evokes deeply negative feelings. *"Though the objects themselves may be painful to see, we delight to view the most realistic representations of them in art, the forms for example of the lowest animals and of dead bodies."*

Interestingly, Aristotle also discusses phenomena psychologists now call "appraisal" and "action tendency." In the *Rhetoric*,[2] he analyzes how speakers appeal to the audience's emotions to influence their behavior. He writes, for instance, about the causes and effects of anger and fear.

"Anger may be defined as an impulse, accompanied by pain, to a conspicuous revenge for a conspicuous slight directed without justification towards what concerns oneself or towards what concerns one's friends. (...) It must always be attended by a certain pleasure—that which arises from the expectation of revenge."

"Fear may be defined as a pain or disturbance due to a mental picture of some destructive or painful evil in the future (...). Fear sets us thinking what can be done."

Fast forward to the twentieth century. Today's psychologists have developed a renewed interest in the paradox of negative emotions leading to the positive and have proposed a range of explanations for the phenomenon.

1. Aristotle (1909). Mimesis quote from *Poetics*, 4, 1448b10-12.

2. Aristotle (1954). Anger quote from *Rhetoric*, 2.2, 1378a30-32 and 1378b1-2. Fear quote from *Rhetoric*, 2.5, 1382a21-23 and 1383a6-7.

The first set of theories focused on arousal, the physiological activation that accompanies emotions. These theories were clearly not inspired by Aristotle, because they essentially deny that people can enjoy negative emotions at all. What they actually enjoy is the state of arousal, the "rush," that comes once they've managed to suppress or override the negative feelings. A clear proponent of this explanation was Melvin Zuckerman, who investigated why certain individuals, "sensation seekers," enjoy extreme activities like skydiving or watching intense horror films, while others find such experiences purely negative. His theory proposes that people don't actually enjoy negative emotions but can learn to suppress them—leaving only the pleasurable arousal they cause.[3] Over time, sensation seekers become so skilled at suppressing the negative element that they can enjoy experiences others would find unbearable. While the effect might be most visible for these individuals, Zuckerman saw it as the universal explanation for any apparent enjoyment of negative emotions. His work built upon the optimal arousal theory developed by researchers including Donald Hebb[4] and Daniel Berlyne.[5] This theory proposes that people have an optimal arousal level, graphically represented as an inverted U-shape. Too little arousal feels unpleasant because it's boring, while too much feels unpleasant because it's stressful. Somewhere between lies the "Goldilocks zone" of just-right arousal. Zuckerman's contribution was to suggest that this optimal point varies significantly between individuals, with sensation seekers having a much higher threshold.

A second set of theories, which we might call "aftermath explanations," suggested that people seek out negative emotions like fear, disgust, and sadness because they enjoy the relief that follows their release. According to this view, a skydiver experiences utter fear and no pleasure during the dive but enjoys the intense relief upon safely landing. Arousal plays a crucial role here, too: the residual physiological activation from the fear during the jump "transfers" to the relief, intensifying it. Researchers like Richard Solomon and John Corbit[6] and Dolf Zillmann[7] championed these theories. While aftermath explanations acknowledge the crucial role of negative emotions—without fear, there would be no relief—they still don't accept that negative emotions can be enjoyable in themselves.

All of the theories we've discussed so far assume that people can only feel one type of emotion at a time. You're either feeling good or feeling bad—never

3. Zuckerman (1979).

4. Hebb (1955).

5. Berlyne (1960).

6. Solomon and Corbit (1974).

7. Zillmann (1980).

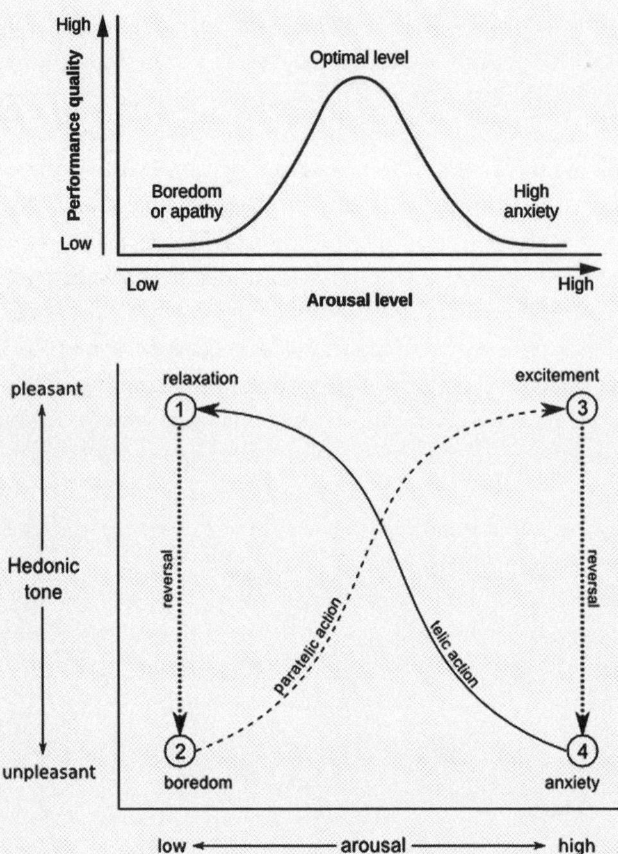

7.7 Optimal arousal theory versus reversal theory

both. However, toward the end of the twentieth century, some psychologists began to question that assumption based on new experimental evidence. When researchers gave people the opportunity to report multiple simultaneous emotions, for instance after watching the bittersweet film *Life Is Beautiful*, participants consistently reported experiencing both positive and negative emotions, also known as *mixed emotions.*[8] The idea of mixed emotions also opens up a possibility that earlier theories had ignored: that positive emotions can emerge within negative ones. Not after them, not instead of them, but in tandem, creating exactly the kind of rich experiences this chapter has explored.

Reversal theory, which gave us the concept of protective frames, goes even further. It proposes that all high-arousal negative emotions have a pleasurable variant, which Michael Apter calls "parapathic emotions." Excitement is the

8. The study was done by Larsen, McGraw, and Cacioppo (2001). Schimmack (2001) conducted similar studies and arrived at the same conclusion.

pleasurable variant of fear, while "parapathic anger" is the pleasurable variant of anger, "the kind of devilish glee one might experience while being objectionable in some social setting, ... or the joyous hate one experiences towards the villain in a cowboy film."[9]

So, which theory is right? Two researchers, Eduardo Andrade and Joel Cohen,[10] decided to test them empirically. They recruited horror film fans and horror film avoiders, and measured their emotions during various horror scenes. The results were revealing: both groups experienced roughly the same level of negative emotion during the scary scenes. But only the fans experienced positive emotions at the same time. In fact, the scarier the scene, the more they seemed to enjoy it. Importantly, the fans' enjoyment didn't come from relief afterward, as the aftermath theories would predict. There *was* relief—but only among the avoiders, who hadn't enjoyed the scenes at all. The fans had enjoyed the fear itself.

In a follow-up study, Andrade and Cohen tested whether they could increase enjoyment among horror avoiders by strengthening the protective frame. They showed the same scary scenes again, but this time included photos and information about the actors, emphasizing that none of it was real. The result: people still felt fear but they also reported more positive emotions. The detachment frame had worked. Even people who usually hated horror were able to enjoy the experience.

These findings support the theories that people can experience multiple emotions simultaneously and that negative emotions can indeed be enjoyable in their own right. And they demonstrate that Aristotle—thousands of years before scientific research existed—had already arrived at the correct conclusion.

9. Apter (2007, p. 119).

10. Andrade and Cohen (2007).

8

LAYERS OF *Experience*

"To be happier, change what you do—not what you have."

This deceptively straightforward suggestion comes from positive psychology, a relatively young branch of psychology dedicated to understanding the nature of human happiness. While traditional psychology often focuses on fixing what's broken, positive psychologists focus on building what *works*. They have spent the past twenty years systematically uncovering the conditions for genuine human flourishing. Their insights inform people on how to build lives that support lasting happiness. Increasingly intrigued throughout our careers, our curiosity has been sparked by what we have found in this field. "Can the science of happiness inform design practice?" we often wondered. Wouldn't that be fantastic: designing for true happiness?

So, what does the science of happiness actually say? Well, for starters, humans tend to look in the wrong direction. In a person's pursuit of happiness, they instinctively focus on the shortcomings of their circumstances, falling into the "if only" fallacy. If only I got that promotion. If only I could afford a bigger home. If only I had more followers online. These external circumstances do matter, but far less than you might expect. What is much more important is how you engage with life, which means you need to look at your *activities*. This insight crystallized into what researchers call the "activity recommendation": genuine well-being comes from actions, not from possessions[1]. Playing music, cooking from scratch, spending quality time with friends, and rescuing a cat from a tree—these activities, not material things, are what truly support our flourishing.

So, here we designers are, faced with an uncomfortable question: does stuff even *matter?*

Apparently not, according to happiness research. To a designer, this feels like an existential crisis. If happiness isn't about stuff, where does that leave us? After all, we're primarily in the business of creating things: products and services aimed at improving people's circumstances. A dark cloud seemed to gather over our profession. Were we merely creating seductively enjoyable distractions—but failing to deliver on their implicit promise of a better life?

Instead of setting the issue aside, we saw it as an invitation to rethink our role. What if design didn't just facilitate moments of enjoyment, but also actively supported happiness? This question interested us so much we founded the Delft Institute of Positive Design, a research institute to investigate this possibility.[2] One of its first projects was a student challenge: design something that stimulates happiness-boosting activity. Hans, one of our students, tackled

1. See Lyubomirsky, Sheldon, and Schkade (2005) for the empirical basis of this principle. Although aspects of their model have since been debated (e.g., Brown & Rohrer, 2020), the key role of intentional activities in well-being remains well-supported.

2. See https://diopd.org

8.1 TinyTask by Hans Ruitenberg and Emotion Studio

the challenge in his master's thesis project. He began by immersing himself in the happiness literature, compiling an overview of research-backed activity recommendations. Armed with this overview, he developed TinyTask, a product specifically designed to help people integrate happiness-boosting activities into their daily routines (see image 8.1).

The heart of the design is a set of 30 colorful tokens, each of which stands for a small, simple act. Here are a few examples:

- Take a completely different route home today. Have a good look around—what new places did you discover?
- Next time you're home alone, put on your favorite upbeat music and dance! How crazy do you dare to get?
- Who haven't you seen in a long time? Reach out and arrange to catch up over coffee or lunch.

Designed like an advent calendar, TinyTask features 30 doors, each hiding a single token.[3] When you open a door, you take out the token, attach it to your keyring, and thereby symbolically commit yourself to the task. Every time you reach for your keys, you're reminded of your intention. After completing the task, you can either keep the token as a memento or pass it along to someone else. When you're ready, you open the next door and continue the journey. By transforming abstract advice into tangible, cheerful prompts, TinyTask helps users cultivate happiness-boosting habits—one small act at a time.

3. Calendar illustration by Levi Jacobs; drawings on the tokens by Jin Li.

To find out if *TinyTask* really increases happiness, we designed a six-week study with 120 participants, divided equally into three groups of 40.[4] Participants reported their level of happiness every day, enabling us to precisely track changes in their well-being over time. The first group received 42 *TinyTask* tokens—one for each day of the study. Each token indicated a different happiness-boosting act. The second group received identical tasks, but each was printed on a sheet of ordinary paper.[5] The third group received no instructions, serving as our control. This experimental setup was designed to examine two main questions: do small daily activities actually increase happiness over time? And, do the *TinyTask* tokens make a difference compared to simple paper instructions?

The results were illuminating. The *TinyTask* group became significantly happier than the group who received nothing, confirming that daily actions do have a positive impact. But more surprisingly, we also found that the people in this group were significantly happier than the group who received the same tasks on paper.

It turned out that stuff *does* matter—or at least it *can*. At the heart of *TinyTask*'s impact were the happiness-boosting activities. However, the study indicated that the physical design did introduce something substantial: motivation. Activities only have an impact if you actually do them. While the design is simple, TinyTask made a difference because it orchestrated a layered emotional journey that, in a subtle but consistent way, motivated and supported participants to follow through. It was so effective that we still use *TinyTask* today.[6]

Throughout this book, we've explored how emotion psychology can inform design. In this final chapter, we turn the lens on design itself. How *do* products evoke emotion—not just at a particular moment but, rather, over time, throughout the usage journey? We introduce a framework with four layers of emotional impact in design. And as you'll see, *TinyTask* reaches all four.

Emotional Triggers: The Building Blocks of Experience

"I'm in love with my new headphones, but my smartphone is driving me crazy!" People often talk about their emotional responses to products as if they pertain to the object as a whole. But as we discussed in Chapter 2, that's not how people actually experience them. Human emotions unfold as a continuous stream of micro experiences: subtle, short-lived feelings that often stay below the threshold

4. For full study details, see Desmet and Sääksjärvi (2016).

5. Both the *TinyTask* group and the paper group received seven tasks each week, delivered by postal mail in an envelope.

6. Over the years, we've continued to refine the design—adding features like the advent calendar format and a new visual identity—but the core idea remains remarkably close to Hans' original concept. For more information, see https://tinytask.nl/en/.

of awareness. Even mundane products, such as laundry detergents, can generate dozens of emotional moments across their usage journey. While these findings reveal the nuances of our emotional lives, they leave one important question unanswered: what, exactly, *triggers* these emotions?

To answer this question, let's return to a fundamental emotional principle: emotions are *always* responses. Any emotion is a reaction to "something" the mind has appraised as relevant to a person's needs. Psychologists call these triggers "emotion antecedents" or "emotion elicitors": the stimuli that set human emotional machinery in motion. What's remarkable about emotional stimuli is their specificity. People don't respond emotionally to a situation or object as a whole; they respond to particular elements within it. The joy of running a marathon isn't spread evenly over all 42.2 kilometers. It's sparked by the moment you spot a friend cheering in the crowd, a stranger handing you water just when you need it, and, of course, the surge of crossing the finish line.

This specificity principle applies equally to people's interactions with products and services. Think back to the last time something delighted, worried, or frustrated you. It probably wasn't the entirety of the product or service experience that triggered your emotion—it was a specific moment of interaction: the reassuring click conveying craftsmanship, the app delay creating uncertainty, or the wobbly button signaling poor quality. These emotion-triggering moments often unfold too quickly for conscious recognition, yet they leave behind the somatic markers we discussed in Chapter 2: the emotional memory traces that guide future decisions.

So why do people end up attributing these specific emotional moments to the whole product? The answer lies in how human memory is organized. In the early 1970s, psychologist Endel Tulving introduced the now-classic distinction between episodic memory and semantic memory.[7] Episodic memory captures the details of specific experiences: what happened, where it happened, and how it felt. Semantic memory distills these experiences into more abstract knowledge, stripped of time and place. You might, for example, remember a specific morning when you enjoyed breakfast on a sunny terrace (episodic), which contributes to your general belief that "breakfast is enjoyable" (semantic).

When we interact with products and services, specific trigger moments create episodic memories linked to somatic markers. Over time, our minds consolidate these episodes into semantic knowledge: an overall emotional impression of the product: "I love my headphones" or "This app is frustrating." Such mental shorthand is efficient, but it is misleading from a design perspective. It makes a person believe they are reacting to products as coherent wholes when, in fact, they are reacting to a constellation of discrete moments

7. See Tulving (1972).

experienced throughout the journey.

This insight has important design implications. We designers cannot directly design the unified, lasting impression a product evokes—we can only design the building blocks that contribute to it: the individual moments that trigger the constellation of micro experiences. These are what we call *emotional triggers*: a delightful sound, an unexpected discovery, a brief moment of confusion followed by clarity, and so on. Each trigger may seem small or even trivial on its own, but together, they form the emotional signature of a product. For designers, they are the true building blocks of emotional design.

This perspective brings a practical challenge. Once you've begun to look for emotional triggers, you'll start noticing them everywhere—in every transition, every gesture, every micro interaction. The sheer number and variety can feel overwhelming. How do you work with such variety without losing track of the overall product experience?

What helps is to recognize that emotional triggers operate at different levels of engagement when it comes to real-world products and services. Some relate to direct sensory contact, others to interactive behavior, and still others to broader patterns of use that can eventually shape a person's identity and lifestyle. Rather than treating every trigger as equivalent, you need a framework that acknowledges these different levels of influence and impact. This insight leads to the eighth law of emotional design.

THE EIGHTH LAW OF EMOTIONAL DESIGN

Design has emotional impact across four layers of user experience: perceiving, using, doing, and becoming

To help us implement this law, we have devised a framework comprising four layers of emotional triggers: perceiving, using, doing, and becoming.[8] Table 8.2 shows the core principles of these layers. Each layer represents a different scope of user engagement with products and services, from immediate sensory impressions to long-term identity effects. While these layers often build

8. This shares principles with Hassenzahl's (2010) three-tier goal hierarchy in human-technology interaction: motor-goals (operations), do-goals (activities), and be-goals (psychological needs).

Layer	Core focus	From the user's perspective	Relationship to other layers
Perceiving	Immediate: at first sight, touch, or other sensory contact	I experience emotions from how the product looks and feels, and what it means to me.	Forms the first impression that sets expectations for all subsequent layers.
Using	Short-term: during direct interaction with the product	I experience emotions from how the product responds to my actions and how it behaves.	Builds on initial perception by adding dynamic behavior and responsiveness.
Doing	Medium-term: throughout the activity enabled by the product	I experience emotions from how well I can achieve my goals and how the activity unfolds.	Extends beyond operation to encompass the activity enabled by the product.
Becoming	Long-term: the product influences lifestyle and identity	I experience emotions from how the product changes who I am and how I live over time.	Transforms momentary experiences into lasting changes in identity and lifestyle.

8.2 Framework of four layers of emotional triggers

upon each other, they aren't strictly sequential—perception remains important throughout usage, and identity effects can sometimes emerge quite rapidly, for example. Understanding these different layers helps designers organize and prioritize the multitude of possible emotional triggers available to them. The insets in the following sections show product examples for each layer.

1. Perceiving: Emotional Impact from First Impressions

Imagine visiting a friend and instantly feeling drawn to a particular object in their living room before even knowing what it is or what it does. Perhaps you're struck by its elegant contours or captivated by its vibrant color, which stands out from everything else in the room. This kind of emotional response happens in the blink of an eye, before any rational assessment takes place. It is a classic example of an emotional trigger at the perceiving layer.

Products can trigger your emotions instantly, even before you begin using them. You engage with them first through your senses: predominantly sight, but also touch, sound, smell, and occasionally taste. These sensory qualities are the most immediate pathway to emotion. Think of the cool smoothness of brushed metal, the inviting texture of soft leather, or the crisp click of a well-fitted lid. Even without knowing what a product does, these qualities can spark feelings—

delight, aversion, fascination, curiosity—purely through sensory perception.

At the same time, you instinctively interpret what you perceive. You "read" a product's character in much the same way as you read a person's body language. Is it playful or formal, rugged or refined, bold or modest? Consider the *Roller Radio* and the *T3 Radio* in the inset. The first signals youthful energy and fun, while the second suggests elegance and precision. These perceived "personalities" trigger emotions depending on how they align with your needs or expectations.

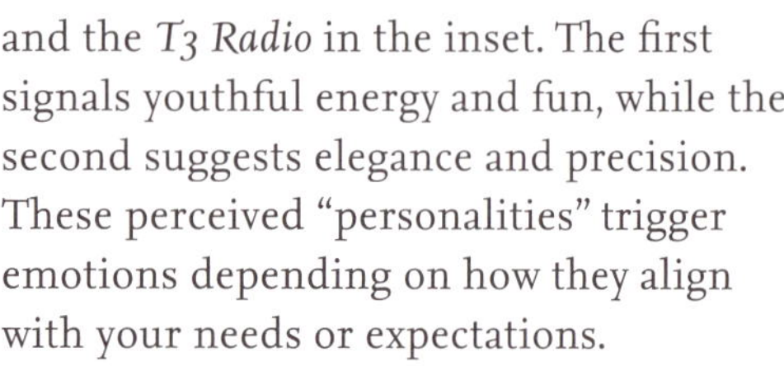

The **Roller Radio**, *launched in 1986 by Philips, was designed to appeal to a younger audience. Its bold, colorful, and toy-like appearance instantly evoke curiosity and youthful energy.*

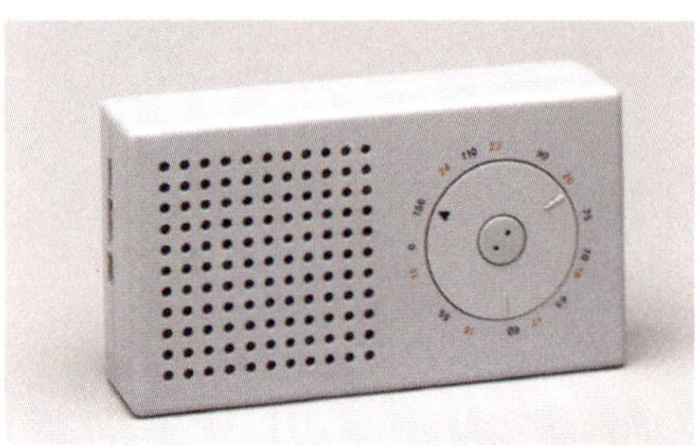

The minimalist **T3 Radio**, *launched in 1958 by Braun and designed by Dieter Rams, became an instant icon. Its clean lines, neutral colors, and balanced proportions, exemplify clarity and functional elegance.*

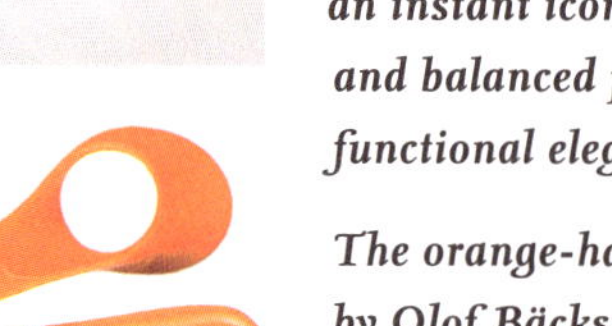

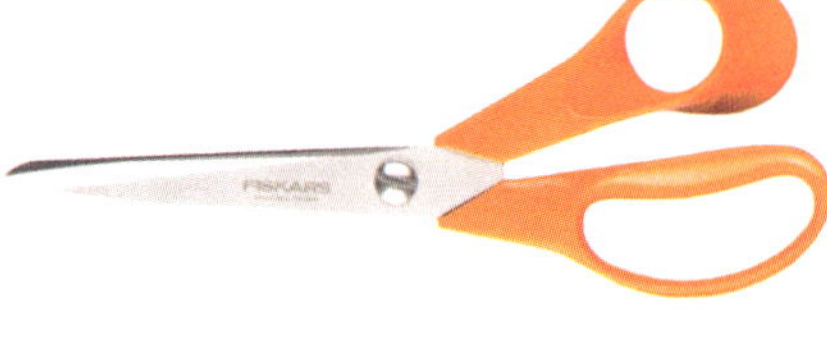

The orange-handled **Classic Scissors**, *designed by Olof Bäckström and launched by Fiskars in 1967, combine visual simplicity with tactile comfort, making them an instant classic.*

Swatch Watches, *designed in part by Marlyse Schmid and Bernhardt Müller, were launched in 1983. Their playful patterns and fashion-forward designs made them an expression of personality.*

Some emotional triggers also tap into cultural symbolism—visual cues, references, or materials that evoke shared meanings. The *Classic Scissors* and *Swatch Watches* in the inset illustrate this well. The scissors' timeless design signals enduring quality and craftsmanship. The bold graphics of the watches connect to youth culture and creative freedom. These symbolic cues may inspire a sense of pride, nostalgia, belonging, or perhaps even discomfort, depending on whether the user identifies with the underlying message. As associations differ between people, so will the meanings they attach to designs. The minimalist aesthetic that signals elegant sophistication to one person might appear cold and unwelcoming to another. A retro quality may feel appealingly nostalgic to one person but fusty to someone else.

These different types of triggers—sensory qualities, design character, cultural symbols, and so on—combine to shape a person's first impressions. Perceptual triggers operate rapidly, often unconsciously, and set the emotional tone for what follows. Even before any interaction occurs, these triggers shape expectations and lay the foundation upon which all subsequent layers of experience are built.

2. Using: The Dance Between Human and Object

Pick up your favorite kitchen tool or open an often-used app on your phone. Notice what happens next: your fingers find their familiar positions, buttons respond to your touch, and mechanisms start to move. This dance between human and object is where the second layer of emotional experience unfolds.

Most products fulfill their purpose through interaction. Unlike the first layer, which concerns the user's initial impression, this layer captures how people feel during product use. The emotional triggers in this layer take several forms. Some arise from how the product responds to people's actions: the precision of a control dial or the effortlessness of a complex feature, like the *Nest Thermostat's* smooth rotating interface. They can also arise from satisfying feedback that confirms that input was received, like the distinctive flipping mechanism of the *Zippo* lighter.

Table Alarm Clock, *designed in 1939 by Arne Jacobsen for Lauritz Knudsen. The updated version has an invisible sensor that activates light and snooze functions, supporting elegant user interactions.*

Zippo lighter, *launched in 1933, designed by George Blaisdell. The signature clicking sound and flipping mechanism create an interaction that is both deliberate and nonchalant (which has made it a favorite prop in countless films).*

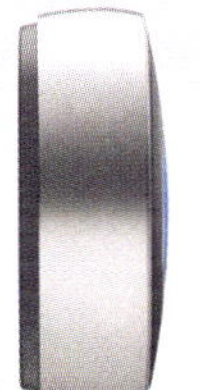

Nest Thermostat, *launched in 2011, designed by Tony Fadell and team. Its rotating dial offers smooth, responsive feedback, turning temperature control into a satisfying gesture.*

Muji CD Player, *launched in 1999, designed by Naoto Fukasawa. Its pull-cord operation mimics turning on a ventilation fan, transforming music playback into a playful and intuitive interaction.*

Other triggers come from how the product directs people's actions: whether it provides clear pathways for people to fulfill their intentions or leaves users uncertain about what to do next. The *Muji CD player's* pull-cord operation mimics a ventilation fan, making it easy to use. A well-designed interface gently leads users through difficult tasks, making people feel competent and in control; a poorly designed one creates confusion and second-guessing, triggering frustration or anxiety—even when our goal is technically accomplished.

Physical comfort also plays a role. Products that accommodate human bodies create different emotional responses than those that force awkward postures, grips, or movements. For example, consider the pen that allows hours of writing without cramping or the knife handle that doesn't press uncomfortably against your palm during extended use. Or consider the *Table Alarm Clock* that responds to simple hand gestures, eliminating the need to fumble for buttons in the dark. These physical qualities translate directly into emotional experiences during use.

Where the perceiving layer involves our response to static qualities like color and material, this layer is about the product's dynamic character. The emotions that surface—confidence when something works just right, relief when a potentially challenging process turns out to be simple, frustration when an interface behaves inconsistently—reflect our needs in the ongoing relationship with the product as we engage with it.

3. Doing: Meaningful Moments in Everyday Activity

We rarely use products just for the sake of using them. Every interaction implies a purpose: a meal to prepare, a message to send, a space to organize. This third layer of emotional experience emerges not from the product itself but from the activity it enables.

Consider why you pick up a pen. Unless you're a professional pen tester, you do this not to experience the sensation of writing but to capture your thoughts, to create a to-do list, or to sign a document. The product becomes a bridge to something more meaningful: the activity itself. You're simply focused on what you are doing rather than how you are doing it. And it's in the activity that many of the relevant emotional triggers emerge.

In this third layer, emotions are triggered in how the activity unfolds in relation to a person's goals and expectations. They are signs that the activity is progressing well or not. There is satisfaction when your carefully prepared meal turns out just right, frustration when your drawing doesn't capture what you see in your mind's eye, or relief when your presentation flows smoothly despite your nervousness. In each case, the product enables the activity, and the emotions connect to needs beyond the product. The *Recipe Journal* enables cooking and documentation, but the emotions come from creativity, accomplishments, and preserving memories.

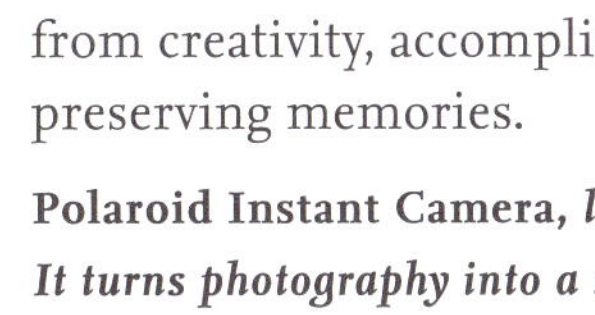

Polaroid Instant Camera, ***launched in 1948. It turns photography into a shared anticipatory activity. As users watch, the image slowly appears—transforming a solitary act into a social ritual.***

Tree Tent, ***launched in 2012 by Tentsile and designed by Alex Shirley-Smith. Its suspended, hammock-like structure evokes a sense of adventure and playful engagement with the outdoors.***

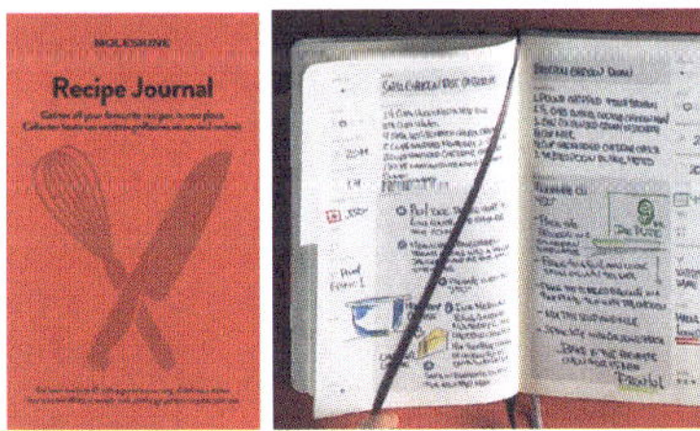

Recipe Journal, ***one of eight "passion-themed" journals available from Moleskine. It transforms cooking into a personal practice by inviting users to document and reflect on their favorite meals.***

Chemex Coffee Maker, ***launched in 1941, designed by Peter Schlumbohm. Its transparent, hourglass shape turns manual coffee brewing into a mindful morning ritual.***

Different people bring different goals to the same activity, creating distinct emotional experiences. A professional chef preparing dinner service experiences the act of cooking differently than a parent hurriedly assembling a weeknight meal or a novice attempting a challenging recipe for the first time. Taking pictures with a *Polaroid Camera* creates different experiences depending on whether you're alone or sharing the anticipation with others. Same activity—different emotional landscape.

The rhythm of an activity also affects how emotions unfold over time: the anticipation of beginning, the focus in the middle, and the satisfaction or disappointment upon completion. Products that support transitional moments support a smooth and coherent experience across the entire activity. Consider a piano that helps maintain flow during rehearsal, a project management tool that celebrates completed tasks, or the *Chemex coffee maker* which turns brewing into a deliberate ritual with clear stages.

In this layer, the product often recedes into the background. When you're fully engaged in writing, you don't think about the pen; when you're immersed in cooking, you barely notice the pan. Once a camper is settled in the *Tree Tent* and enjoying the outdoor experience, the tent itself fades from awareness. It isn't the product that brings out the emotion; it's your progress toward a goal that matters to you—be it creating something, solving a problem, connecting with others, or expressing yourself.

4. Becoming: When Products Shape Identity, Lifestyle, and Relationships

Products don't just enable isolated activities. They also influence what we do regularly, how we see ourselves, and how others perceive us. Over time, they shape our routines, our sense of identity, and the roles we inhabit. These are ripple effects that extend beyond individual moments of use.

The emotions triggered in this layer emerge neither from the product nor from the immediate activity it supports but, instead, from the change product use has brought to your life. Some effects are relatively small: going outside more often because you have a good waterproof backpack. Others are more significant: picking up a circular saw and gradually becoming someone who builds their own furniture.

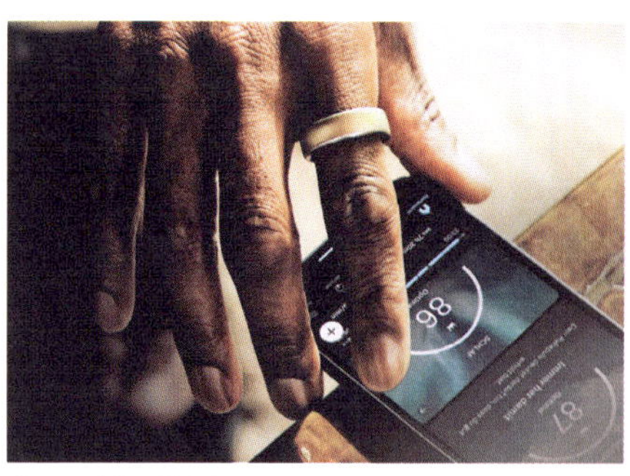

Oura Ring, ***launched in 2015, designed by Kari Kivelä and Petteri Lahtela. It transforms wearers into data-aware optimizers of their sleep and health, supporting long-term lifestyle awareness and self-improvement.***

Valentine Typewriter, ***launched in 1969 by Olivetti, designed by Ettore Sottsass and Perry King. Its bold color and portable casing signified youthful rebellion and individuality, embodying a countercultural identity.***

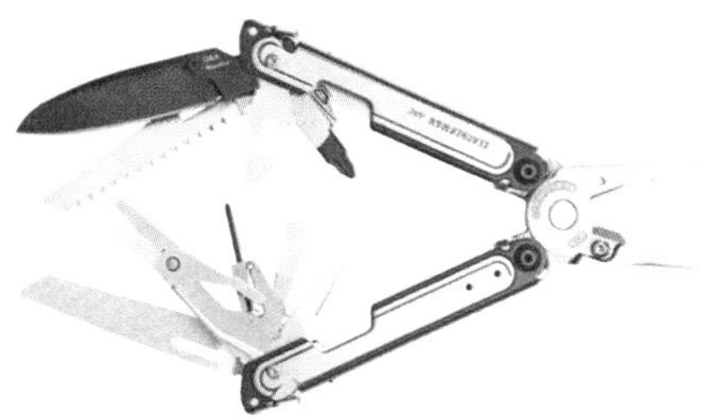

Leatherman Multi-tool, ***launched in 1983, designed by Tim Leatherman. It symbolizes self-reliance and becomes part of the user's identity as a problem-solver and do-it-yourselfer.***

Harley-Davidson Motorcycles, ***founded in 1903. The brand represents a lifestyle of freedom, strength, and community, becoming deeply intertwined with users' self-image and group identity.***

These emotions surface when something happens that makes you aware of such change. Perhaps you've received a compliment from a neighbor about your garden, you're standing back to admire your just-finished self-built project, or you just realized that carrying a *Leatherman multi-tool* makes other people recognize you as the problem-solver in the group. These moments show how products can facilitate new practices and perspectives.

This layer also has a strong social dimension. Products can connect us to communities, traditions, or shared practices. They can help signal membership in groups or alignment with particular values. *Harley-Davidson motorcycles* connect riders to a broader culture and shared identity. Examples include the specialized tools that mark membership in a craft or hobby group, the inherited objects that link generations, and the sustainable products that express environmental values and connect users to like-minded others. Through these connections, products can evoke feelings of belonging, contribution, and shared experience.

The timescale of this layer extends beyond the immediate or daily experiences of the previous layers. These emotional impacts unfold over longer periods as products gradually influence your routines, skills, relationships, and self-image. A journal doesn't just help you write down thoughts today; over time, it might become part of how you process experiences. Similarly, the *Oura Ring* can gradually transform habits and self-awareness around health and sleep. While the previous layers unfold in moments or hours, this layer emerges over weeks, months, or even years. It represents the deepest and most lasting emotional impact products can have—contributions to a life well-lived.

Connecting the Dots: The Complete Emotional Picture

The ingredients in our framework are not new. For decades, researchers and designers have developed theories about product experience, exploring everything from visual aesthetics to usability, from symbolic meaning to behavior change. The section *Further Reading* (pages 260-263) offers a curated overview of core concepts from the design research literature. Each perspective offers insights and tools for designers. Still, in our own design projects, we kept running into the same issue: the theories were insightful but fragmented. Each illuminated one part of the picture but left the rest in the dark. It's a bit like having different medical specialists examine the same patient: the cardiologist focuses on the heart, the neurologist on the brain, and the dermatologist on the skin. Each provides crucial information but rarely gives a more complete picture of the person's health.

The four-layer framework aims to provide an overarching structure that connects all the dots. By organizing emotional triggers according to where they occur in the user's experience, the framework helps designers understand how different elements work together to shape a complete emotional journey. To make this more concrete, let's look at *TinyTask* as an example of how the framework is helpful (see image 8.3 for a visualization).

TinyTask in Action: The Four Layers at Work

Layer 1. Perceiving: *TinyTask* presents itself as a playful object. Its advent calendar format—thirty numbered doors in a compact display—immediately suggests a sequence of small surprises. The illustration of a head as a garden (see image 8.1) hints at personal growth. This visual framing positions the project as a series of actions, one per door. The tokens inside are brightly colored, pleasant to touch, and feature simple pictograms, making the tasks feel approachable. Together, these design choices convey that this is not a serious commitment; it's something to explore step by step.

Layer 2. Using: Interacting with *TinyTask* is straightforward. The numbered doors suggest a natural order, and the process—opening, discovering, attaching—feels intuitive. Behind the first door is a carabiner clip, emphasizing that the tokens are meant to be carried with you. Behind the next is a task token with a pictogram and a brief explanation. The act of opening a door along its perforated edges produces a satisfying tactile and auditory reward. Attaching the token to your keychain, however minor, feels deliberate: a commitment to the task. Later, removing it after completing the task creates a sense of completion.

8.3 TinyTask in action

Layer 3. Doing: The tokens prompt modest, achievable activities—actions that fit easily into daily life. Carrying a token around, for instance on your keychain, acts as a subtle reminder. The calendar hanging in a visible spot reinforces intention without pressure. There's also an ongoing curiosity about the next door, which keeps the engagement fresh. The flexible pace—you choose when to open a new door—helps maintain a sense of autonomy rather than obligation.

Layer 4. Becoming: Over time, *TinyTask* can influence how users see themselves. The accumulation of completed tokens becomes a visible trace of effort. For some, it creates a sense of continuity or even a personal archive of positive actions. Users may also pass tokens on to others, thereby creating shared experiences. These patterns support an emergent self-image—someone who invests in well-being or cares for others. The design doesn't prescribe this identity; it quietly makes room for it to take shape.

TinyTask is, admittedly, an unusual example—a specially designed happiness intervention rather than an everyday product or service. But the four-layer model offers a lens through which to examine any product, from kitchen utensils to digital interfaces, and uncover its emotional architecture. Learning to see products this way is like acquiring a new language or looking through a microscope for the first time and discovering that something that seemed simple has a number of intricate components. Apply this lens to the objects around you, and the everyday world becomes rich with emotional triggers.

Consider your coffee machine with all of the above in mind. No longer just a functional appliance, it has become a complex arrangement of sensory impressions, interactions, activities, and identity markers. There's the warm, tactile sensation of the handle against your fingers and the reassuring gurgle as water begins to flow through the machine. The morning ritual created by using it structures your day and helps you transition from sleep to productivity. Perhaps it even contributes to your self-image as a coffee connoisseur, a gracious host, or someone who values small pleasures.

Seen this way, every product becomes an emotional landscape. To make this more concrete, we have applied the framework to two familiar products—the turntable and Google Maps. The insets on pages 211 and 213 show what there is to discover when you unpack a product through the lens of the four layers.

Crafting Emotional Journeys

We have seen how the four experience layers can help examine the emotional impact of products. The framework proves particularly useful when analyzing the results of a Micro-Emotion Scan (Chapter 2). For each emotion captured during the scan, you can trace it back to its specific trigger and determine which experience layer it belongs to. Different products will show different patterns. Some create their strongest emotional impact through activities (doing) or identity development (becoming). Others evoke emotions mostly through usability (using) or visual appeal (perceiving). The framework provides a structured way to map these emotional patterns and understand where a design creates its impact.

But how can you use this framework in the design process? This is where it shows its full potential. It provides a structure for deliberately designing positive (or rich) emotional triggers across each layer. For each layer, you can explore which emotional triggers to create. To guide this process, the thirteen fundamental needs we explored in Chapter 1 offer additional direction. After all, every positive emotion signals need fulfillment.[9] Imagine, for example, fulfilling Stimulation with unexpected tactile contrasts (perceiving), Competence via perfectly timed feedback (using), or Purpose by supporting someone's journey towards becoming more mindful (becoming).

At the same time, a layer-by-layer approach doesn't guarantee coherence. To create a meaningful whole, something additional is needed: an overarching

9. This builds on the "Needs as Design Seeds" design opportunity discussed in Chapter 1, but maps specific needs to particular experience layers.

EMOTIONAL JOURNEY 1
Sarah and Erik share an evening playing vinyl records

1. *The Perceiving Layer*

Feeling the wood – Erik runs his hand along the wooden base of the turntable, feeling its smooth, polished grain. "*This feels so much more substantial than my plastic Bluetooth speaker,*" he thinks.
Turning the knobs – Sarah reaches for the oversized volume knob. "*These big turning buttons,*" she says, "*they're just like the ones on my parents' stereo in the '70s. I didn't even realize I missed that.*"
Watching the meters glow – "*Look at that!*" Erik points to the vintage-style VU meters on the amplifier, their warm amber glow pulsing gently even before any music plays. "*Those analog meters look so much cooler than digital displays.*"

2. *The Using Layer*

Balancing the tonearm – Erik carefully lifts the tonearm, feeling that perfect balance as it responds to his touch. "*It's like the player is meeting me halfway,*" he says as he guides it toward the spinning record.
Changing the speed – When Erik adjusts the speed selector from 33 to 45 RPM, the immediate visual feedback of the record spinning faster gives him a sense of control that digital streaming doesn't provide.
Repositioning the needle – Sarah winces when the needle catches on a scratch. "*Here, let me,*" she says, lifting the tonearm and precisely repositioning it just after the damaged groove. "*That little bit of trouble makes you pay attention in a way that hitting 'next' never does.*"

3. *The Doing Layer*

Adjusting the sound – Erik leans back in his chair as Sarah adjusts the equalizer, boosting the bass just a touch. "*There!*" she exclaims as the sound fills the room more completely, giving them both a sense of having crafted the perfect audio environment.
Flipping the record – "*This player makes switching sides feel like an event,*" Sarah remarks as they both stand up at the end of Side A. Erik carefully flips the record, and they share a moment of anticipation before lowering the needle again.
Taking turns – Sarah notices how they've naturally fallen into taking turns choosing records. "*The player kind of forces you to be present with each other,*" she observes. "*We're not just streaming something in the background while staring at our phones.*"

4. *The Becoming Layer*

Listening differently – "*You know what's weird,*" muses Sarah, "*I've started really listening to entire albums instead of just skipping to the hits. Your turntable has changed how I experience music.*"
Changing friendship rituals – Sarah realizes that since Erik got his record player, their friendship has evolved to include regular listening sessions. "*This player has changed how we hang out.*"
Rearranging the space – Erik notices his apartment has gradually been rearranged around the record player, with the most comfortable chairs now facing it and shelving added nearby for his growing collection. "*This turntable has become the center of my living space.*"

vision of the user experience. The framework gives you the ingredients, and the vision helps you decide what to focus on and how everything fits together. This is especially important once emotional triggers start multiplying into dozens or even hundreds of small design decisions. Without a unifying vision, these can easily lead to a fragmented experience. Emotional design, like all design, is an integrative activity. The key is ensuring that individual triggers work together to create a coherent experience.

Designers use a variety of methods to articulate and refine their vision on the overall experience. Some work with interaction visions—conceptual directions like "serious guidance" or "playful exploration" that anchor design decisions in the using layer. Others create style collages or mood boards for the perceiving layer. Some use personas and narrative roles (like "the discoverer" or "the caring leader") to guide longer-term identity experiences in the becoming layer. These methods guide design without dictating it. Like a compass, they offer orientation without locking you into a fixed route.

In our design practice, we often create *experience metaphors*. An experience metaphor links the emotion you are targeting to a familiar context: something that already embodies those qualities. "A road trip with friends," for example, carries a sense of adventure, spontaneity, and fun. "Setting up camp before a storm" represents urgency, focus, and preparation. A strong metaphor does two things: inspire and align. It opens up creative directions while helping designers stay grounded in a shared emotional intent. It can help unify diverse needs or requirements that may otherwise feel disconnected.

We've used this approach throughout our careers. Do you recall *Morning Tapas*, the redesigned airline breakfast from Chapter 4? The guiding metaphor for its design was "a morning stroll in the park." Obviously, we weren't trying to recreate a park inside the aircraft cabin. Instead, the metaphor captured the experience we were after: a calm start to the day, a quiet focus, a self-paced rhythm, simple choices, and a bit of freshness to gently awaken the senses.

Another example comes from the NOS News format redesign we discussed in Chapter 5. The guiding experience metaphor was "the news presenter as a travel guide who takes you through the story." That framing gave direction to everything from the studio layout (as a space to move through), to the presenter's position (in motion, rather than static), and the viewer's perspective (as the witness of unfolding events, rather than passive observer). These metaphors didn't make any design decisions for us—but they gave us a shared emotional vision that made sure the design team was heading in the same direction.

EMOTIONAL JOURNEY 2
Alina and Mark use *Google Maps* to look for a nice restaurant in an unfamiliar part of their city

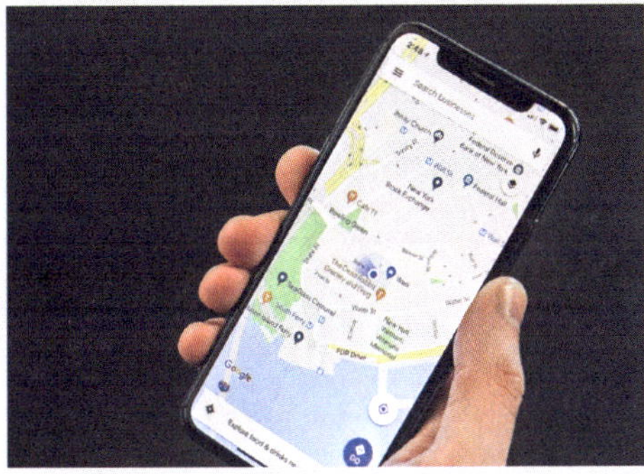

1. The Perceiving Layer

Seeing the whole – As Alina opens the app, the map fills most of the screen, with just a few buttons tucked along the edges. "*It's immediately clear what this app is for,*" she thinks. "*I like that it doesn't get in its own way.*"

Noticing the color scheme – Alina notices the clean color scheme. "*It's so crisp and organized,*" she thinks, already feeling more confident about finding their dinner spot.

Distinguishing road hierarchy – Mark appreciates the visual hierarchy of the interface—the bright colors of main roads contrasting with the muted tones of smaller streets. "*Even before I start navigating, I can see which routes matter,*" he notes.

2. The Using Layer

Experiencing search prediction – Alina types "*Thai food*" and feels a small thrill when suggestions start appearing instantly with each keystroke. "*It's like it's reading my mind,*" she laughs.

Waiting for loading – Alina taps on a restaurant icon and frowns when it takes an extra second to load. "*That tiny delay makes me irrationally annoyed,*" she admits, revealing how accustomed she's become to instant response.

Smooth zoom – Mark pinches the screen to zoom in, and the map glides smoothly into a close-up of the neighborhood. "*I love how precise this feels,*" he says. "*Like I'm in control, not just dragging pixels around.*"

3. The Doing Layer

Discovering the detour – "*Yes!*" Alina says when Google Maps suggests a route that avoids the construction she'd forgotten about. "*We would have been stuck in traffic for ages if we'd gone the usual way.*"

Following the location dot – Mark feels a wave of relief when he spots the blue dot moving along their route. "*We're definitely heading in the right direction,*" he confirms, the real-time tracking giving him confidence in an unfamiliar part of town.

Reading the reviews – "*4.5 stars with over 200 reviews,*" Alina notes, scrolling through the restaurant information. "*I always feel better about trying somewhere new when I can see other people liked it.*"

4. The Becoming Layer

Abandoning pre-planning – Alina realizes she's stopped keeping mental maps of new cities she visits. "*Google Maps has changed how my brain works,*" she tells Mark. "*I don't memorize routes anymore – I just trust it'll get me there.*"

Exploring unfamiliar areas – Alina notices how her exploration habits have changed. "*I'm much more adventurous about trying restaurants in unfamiliar neighborhoods now,*" she says. "*Before Google Maps, I stuck to places I already knew how to get to.*"

Filtering by ratings – Mark realizes he now judges places differently. "*If it doesn't have good reviews on Google Maps, I probably won't try it,*" he admits. "*The app has completely changed my criteria for where I'm willing to eat.*"

Stickz: Bringing the Forest into the Hospital

While the news broadcast and airline meal redesigns both adapted existing experiences, some design processes begin only with an abstract goal. The *Stickz* project is a good example (see image 8.4).[10]

For children undergoing cancer treatment, a hospital stay involves more than medical treatment. It often involves long periods of inactivity. Environments are clean but sterile. Spontaneous play—so central to childhood—is rare. And yet, physical play isn't a luxury; it's a vital part of development. It helps children explore, express themselves, develop physical skills, and maintain social bonds. When illness confines them, these opportunities disappear at a critical time in their lives.

The Princess Máxima Center, a leading pediatric oncology hospital in the Netherlands, challenged PhD candidate Boudewijn to address this. The brief was open, but the constraints were tight: limited space, strict hygiene, and suitable for children with reduced physical strength. Boudewijn grounded his design concept in a metaphor: "Playing in the woods," not because forests are practical, he reasoned, but because they embody the emotional qualities he wanted to recreate, such as freedom of movement, imaginative storytelling, and unstructured building. This resulted in *Stickz*, a set of large, colorful, branch-like elements. The oversized pieces invite full-body creative play without screens, rules, or instructions. In the hands of children, the elements become magic wands, animal legs, bridges, wings, or whatever their imagination can dream up. Soft, safe, and open-ended, they offer endless possibilities for exploration, movement, and shared invention—all within the walls of a hospital.

The experience metaphor resulted in shapes and interactions that support the movement-rich, imaginative play of being in the woods, like dragging branches across the forest floor and building forts with fallen limbs. Crucially, the metaphor wasn't applied literally across all layers. Deliberate adaptations were made to fit the hospital context. For example, natural colors were replaced with bright, cheerful colors that immediately signal "this is a toy" in an environment where children are often unsure what they're allowed to touch. Rough textures and breakability—qualities of real branches—were replaced with strong cores and soft foam exteriors. This makes them feel substantial but safe: no risk of splinters or bumps. Strong inner cores and soft outer layers also provide both safety and substance. Subtle connection points and nesting shapes support construction without dictating outcomes.

The *Stickz* project illustrates the effectiveness of designing on two levels: the overarching emotional experience you want to create, and the specific emotional triggers that bring it to life. The metaphor provides direction, and the four

10. See Boon (2020) for the full development of *Stickz* as part of his PhD research on *Playscapes*.

8.4 Stickz by Boudewijn Boon

layers help translate that vision into moments of emotional impact—each one tailored to the situation. The result is a product that does more than enable play: it creates a space for movement, meaning, and escape right in the middle of the clinical world of the hospital.

Why Stuff Matters After All

Now that we have explored the four-layer model of emotional experience let's return to where we began this chapter: *does stuff even matter?* Is emotional design merely creating enjoyable distractions—delightful but not genuinely fulfilling?

The outcome of the *TinyTask* experiment offers a nuanced perspective. At the end of the study, the physical tokens group was significantly happier than the paper group, even though both versions included the exact same activities. The paper instructions simply couldn't match what the tokens achieved.

It seems then that *stuff does matter*—but not as the objects of desire. *TinyTask*'s happiness impact doesn't come from ownership; it comes from how using it *supports* daily happiness activities. The tokens create an emotional journey dotted with small moments of pleasure that support and reinforce these activities; it is filled with positive reminders, small motivations, and tiny successes. These motivate participants to *engage* in the activities as well as sustain them over time.

The paper version in the study addressed only the doing layer: the activities themselves. But without the motivational bridges created by positive emotions across the other layers, it provided no means of sustaining engagement. It's a bit like being handed a shopping list for a recipe versus receiving a beautifully illustrated cookbook with the same recipe and set of ingredients. The cookbook doesn't just tell you what to buy—it inspires you to cook.

This is what we call "emotional frontloading"—a concept we use to describe the strategic placement of positive emotional triggers in the earlier layers of experience that help people get started, and which foreshadow the need satisfactions to come later in the usage journey. Likewise, "emotional backloading" involves emotional triggers that create lingering positive impact—often located in the later doing and becoming layers. These include reflection, pride, meaning, nostalgia, or a strengthened sense of identity after the core activity has ended. These aren't just nice-to-have enjoyments; they act as powerful motivators. They help users work their way up to doing the activity by creating a sense of anticipation and emotional momentum.

This brings us back to the foundation of this book: the 13 fundamental needs. These needs are sources of joy for a deeper reason: they are essential to a fulfilling life. That's where emotion and happiness align. And that's how we can resolve the paradox in the introduction: Products matter to our happiness, not because we can possess them, but because they are vehicles for moments of engagement that gradually, sometimes collectively, lead to the fulfillment of fundamental needs.

It turns out that the recommendation to focus on activity isn't at odds with emotional design after all. Good design doesn't replace meaningful activities—it makes them more likely to happen, and more impactful when they do. It's not just that stuff matters. It's *how* it matters: it shapes the activities that fill our lives. And that's something both designers and psychologists can celebrate.

THEORETICAL DEEP DIVE:

Understanding Emotional Triggers

Are there design features that always trigger positive emotions?

We have probably been asked this question more often than any other by students, designers, and executives alike, all hoping for a formula. Will rounded corners instead of sharp edges make people feel joy? Does the color blue reliably instill a sense of calm? Are natural materials emotionally superior to synthetic ones? These questions reflect a tempting but ultimately flawed assumption: there is a direct, one-to-one relationship between design features and emotional responses. After decades of research, we know that this isn't how emotions work.[1]

Some sensory stimuli do generate universal *like* or *dislike*. People tend to enjoy sweet tastes, gentle touches, and relief from discomfort. Humans are born with these preferences. Similarly, certain events in a social context seem to evoke hardwired feelings within humans—like feeling affection when someone you love shows care.[2] On the negative side, pain, sudden loud noises, extreme temperatures, and hunger are universally disliked. These responses appear consistent across cultures and individuals.

But the catch is that these preferences are not yet emotions. They are basic responses of pleasure and displeasure. Emotions require cognitive appraisal: an interpretation of what something means relative to a person's goals and needs.[3] Although the taste of sugar is universally pleasant, it may trigger joy in one person, guilt in another, and nostalgia in a third, depending on their needs. Even physical pain, a seemingly straightforward negative stimulus, can evoke pride in an athlete who interprets it as evidence of pushing boundaries (an example of a Self-Sacrificing rich experience, see page 181)—while another person experiences only distress from the same sensation.

Moreover, emotions and their triggers never occur in isolation. They happen within a rich context of personal history, cultural meanings, and specific situations. The same "universal" stimulus can trigger entirely different emotions depending on where and when it happens, what preceded it, and what the person expects to happen next.[4] For design, this means you cannot rely on supposedly universal stimuli. Pleasant sensory qualities don't guarantee positive emotions, just as avoiding unpleasant sensations doesn't prevent negative ones. The emotional impact always depends on understanding specific users in their unique contexts, with their particular needs, values, goals, and expectations.

Why does the joy of products wear off after time?

A common misconception is that products generate stable emotional states. We often see design briefs asking the designer to "make the product feel joyful" or "create a sense of calm." It sounds straightforward enough. But this view overlooks a fundamental principle from emotion psychology: emotions aren't evoked by stable states but by *change.*

Emotion psychologist Nico Frijda formulated this as the Law of Change: "Emotions are elicited not so much by the *presence* of favorable or unfavorable conditions but by actual or expected *changes* in favorable or unfavorable conditions."[5] A comfortable chair doesn't make you feel grateful all day long. But the moment you shift from a hard bench into it, the gratitude or relief is triggered.

This principle has profound implications for how we understand emotional responses. Consider an intimate relationship. Being in a loving relationship satisfies your need for Relatedness (and probably several others) but you don't experience constant joy simply because the relationship exists. Instead, specific moments within the relationship—a supportive gesture when you're struggling, a shared laugh over dinner, or a meaningful conversation late at night are what evoke your emotions. These moments stand out against the backdrop of the overall relationship.

Similarly, products don't generate permanent emotional states by their mere presence. Instead, they create the possibility for moments in which changes happen that our emotional system picks up on. Your brain functions as a change-detecting instrument; some of its neural pathways have evolved to pick up on environmental shifts that might signal good or bad news for your well-being. This makes perfect sense from an evolutionary perspective. Emotions evolved primarily to help us adapt to changing situations requiring new responses.[6] Feeling continuous emotion about unchanging conditions would waste precious mental and physical resources. By focusing on moments of change, our brains efficiently direct attention to what matters most—situations that might require adaptation.

According to the First Law of Emotional Design (Chapter 1), a product only evokes a positive emotion if it fulfills a genuine user need. But as Frijda's Law of Change reminds us, need fulfillment has to stand out in some way. The user or consumer must notice it as a change. Changes come in several varieties: something that either satisfies a previously unfulfilled need (receiving recognition after hard work), removes a source of need frustration (the office bully finally retires), shows progress toward need satisfaction (seeing muscle develop after weeks of exercise), or opens new opportunities for future need fulfillment (learning a valuable skill). Table 8.5 provides an overview for both positive and negative emotions.

Positive emotions *Evoked by triggers that signal:*	**Negative emotions** *Evoked by triggers that signal:*
• Need fulfillment • Progress towards need fulfillment • Opportunities for future need fulfillment	• Need frustration • Progress towards need frustration • Threats that signal future need frustration
• Removal of need frustration • Progress towards removing need frustration • Opportunities for future reduction of need frustration	• Decline of need fulfillment • Decline of the progress towards need fulfillment • Threats that signal future decline of need fulfillment

8.5 Triggers for positive and negative emotions

A product may continuously fulfill a need, but it won't evoke ongoing emotional responses unless it creates moments where something shifts: a small success, a moment of relief, a sign of progress. Your dishwasher supports your needs for Autonomy and Ease, but you don't feel joy simply because you own it. The emotion comes at specific times: when it rescues you just before guests arrive, for example, or takes care of a particularly grimy load you had been dreading to do by hand, or after returning from a week of camping where you had nothing but a sponge. Products don't generate sustained emotion. They create the conditions for emotional moments, when something changes in a way our emotional system registers as meaningful.

Why does the same event evoke different emotions at different times?

Two capuchin monkeys are doing the same simple task—handing objects to a researcher. Both initially receive cucumber slices as rewards, and each seems content with this arrangement. Then something changes: one monkey starts receiving grapes—a far superior treat—for the same amount of work. What happens? The cucumber-receiving monkey becomes visibly agitated. He throws his cucumber slice back at the researcher, refusing to accept what was perfectly satisfactory just moments before.[7]

This seminal experiment reveals something about primate emotions that is also fundamental about human emotions: they depend heavily on frames of reference. Emotional triggers are not absolute. The monkey's reaction changed not because the cucumber changed, but because his reference point shifted. What once seemed fair suddenly felt deeply unfair when contrasted with his companion's superior reward.

We all carry frames of reference that strongly influence our emotional responses. These frames arise from our past experiences, our expectations, and what we observe happening around us. Consider getting a raise in salary. Good news, right? Usually. But what if it's significantly smaller than you expected? Or your coworker, who has fewer responsibilities, received the same increase? Suddenly the same "positive" event triggers disappointment or even anger. Our reference points are shaped by past experiences, cultural norms, marketing, peer behavior, and more. As Daniel Kahneman and Amos Tversky showed in their revolutionary research, humans don't evaluate outcomes in absolute terms—they evaluate them relative to expectations.[8]

Product experiences work the same way. Different people apply different frames of reference to the same product. You might be delighted with your new headphones because they sound substantially better than your old pair. But your emotion might change to disappointment after comparing them to a high-end set you try in a store. Same product, different emotions—all due to shifting reference points. Without knowing someone's frame of reference, you can't reliably predict their emotional response to your design. The physical product may be constant, but the emotional experience it generates depends on the invisible reference points each user brings to the interaction.

1. Desmet and Hekkert (2007).

2. Ekman and Friesen (1978).

3. Frijda (2007).

4. Hassenzahl (2010); McCarthy and Wright (2004).

5. Frijda (2007, p. 10), emphasis added.

6. Ledoux (2012); Tooby and Cosmides (2008).

7. Brosnan and De Waal (2003).

8 .Kahneman and Tversky (1979).

Epilogue

Early in our consulting careers, we took a six-hour train journey from Rotterdam to Hamburg for what seemed like a breakthrough opportunity: present emotional design at the European headquarters of a multinational consumer goods company. The CEO had heard of our work and was curious enough to invite us in. Armed with a 45-minute slideshow, we arrived ready to inspire.

The boardroom was impressive: mahogany table, floor-to-ceiling windows. Research directors, marketing chiefs, and product managers settled in to hear our story. We delivered our presentation with practiced precision: micro emotions, rich experiences, fundamental needs, and all the innovation opportunities that emotional insights could unlock. We finished, and the room filled with silence. Then the CEO stood up. "Thank you," he said. "I have one question. How will this help me sell more products next quarter?"

For a moment, the question hung in the air. We exchanged glances—who would field it? What followed was a fumbled response about happy customers and long-term value that rang hollow, even to us. The CEO thanked us with the polished courtesy that executives master. He would call, he said, when a suitable project emerged. Ten minutes later, we were on a bus back to the station. The call never came.

During the long train ride home, we dissected what had gone wrong. Somewhere between Osnabrück and Amersfoort, it hit us: we had crafted an elegant answer to a question no one in that room was asking. Our entire presentation focused on the mechanics of emotional design—the what and the how—while completely overlooking the real question in the room: return on investment. They wanted to know whether emotional design could drive business results. We had offered them tales of improved experiences and our passion for methodological elegance.

Worth the Investment

Emotional design requires investment. Conducting a Micro-Emotion Scan means spending hours with users in their natural environments. Laddering needs requires new skills. Targeting specific user emotions adds new challenges to the design process. These approaches aren't necessarily more expensive than other research methods—they are just different. Any shift in process requires training, adjustment, and financial investment. So maybe, while reading this book, the German CEO's question also crossed your mind: is emotional design worth the investment?

The answer is a clear yes. And the evidence is well established.

In 1982, researchers Morris Holbrook and Elisabeth Hirschman published a paper that challenged how consumer research understood decision-making. At the time, the dominant view was that people are rational problem-solvers, methodically weighing features and benefits when buying products. They proposed something more human: people choose products not just for what they accomplish, but for how they make them feel.[1] What seemed radical in 1982 now stands as one of the most thoroughly validated findings in consumer psychology.

As it turns out, the researchers had understated their case. Emotions don't just influence purchasing decisions—they are the primary driver. A recent meta-analysis of 82 studies across 34 countries found that emotional value is the strongest predictor of consumer behavior.[2] These effects extend far beyond buying decisions. Customers who feel emotionally connected to brands remain loyal and become ambassadors, generating 50% more value over time than customers who are merely satisfied.[3] The flip side is equally striking: one in three customers will abandon a brand permanently after just one negative interaction[4]—revealing both the power *and* fragility of emotional connections.

The financial impact is just as compelling. Organizations that invest in emotional engagement report return on investment gains of 40% or more.[5] One longitudinal study tracked companies for sixteen years and found that those excelling in customer experience delivered stock market returns more than double the average.[6] This isn't a short-term bump—it's sustained competitive advantage that builds over time. The numbers are clear: emotional engagement is one of the most reliable and evidence-backed business investments a company can make.

Emotions in the Boardroom

The evidence speaks for itself. Even so, we never lead with the numbers during conversations with our clients. And you may have noticed that we managed to write eight chapters on emotional design without mentioning business results even once. Have we learned nothing from the Hamburg debacle?

The answer is both yes and no. Our roots lie in human-centered design, where the goal is to create products that genuinely enhance people's lives. The business

1. Hirschman and Holbrook (1982).
2. Mason et al. (2023).
3. Bjørnland et al. (2015).
4. Merritt (2018).
5. Harvard Business Review found 40% new account growth (Magids, Zorfas, & Leemon, 2015) and McKinsey customer experience studies found up to 800% improvements in customer satisfaction metrics (Arnous, 2023). Both studies were based on documented business improvements.
6. As compared to the S&P 500, which is a benchmark representing 500 of America's largest corporations. See Watermark Consulting (2023).

case for emotional design isn't our driving force, it's our license. We focus on understanding people and improving their lives, knowing that the financial case is strong enough to speak for itself. We wrote this book to provide the methods and tools to make that understanding actionable.

There is another reason the executives weren't convinced by our presentation. They were expecting a one-size-fits-all solution they could easily implement. But emotional design is not a silver bullet; it's a comprehensive toolbox. Which approach works best depends entirely on the challenge at hand. The laundry detergent required micro-emotion analysis. The airline breakfast project demanded contextual emotion mapping. The news show benefited from understanding viewers' clashing needs. To identify the right approach, try to deeply understand the product, the context, and the users. This is best done in collaboration with stakeholders, whether clients or colleagues, since they bring context and domain expertise.

And frankly, applying individual tools to isolated projects is just the starting point. The biggest impact is achieved when emotional design thinking becomes woven into the organizational fabric: when research methods, design processes, and decision criteria all reflect emotional insights, and when teams possess both the skills and support to implement them effectively. Of course, that level of organizational change requires investment and leadership commitment.

If that's not immediately feasible, not all is lost. Start out small, by integrating emotional insights into work you're already doing, and build from there. In interviews, take a few extra minutes to ladder needs. In design reviews, introduce fundamental needs as evaluation criteria. When getting feedback, watch for emotional signals—frustrations, delights—that hint at deeper needs. These steps may seem modest, but they often yield surprisingly valuable insights. You can start where you are without disrupting existing workflows; over time, these small changes create opportunities for deeper integration.

Design for the Real World

Return on investment matters, but it's not the sole measure of impact in the world. Design increasingly tackles challenges where success extends far beyond quarterly returns. The field has evolved dramatically since we started this research in the early 2000s.

This evolution is playing out across multiple fronts. For starters, today's designers are grappling with the political dimensions of their work. Who decides what counts as good design? Who gets to participate in design decisions? Whose needs are seen, and whose perspectives are overlooked? Alongside this political awareness, designers are envisioning alternative futures through *speculative design*, asking not just what people need, but what kind of world we want to create.

Systems thinking has similarly pushed designers beyond standalone solutions toward addressing complex, interdependent challenges like climate change and healthcare access. *Generative AI* introduces another layer to this complexity, making design tools faster and more accessible while raising questions about how to meaningfully guide creative processes. Even the boundaries of who designers are designing for are shifting. *More-than-human design* is pushing the field beyond its anthropocentric roots, recognizing ecosystems, animals, and even rivers and forests as legitimate stakeholders.

Emotions remain fundamental across all these developments. The heightened awareness of design's political dimensions requires understanding how people feel about participation and power. Speculative futures depend on our emotional responses—what scares us, what excites us, and what futures we're willing to imagine. Systems interventions succeed when they address where frustration accumulates, where trust erodes, and where hope takes root. Even more-than-human design draws on emotions like care, awe, and grief in how we relate to the living world.

AI collaboration particularly benefits from emotional design thinking. While AI can reveal emotional patterns across thousands of interactions, it cannot empathize or understand context the way humans do—at least not yet. The introduction of AI in the design process makes emotional design skills more important, not less.

These developments raise new questions for emotional design. How do emotions function in collective action? How do emotional responses shape people's willingness to imagine alternative futures? What emotional dynamics emerge in complex systems interventions? How do we ensure AI tools enhance rather than manipulate human emotional experiences? These questions compel us to develop new methods and frameworks to understand emotions in these expanded design contexts.

At the same time, there's something profoundly reassuring about the universality of emotional principles. Fundamental needs don't change when the context shifts from designing a payment app to facilitating community dialogue. The way people appraise situations emotionally remains consistent whether you're working on product interfaces or climate interventions. The challenge isn't that emotions work differently—it's developing the tools to understand and apply emotional insights in these new domains.

From the Boardroom to the Dinner Table

Not long ago, a workshop participant told us he now uses our overview of fundamental needs with his teenage daughters during dinner. The framework happened to be on the table one evening and sparked a conversation. Since then, he said, they pick a random need as an entry point to talk about their day. Their conversations have become less superficial—and much more positive.

Once you begin perceiving the emotional dimension of design, you encounter it everywhere. The coffee shop that makes you feel welcome versus the one that makes you feel rushed. The parking meter that clearly displays remaining time versus the one that leaves you guessing. The playground that invites exploration versus the one that feels sterile and forbidding. The waiting room that soothes versus the one that heightens anxiety. Once you see it, you cannot unsee it. And once you care about it, you can ignore it no more.

What energizes us is how this awareness spreads beyond design disciplines. We've collaborated with teachers, healthcare providers, young people, and community organizers—all of whom discovered ways to apply emotional design thinking to their unique contexts. The ripple effects extend beyond products and services, touching how people relate to each other and navigate their daily lives.

You don't need psychology training to recognize that people have fundamental needs. You don't need expensive research infrastructure to notice the micro emotions that flow through everyday interactions. You don't need massive budgets to create beloved experiences or to explore how your work might contribute to human flourishing.

We want to continue making the emotional design toolbox accessible and useful for anyone who wants to create more meaningful experiences—whether that's a designer creating an interface, a teacher connecting with students, a policymaker addressing the energy transition, or a parent navigating family dinners. Each person who applies these ideas extends the circle of more thoughtful human interactions.

As accessible as a simple black pencil—and just as likely to be there when you need it most.

TOOLS
& TECHNIQUES

This section brings together all the practical tools, measurement instruments, and step-by-step methodologies introduced throughout the book. Here you'll find everything from interview guides and measurement scales to analysis frameworks and design templates. These approaches been refined through years of application in academic research and real-world projects.

Every resource includes clear instructions, practical tips from our experience, and examples to help you adapt the approaches to your specific context. Some can be implemented immediately, with minimal resources, while others may require more preparation and practice.

Think of this section as your workshop manual. Whether you're a seasoned researcher looking to add emotional insights to your toolkit, or a designer taking your first steps into emotion-driven work, this section is a resource to revisit as you develop your emotional design practice.

T&T 1 — FUNDAMENTAL NEEDS IN DETAIL

The table below defines the thirteen fundamental needs and gives an overview of their related sub-needs. Sub-needs are either components of the overall need (like physical comfort and rest for Fitness) or common manifestations of it (like expressing views for Autonomy). Sub-needs aren't universal but are widely recognized ways to fulfill fundamental needs. Reflecting on them helps deepen understanding of the broader needs.

We have created an online resource that presents the thirteen needs with additional examples and details. The website includes short videos for each fundamental need, providing visual demonstrations of how these needs manifest in people's daily lives. For more information, please visit https://needtypology.com.

Definition	Sub-needs
1. Autonomy: Having the freedom to make choices and do things your own way, rather than being constrained in what you do and who you are by other people or things.	• Having the freedom to make your own choices. • Having the freedom to be yourself. • Being independent and self-reliant. • Having the freedom to express your views and opinions.
2. Beauty: Experiencing beauty, elegance, and sensory harmony in your daily life, rather than experiencing ugliness, chaos, or distaste.	• Experiencing order and balance. • Experiencing elegance and refinement. • Enjoying artistic and cultural expressions. • Experiencing grandeur and splendor.
3. Community: Being part of and accepted by a social group or entity that is important to you, rather than feeling you do not belong anywhere and have no social structure to rely on.	• Identifying with a group, team, subculture, or culture. • Feeling that you are part of and accepted by a group. • Having a sense of your roots and traditions. • Seeing others share your sense of community.

Definition	Sub-needs
4. Competence: Using your skills to master challenges, seeing yourself improving, and having control over your environment, rather than being incompetent or ineffective.	• Using your skills to master challenges. • Developing your skills and strengths. • Having and acquiring knowledge and understanding. • Having control over the state and events of your surroundings.
5. Ease: Experiencing things as simple, convenient, and clear, rather than experiencing them as hard, effortful, or overstimulating.	• Experiencing tranquility and peace of mind. • Experiencing simplicity and clarity. • Experiencing perspective and structure. • Experiencing convenience.
6. Fitness: Having and using a body that is healthy, rested, and energetic, rather than feeling ill, listless, or weak.	• Doing physical activity and getting exercise. • Getting enough rest and recovery time. • Being physically comfortable. • Being in an environment that is healthy and hygienic.
7. Impact: Noticing that your actions or ideas affect the world and contribute to something, rather than experiencing your actions as insignificant.	• Creating, building, or growing things. • Working towards leaving a legacy. • Seeing that your actions have an influence on people and things. • Having the power to shape outcomes.
8. Morality: Feeling that the world is a moral place where you can act in line with your values, rather than feeling that the world is immoral or your actions conflict with your values.	• Being able to act in line with your values. • Fulfilling your responsibilities. • Being treated by others according to your norms and values. • Living in a society that aligns with your norms and values.
9. Purpose: Having a clear sense of what makes your life meaningful and valuable, rather than lacking direction or meaning in your life.	• Engaging in activities that are meaningful to you. • Having aspirations and life goals. • Undergoing personal growth. • Engaging in spirituality or religion.

Definition	Sub-needs
10. Recognition: Getting appreciation for what you do and respect for who you are, rather than being disrespected, underappreciated, or ignored.	• Having status and a good reputation. • Being appreciated and valued for who you are. • Being taken seriously and treated with respect. • Being popular and liked by others.
11. Relatedness: Building and having warm and mutual relationships with people who you care about, rather than feeling isolated or being unable to form meaningful bonds.	• Spending time with friends and loved ones. • Providing care and support to others. • Experiencing love, tenderness, and intimacy. • Receiving care and support from others.
12. Security: Being safe from harm and threats, rather than feeling vulnerable, threatened, or insecure.	• Feeling physically safe. • Living in a stable society. • Feeling financially secure. • Conserving the things in life that are important to you.
13. Stimulation: Having new and exciting experiences that engage your mind and body, rather than feeling bored, indifferent, or stuck in monotony.	• Engaging in playful activities. • Experiencing thrill and adventure. • Experiencing bodily sensations. • Experiencing novelty and variety.

T&T 2 — THE FUN SCALES: Measuring Need Fulfillment in Design

The *Fundamental User Needs* (FUN) Scales research tool assesses how well a design supports or frustrates fundamental human needs.[1] Developed at the Delft Institute of Positive Design, the FUN Scales respond to a growing interest in the psychological impact of products, services, and environments. The core idea is simple but powerful: the more a design satisfies people's fundamental needs, the more positive their experience is likely to be.

Based on the typology of thirteen fundamental needs introduced in Chapter 1, each need is assessed across two sub-scales: one for satisfaction and one for frustration. This dual approach recognizes that positive experiences are both about fulfilling needs and avoiding the frustration of those needs.

The instrument includes 78 items total, grouped into 26 sub-scales (13 needs × 2). Each sub-scale consists of three statements. For example, Autonomy satisfaction is measured with statements such as "I can do things my way," while Autonomy frustration measurements include "My self-expression is constrained." Respondents rate how true each statement is for a particular experience or interaction, typically on a 7-point Likert scale.

The scales can be used in full or selectively, depending on the context and goals. The results offer a rich picture of how users experience a design: which needs it fulfills, which it compromises, and which are left untouched. The scores can be analyzed per need, aggregated into overall satisfaction or frustration scores, or converted into percentages for easier interpretation.

The FUN Scales have been tested in academic settings and applied in professional ones, where they have been used to evaluate healthcare environments and digital interfaces to explore how new products support well-being. Because the items focus on subjective experience rather than product qualities, the scales are versatile and applicable across domains.

The complete FUN Scales, scoring instructions, and background materials are freely available via the Delft Institute of Positive Design: https://diopd.org/fun-scales/

1. Huang, Desmet, and Mugge (2025).

Top row (positive): joy, admiration, pride, hope, satisfaction, fascination, desire
Bottom row (negative): sadness, fear, shame, contempt, dissatisfaction, boredom, disgust

T&T 3 — PREMO: A Visual Tool for Measuring Emotions

PrEmo is a research tool designed to measure people's emotional responses to products, situations, and services. We developed it with a specific challenge in mind: many people struggle to express their emotions in words, especially when asked to describe subtle or fleeting feelings. PrEmo sidesteps this challenge by using a set of expressive cartoon characters to represent emotions—allowing people to simply point to what they feel.

The first version of PrEmo was developed in 2002.[2] Since then, it has undergone considerable evolution over the past two decades of application and refinement. The current version includes fourteen emotions: seven positive and seven negative. These emotions represent a meaningful cross-section of the human emotional repertoire, covering a broad range of valence (positive/negative) and activation (from calm to intense). Each emotion is depicted as a short animation. While originally developed as animated clips, the characters are also often used as still images on printed cards, in physical workshops, or during interviews when screens are not present. PrEmo is available in both female and male character versions. Because it relies on images rather than language, it can be used across cultures and user groups. Over the years, PrEmo has been applied in both academic and commercial settings, from public transportation and digital interfaces to comparing emotional responses to cookies, product packaging, and service journeys.

The full PrEmo set is freely available to student projects and academic researchers at the Delft Institute of Positive Design website: https://diopd.org/premo. PrEmo can be licensed for commercial use at https://premotool.com.

2. PrEmo development is reported by Desmet (2002).

T&T 4 — MICRO-EMOTION SCAN: Conducting the User Interview

A Micro-Emotion Scan captures all the emotions that emerge during a product or service journey, revealing insights that traditional post-experience inquiries tend to miss. Success depends on creating the right conditions for participants to notice and share their micro emotions without disrupting their natural behavior.

Structure your research in two phases to protect the authenticity of the emotional data. In Phase 1, you accompany participants through their entire product journey, focusing solely on documenting each emotion as it emerges. You move to Phase 2 after the complete experience, sitting down for a detailed interview to explore the emotions more deeply and understand their context. This separation prevents analytical thinking from contaminating the immediate emotional responses while ensuring you capture both the raw emotional data and the insights needed to interpret it effectively. The procedure is flexible and can be adapted to fit your needs and resources—but it works best when guided by the following six principles.

Principle 1. Make emotions easy to express: The procedure relies on the participant's ability to express their emotions quickly and easily. While most people have little trouble expressing what they feel, the words they use vary in precision. Someone may say they feel "good" or "bad," which gives some information but not much detail. People typically know more emotion words than they spontaneously use. Offering a set of emotions to choose from helps. As mentioned earlier, we often use PrEmo cards. Participants can simply point to what they feel, which lowers the threshold for expression and requires minimal effort. Let them review the set in advance to ensure a shared understanding.

Principle 2. Capture emotions in the moment: To protect the natural flow of the experience, the procedure is divided into two stages. In the first, you focus solely on capturing each emotion as it arises, along with its intensity and what triggered it. Ask participants to share what they are feeling *in the moment.* Don't interrupt, interpret, or ask for clarification. Just follow the participant and record what comes up. Only after completing the entire experience journey do you sit down with them to discuss their emotions, adding more details and context.

Principle 3. Include every emotion: Encourage participants to express all of the emotions that arise during the procedure—not only emotions about the product, but also those directed at themselves. For example, someone might feel frustrated that their finger is too large for a button or embarrassed that they don't understand a manual instruction. These emotions may not relate to the product directly, but they're still highly relevant for informing design. Participants can have the tendency to censor themselves based on what they think is useful to the research, so make it clear that you're interested in all their emotions.

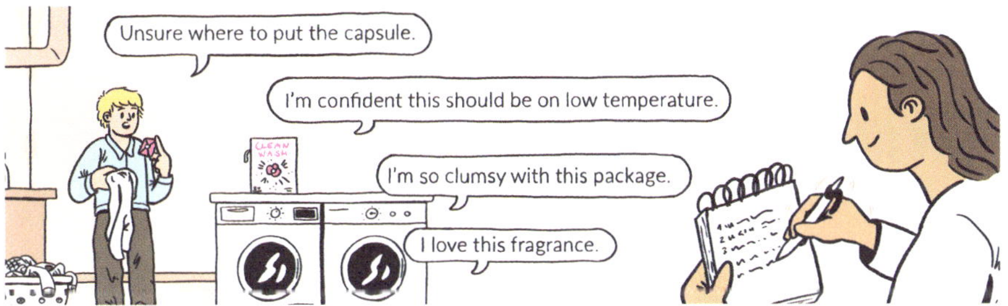

Principle 4. Avoid rationalizations: Most people have a natural tendency to share opinions about the product ("This should be easier to open") rather than their emotions ("I feel disappointed"). This tendency needs to be curbed to preserve the authenticity of micro emotions. This can be challenging because talking about feelings can feel more vulnerable to people than giving opinions. For the same reason, try to prevent people from reviewing the product, as this disconnects them from their immediate feelings. To avoid this, ask respondents to begin each report by naming what they feel and only describe what triggered that feeling.

Principle 5. Keep the experience authentic: It would be ideal for product researchers to be invisible, mind-reading, and omnipresent. Unfortunately for researchers (and fortunately for everyone else), this is not the case. In reality, any type of user research introduces artificial elements. Respondents receive the test product, are observed, interviewed, and compensated for their time. All of this can influence their experiences and, thereby, the reliability of the data. It is important to encourage respondents to act as they would under normal circumstances. We often give respondents the example that if they would not normally read the instructions, they should not do so for the study—and vice versa. Likewise, they should use the product in the setting they normally would—not in a location chosen for the convenience of the researcher. Above all, resist the temptation to direct respondents' attention to particular features or aspects, as this undermines the authentic reactions you're trying to capture.

Principle 6. Slow down and zoom in: There is one important exception to the authenticity guideline: participants should be encouraged to slow down their actions and zoom in on their micro emotions. These moments are easy to miss, not because people are unwilling to share them, but because they fade quickly. Without slowing down, participants may skip over emotions or compress several into one. Essentially, participants need to pay close attention to the stream of emotions with an open mind. For example, consider the sequence of emotions shown in the cartoon. The entire sequence might happen in two seconds. Without slowing down, you might only capture the final emotion. This is why we ask participants to briefly pause after every micro emotion, no matter how short it is, and report it before moving on.

T&T 5 — THE USER NEED CAPTURE APPROACH

The UNC is a set of guidelines for capturing genuine and deep user needs surrounding a product or user situation. It builds on the principles of the Micro-Emotion Scan (MES) described in Chapter 2 and in the previous pages. The guidelines are organized into two sets: one for collecting rich emotional data and one for extracting meaningful needs from that data. Understanding these principles will help you adapt the approach to your research context.

Interview Principles

Principle 1. Build upon the Micro-Emotion Scan: Capture emotions in real time as much as possible, avoid rationalizations, offer respondents a visual tool to express their emotions, and, above all, make sure their behavior and answers are authentic. As with the MES, meaningful results come from genuine emotional responses, not rationalized opinions.

Principle 2. Gather all that is relevant but prioritize quality: UNC doesn't involve specifying every micro emotion, as does a full MES. But it does take time to uncover the needs or needs underlying an emotion. Not every emotion leads to an insightful need ladder, so you'll have to make quick decisions during interviews about where to go deeper.

For a simpler product, capturing a few dozen needs may be sufficient. When working with a more complex product, or when the product plays a major role in the user's life (like a wheelchair), you might need to gather a larger set of needs to get the full picture. For such products, it won't always be possible to capture all emotions in real time. In that case, use tools such as *journey mapping* to help respondents relive their experience, which will naturally reveal an array of emotions.[1]

A broad set of meaningful needs means more need ladders, more precision about users' precise needs, and greater clarity about overarching need themes. Ultimately, it will be project specifics and researcher judgment that determine whether enough relevant needs have been captured to reveal the full picture.

Principle 3. Follow a consistent structure: It is crucial that you structure interviews systematically. Always start with the emotion, then move on to the event. Next, identify the specific need behind it. And finally, uncover more needs to build the ladder. Following the same set of steps makes it easier to

1. Journey mapping (also called user journey mapping, customer journey mapping, or experience mapping) is a design research method that creates a visual timeline of a user's experience with a product or service (see, for instance, Howard, 2014). It can also be used to map broader life episodes, such as a morning ritual or a commute.

compare and analyze results across users. A sample line of questioning might be:

- *Which emotion did you experience?*
- *What happened that made you feel that way?*
- *Why did you feel [emotion] when [event] happened?*
- *Why is [need] important for you?*

Principle 4. Collect rich contextual information: Respondents rarely express their needs in neat, laddered statements like the examples in this chapter. Your job during the interview is to collect enough raw material to build those ladders afterward. This involves four key practices:

- *Be patient and thorough.* The more detail you capture about the event, the setting, the timing, and so on, the better. Rich descriptions give you the material you need to understand not only what happened, but also *why* it mattered to the user.
- *Mentalize the respondent's experience.* As a researcher, you need to step into the shoes of the respondent: clearly document what happened, who did what, and how the situation unfolded. This helps you understand why they felt a particular emotion.
- *Encourage honest answers.* Although you will probe with a lot of "why" questions, you need to make sure that people feel comfortable saying when there is no deeper reason behind a particular need. Otherwise, they might start constructing answers just to please you.
- *Assume nothing.* It's tempting to draw conclusions prematurely. But even when a need seems obvious, stay curious. If you'd assumed that children disliked fragile wheelchairs purely because they might break, you would've missed the deeper insight: they wanted to signal that rough play was welcome (see page 80).

Principle 5. Be mindful of different types of needs: As you work to uncover a person's true motivations, pay close attention to the language they use, because it often gives clues about what type of need they're expressing (see pages 83-90). Goals are typically framed with phrases like "I want to X" or "I'm trying to achieve X." Urges come through in statements like "I'm craving X" or "I could really go for X." Values can be recognized with phrases like, "I should X," or "People ought to X." Preferences show up when people say "I like X" or "I prefer X."

While it isn't essential to categorize every need based on its type, recognizing these patterns can help you ask more targeted questions and uncover the full need ladder more efficiently. It can also guide you towards needs that are worth spending more time exploring.

Data Analysis Principles

Principle 6. Frame needs positively: Formulating needs positively is important because it shifts your focus from problems to possibilities. When a person says they want to avoid something, there is usually a more constructive way to phrase it, one which lends itself naturally to design. Remember the plastic pouch containing the detergent pods in Chapter 2? People expressed negative emotions about the bag looking ragged and messy once opened (see page 62, points 5 & 6). If you were to ladder these needs, you could frame their first-level need in one of two ways: "I don't like the bag to look messy" or "I like the bag to look neat." Although the difference in wording might seem minor, opting for the positive turn is a useful convention.

It is easier and more inspiring to focus on fulfilling what users want than avoiding what they don't want. With the positive turn of phrase, you can take a step further and think, "How could I design the bag to look even neater?" instead of merely preventing it from looking messy after opening.

Principle 7. Cluster similar needs: Once you've gathered a sufficient quantity of needs, the next step is to make sense of them. This chapter features cleanly laddered examples, as though each hierarchy came complete from a single user and emotion. But in practice, you'll often be dealing with fragments. And the most efficient way to assemble and ladder them is by clustering needs that share a general theme together.

Start by grouping specific needs that ladder to the same underlying need. Write this underlying need as a short statement on a note and use it to label the group. This gives you a clear view of how frequently a certain need appears—even if users word things differently. If you end up with too many clusters, you can go one level deeper: try to group them into broader superclusters. One or two levels are usually enough to reveal structure, depending on the volume of needs you're working with. This process turns a chaotic list of needs into something more navigable and far easier to translate into design opportunities. This approach also helps identify common themes across the need groups (see the section about need themes on pages 81-82).

Principle 8. Ladder toward fundamental needs: It's important to cluster your data by fundamental need rather than by event or circumstance. For example, wheelchair user needs wouldn't be clustered under "ergonomic," "transportation," or "aesthetic." The power of need clustering comes from using fundamental, universal human needs as categories. Fundamental needs provide a framework for understanding deeply relevant product-related needs beyond the context at hand.

By following these eight principles, you'll gather a rich collection of user needs anchored in genuine emotional experiences. Unlike needs derived from direct questioning, these emotion-based needs often reveal surprising insights that wouldn't've emerged through traditional research methods. The result is a need profile that captures not just what users say they want, but what truly drives their emotional responses to a product or service.

T&T 6 — MAPPING CONTEXTUAL EMOTIONS

The following guidelines will help you systematically identify and analyze contextual emotions in any use situation. The guidelines build on the MES and UNC approaches. The approach encompasses two key steps: defining context boundaries and determining which contextual emotions offer the greatest design opportunities.

Step 1: Determine context: The first step is defining the boundaries of your context. In some cases (such as the airline breakfast), the context is relatively easy to delineate because the physical and temporal boundaries are clear: there is a place (airplane cabin), an activity (intercontinental flight), and a timeframe (6-12 hours). But most products are used in more fluid settings. A smartphone might be used anywhere from bedrooms to boardrooms, for seconds or hours, alone or in company. A fitness tracker might accompany an intense gym workout, a lazy walk, or a night's sleep. In such cases, context isn't a given; it is a decision. You will have to deliberately choose which settings to include in your research. To guide that decision, consider:

- **Location**: Where is the product used?
  Example: For a fitness tracker, focusing on "gym workouts" versus "all-day wear" creates entirely different research priorities and findings.
- **Activity**: What is the user doing?
  Example: A music streaming service might be used during focused work, relaxation, or social gatherings each has a distinct emotional landscape.
- **Social setting**: Who else is present?
  Example: A cooking app might be used differently when cooking alone versus preparing a meal for guests—the stakes and needs may be different.
- **Life stage**: Where is the user in their broader journey?
  Example: A navigation app might need to address the differing needs of a teenage tourist and a middle-aged one.
- **Time-related factors**: When and for how long is it used?
  Example: A smart lighting system creates different emotional contexts for morning wake-up versus evening relaxation periods.
- **Cultural region**: How do local norms and expectations affect use?
  Example: Gift-giving apps must consider that the emotional context of presenting gifts varies significantly across cultures.

There is a clear trade-off at work here. A narrowly defined context ("young professionals using smartphones during their morning commute on public transport") simplifies your research but limits the range of emotions and needs you'll capture. A broader context ("smartphone use throughout the day") will uncover more emotional variety but will demand more time and resources to study. Broader contexts usually require more extensive data collection and analysis efforts. The challenge, then, lies in calibrating your research scope and resource allocation effectively. This trade-off in scope is often worth discussing with clients or stakeholders to balance your research efforts with the design potential. The goal is not to capture everything, but to map a context wide enough to surface meaningful emotional cues, without spreading your resources too thin.

In some cases, the service *is* the context. Think of staying at a hotel or watching a theater performance. In these situations, the "product" isn't just a part of a larger experience; it forms the container for the experience. A hotel doesn't just offer you a bed; it entirely creates the environment you spend time in, from arrival to exit. Everything from how the lobby feels to the timing of staff interactions, the background music, and the scent in the air is carefully chosen. The boundary between service and context has become fuzzy; the emotional environment itself is what's being designed.

This matters for research. If you're studying a toothbrush, you need to decide which bathroom contexts are part of your scope. But if you're studying a theater performance as a service, the performance *is* the context—and you study all the emotions that arise while it is taking place, including those seemingly unrelated to the show itself (like a noisy neighbor or an awkward seat). These "background" emotions are relevant because the service provider has the power to influence them through design decisions.

Step 2: Choose which emotions to focus on: After mapping the emotional landscape of a context, you'll likely find yourself with a rich but potentially overwhelming dataset. Not all contextual emotions will be equally useful for your design brief. Which ones should you focus on? Here are three strategies that can help guide the selection process:

- **Pick the most common.** Look for patterns that repeat across users. When multiple people report similar emotions in a situation, it suggests a shared need worth addressing. Use the laddering technique (see Chapter 3) to identify patterns across deeper needs.
  In our airline breakfast study (see Chapter 4), both frustration and boredom came up across interviews. They were part of the shared emotional fabric of long-haul flying. The frustration passengers described was tied to a deeper need for Autonomy. Boredom revealed an unmet need for Stimulation.

- **Pick the most feasible.** Not all emotional insights can be turned into viable interventions. Some needs, while real, may lie outside your product's reach due to budget, regulatory, or technical constraints. Be realistic about what your product or service can influence.
  Our emotion map revealed many unmet needs during the long-haul flight: privacy, connection to the outside world, personal space, and so on. But for a breakfast redesign, those needs were out of scope. We focused on needs the breakfast could plausibly address.
- **Pick the most proximate.** Consider when the emotion is felt in relation to the moment your product appears. Emotions experienced just before, during, or immediately after interaction often carry the most weight, even if your product didn't cause them.
  We focused on the frustration and boredom that occurred late in the flight, which is when breakfast was served.

These strategies aren't checklists. They are a framework to guide your thinking process. Every design project has unique considerations that may influence which emotions and needs you prioritize. Sometimes, an insight might come from a single user's experience that reveals something profound about the context, even if it doesn't meet our "most common" criterion. Trust your judgment as a designer, and consider factors specific to your project goals, brand values, and innovation strategy.

T&T 7 — IDENTIFYING CLASHING NEEDS

The following guidelines provide a systematic approach to uncovering and documenting clashing needs in your design research. These methods build directly on the User Need Capture (UNC) approach introduced in Chapter 3, extending it to more deeply reveal the tensions between competing user needs.

Gathering Need Clash Data

To identify useful clashes in needs, you'll need a rich collection of user needs relevant to your specific design context. Begin by capturing the emotions users experience during concrete events (Chapter 3), then work with the participants to ladder downward to the needs underlying these emotions (Chapter 4) while considering the full spectrum of needs relevant to the situation (Chapter 5). As noted in this chapter, clashes tend to show up in two ways: those that users consciously experience (dilemmas) and those that remain hidden. Let's explore how to identify each type.

When the Clash Is Felt: Capturing Dilemmas: Users experience conscious clashes in needs as dilemmas that create emotional tension. These are often both cognitive ("I know I need to finish this report, and I also know I need to attend my daughter's music recital") and emotional ("I'm feeling anxious and frustrated because I cannot fulfill both needs at once"). Clashes sometimes emerge naturally in conversation. Remember, a dilemma often results in a pair of emotions, usually one positive and one negative, each reflecting a distinct need (see page 127). The emotional experience itself varies greatly, depending on the specific needs involved and how important they are to the person. Some dilemmas produce mild frustration or momentary hesitation; others bring anxiety, anger, or even a sense of being stuck. Of course, people rarely spell it out in a sentence like "I want X, but I also want Y." This kind of concise need clash statement is created by the researcher based on what respondents have shared.

When the Clash Is Hidden: Unveiling Unrecognized Tensions: Not all clashes are consciously felt. Some remain under the surface, not explicitly known by the user, yet equally valuable for design innovation (see pages 126-128). Identifying and addressing these hidden tensions can lead to breakthrough products. How can we identify tensions that people aren't consciously experiencing?

Start by analyzing unmet needs, which are signaled by negative emotions. For every unfulfilled need you discover, conduct a thought experiment: what if this need were fully prioritized? What trade-offs would that create? Which other needs might be compromised as a result? Take a user who feels frustrated by the complexity of his RIVO coffee machine (see page 130). If they were to prioritize ease of use entirely, they might end up with something like the FLIK self-heating can—a solution that maximizes simplicity. The frustration is gone. But in return, they've sacrificed their need for fresh coffee. This thought experiment reveals the tension between simplicity and quality—a clash the user might not name directly but still experiences through their choices.

This approach works best when grounded in real data from interviews, observations, and emotion mapping. Once you see the full range of relevant needs, you're not making assumptions about trade-offs. You're letting the user's own behavior and emotions point to the tensions that matter.

Formulating Need Clash Statements

Every clash of needs can be captured in a single sentence: "I want [a], but I also want [b]." This format helps you clearly express the tension between two needs. It's usually not the only information you share as part of your research. You can support it with background information, relevant quotes, stories, and additional context. But a well-phrased statement helps communicate the essence of the tension you've identified.[2]

To help a clash resonate, the tension between the opposing needs should feel vivid and familiar. Adding a touch of context often helps others empathize with the person experiencing the clash. For example:

- *Basic version*: "I want meal prep to be convenient, but I also want to eat healthy."
- *More explicit version*: "I want my meals to be quick and convenient so they fit into my busy schedule, but that shouldn't get in the way of proper nutrition."

If the full tension doesn't fit into a single sentence, a short clarifying note in parentheses can help.

With that in mind, let's look at three common pitfalls to avoid when formulating clashes in needs.

Consideration 1: Ensure both sides are genuine needs: Consider the following examples:

1. "I want to cook a healthy meal, but I don't know how."
2. "I want to switch to a more meaningful job, but I'm afraid it will result in financial insecurity."

2. The approach of formulating needs at different abstraction levels can significantly affect the creative output when designing to resolve dilemmas. Özkaramanlı, Desmet, and Özcan (2017) demonstrated that consciously exploring need formulations at product-focused (concrete), activity-focused (intermediate), and identity-focused (abstract) levels can open up new perspectives on dilemmas that might otherwise be overlooked. Their research found that the "most abstract yet informative" dilemma formulations were often the most inspiring for designers seeking innovative solutions.

3. "I want to buy fresh and locally sourced vegetables for my family, but that option is not available in my area."
4. "I want to get a promotion, but my boss thinks I'm not ready for the responsibility yet."

In all these statements, the phrase after "but" doesn't describe a need: it points to a knowledge gap, an emotion, a situational constraint, or someone else's judgment. Though these aren't explicit clashes on the surface, there may be genuine clashes hidden within them that can be reformulated. Consider these alternatives:

1. "I want to cook a healthy meal, but I also want cooking to be effortless (especially after a long day at work, when I don't have the energy to learn new recipes)."
2. "I want to switch to a more meaningful job, but I also want to maintain the financial security that my current position provides."
3. "I want to buy fresh and locally sourced vegetables for my family, but I also want to complete my grocery shopping at a convenient distance from home."
4. In this case, there is no clash, just a single unmet need (professional advancement), with an external factor (the boss's evaluation) standing in the way.

Consideration 2: Clarify how the needs create tension: Consider this statement: "I want to enjoy a healthy meal, but I also want to be home on time."

The formulation doesn't make clear *why* the needs conflict. Why can't the user enjoy a healthy meal and arrive home promptly? When the tension is unclear, the clash can be misread or dismissed.

This can be avoided by adding a bit of contextual information: "I want to enjoy a healthy meal, but I also want to eat on-the-go so I'm home on time (and my on-the-go options are typically unhealthy)."

Consideration 3: Frame both needs positively: A strong need clash statement frames both sides as positive desires—things the user wants, not things they want to avoid. We offered a similar guideline on page 241 for individual need statements. The reason is simple: when needs are negatively framed ("I don't want..."), the solution space shrinks. Compare:

- "I want to walk to work (in the rain), but I don't want to get wet."
- "I want to walk to work (in the rain), but I also want to arrive looking presentable."

In the first example, the solution space only includes options that prevent getting wet, such as an umbrella. The second, improved version reveals what the person truly wants: to arrive at work looking neat and professional. This opens up a broader solution space that includes both preventive solutions (umbrellas, raincoats) and remedial ones (perhaps a clothing dryer at the workplace entrance or a change of clothes kept at the office).

Negative framing becomes particularly problematic when it creates direct contradictions. For instance, "I want a portable laptop with a small screen, but I don't want it to have a small screen." This clash statement obviously provides zero solution space—no single device can simultaneously have a small and *not* have a small screen. This impasse can likely be resolved by laddering the needs. Why does this person want a small screen? Perhaps because it is easy to carry while commuting on the train? Or because it fits on cramped café tables where they often work? And why *don't* they want a small screen? Because they want to view multiple documents side-by-side when writing reports? Or because it reduces eye strain during long work sessions?

We saw a similar tension in Chapter 3 in the wheelchair handle design, with the difference being that it existed between two entities: the children who wanted no handles and the parents who wanted large ones. Uncovering the laddered needs will give you a direction to move in and open up the solution space to innovative solutions such as foldable displays, external monitor setups, or cloud-based workspace continuity between devices—none of which would be apparent from the contradictory original statement.

T&T 8 — SPECIFICS OF TEN POSITIVE EMOTIONS

The following table provides the key components of ten positive emotions. The appraisal theme column shows the meaning a person makes of a situation—the holistic evaluation that gives rise to each emotion. The appraisal components column breaks this down into specific evaluative criteria that determine when each emotion occurs. For instance, fascination requires a person to interpret the situation as novel, comprehensible, and relevant. The action tendency column shows how each emotion naturally moves people to behave, and the final column explains the lasting personal resources that develop over time. Together, these elements form a complete picture of how each positive emotion works and what it contributes to human flourishing.

Emotion	Appraisal components	Action tendencies	What it helps us to grow
Amusement Encountering something funny, silly, or witty that feels safe and lighthearted.	**Incongruity**: Breaks with expectations or norms. **Non-threatening**: Feels harmless, lighthearted. **Playful context**: Encourages a playful and creative mindset.	• Play • Share humor • Disrupt seriousness	A playful, flexible mindset and stronger bonds through shared humor.
Serenity Feeling at peace when needs are met and nothing demands immediate action.	**Fulfillment**: Matches what you want or expect. **Absence of urgency**: No pressing tasks or stressors. **Stability**: Feels safe and predictable.	• Reflect • Bask in the moment • Slow down	Inner calm and a deep sense of what matters most.
Gratitude Recognizing someone's intentional kindness or helpful action.	**Intentionality**: The act was done on purpose. **Beneficence**: The action brought a personal benefit. **Exceeding expectations**: It went beyond what was needed.	• Express appreciation • Give back • Pay forward	Trusting relationships and a greater sensitivity to the good in daily life.
Affection Feeling connected and caring towards someone significant in your life.	**Positive regard**: Seeing the other person as likable. **Closeness**: Emotional attachment or connection. **Reciprocity**: The relationship feels mutual.	• Nurture • Express warmth • Give undivided attention	Supportive connections and emotional skills for nurturing closeness.

Emotion	Appraisal components	Action tendencies	What it helps us to grow
Elevation Witnessing actions that reflect moral excellence and inspire positive change.	**Virtuous action**: Behavior reflects moral excellence. **Inspiration**: Motivates upholding similar values. **Altruistic impact**: Benefits others more than the self.	• Adopt higher standards • Reflect on values • Act selflessly	Moral clarity and a stronger drive to contribute.
Admiration Recognizing and valuing someone's exceptional abilities, qualities, or accomplishments.	**Excellence**: Outstanding skill or accomplishment. **Relevance:** Aligns with your values or interests. **Deservedness:** Success is earned fairly.	• Study excellence • Aspire to improve • Reflect on role models	A clear vision of your potential and pathways for personal growth.
Pride Acknowledging one's own meaningful accomplishments.	**Achievement**: Completing something challenging. **Social recognition**: Acknowledgment by others. **Alignment with values**: Reflects personal or cultural ideals.	• Stand taller • Share achievements • Set higher goals	Self-confidence rooted in real accomplishments and a stable sense of self-worth.
Determination Facing a challenge with the belief that persistence will lead to success.	**Challenge**: The task is difficult but achievable. **Self-efficacy**: Beliefs in one's ability to succeed. **Goal Relevance**: The task matters personally.	• Focus attention • Resist distraction • Push through	Grit, resilience, and the capacity to stay on course despite setbacks.
Fascination Being drawn to something novel or complex that sparks curiosity and attention.	**Novelty**: Unfamiliar or unexpected. **Comprehensibility**: Complex but not overwhelming. **Relevance**: Personally meaningful or aligned with interests.	• Examine closely • Explore new ideas • Ask questions	A rich knowledge base and the ability to connect ideas in novel ways.
Hope Envisioning a desirable future outcome despite uncertainty.	**Possibility**: The desired outcome could happen. **Desirability**: The outcome is highly valued. **Lack of control**: It's not entirely under one's control.	• Envision possibilities • Stay optimistic • Plan steps forward	Optimism, endurance, and the mental habit of seeing possibilities.

T&T 9 — CREATING A POSITIVE EMOTION BLUEPRINT

The emotion blueprint transforms abstract psychological insights into concrete design inspiration. This step-by-step process walks you through creating your own blueprint—from selecting your target emotion to gathering user insights that reveal how universal emotional patterns play out in your specific context. More than just a document, the blueprint helps keep emotional intent alive in your process—giving direction without dictating outcomes.

Step 1. Identify your target emotion: Start by selecting the positive emotion you want to design for. Let your design goal guide the choice: Are you aiming for emotional consistency across touchpoints? A memorable moment? A shift in user behavior? You can use the last two columns of the table on the previous pages to understand the impact of each emotion on behavior, mindset, and personal development.

Step 2. Break the emotion into its core components: Use the appraisal theme and components in the table on the previous page to understand what gives rise to the emotion. You can also include action tendencies—what the emotion typically moves people to do. This helps you pinpoint what your design should enable or evoke.

Step 3. Gather context-specific insights: This is where the universal meets the specific. Use fieldwork—interviews, creative workshops, quick observations—to explore how the appraisal components show up in your users' reality. What do small acts of care look like? When does curiosity spark? Gather quotes, images, anecdotes, and so on. You can also look for existing situations, products, or places that already evoke your target emotion.

Step 4. Build your Emotion Blueprint: An Emotion Blueprint usually takes the form of a poster or digital canvas. It should bring the findings together in one space: emotion definitions, appraisal components, action tendencies, user quotes, visual references, and inspirational examples. Some designers structure it like a collage; others use a more modular format, with separate sections for things like user quotes, triggers, and appraisal components.
A strong blueprint is:

- *Flexible:* It can evolve as new insights emerge.
- *Engaging:* It combines words and visuals to inspire diverse team members.
- *Portable:* It stays visible and accessible throughout the design process.

T&T 10 — SPECIFICS OF NINE RICH EXPERIENCES

The following table lays out the specifics for nine categories of rich experience. The appraisal column shows what type of trigger evokes the negative emotion. The adjacent column indicates which protective frames can shield the user from the emotion, transforming it into a rich experience. A frame marked with (Required) indicates that the protective frame is required for that specific experience to work effectively. For instance, a Self-Sacrificing rich experience has to include a Perspective frame because, without it, people will not be able to perceive the broader implications of their hardship or sacrifice. Every rich experience has to have at least one protective frame present, regardless. The final column details the kind of experience and the action tendency that the emotion produces.

Rich experience, emotions & appraisal	Protective frames	Resulting experience & action tendency
The Thrilling Fear + Exhilaration ---- *A danger or risk.* Instances include physical danger (falling, sharp objects), psychological danger (being chased, failure), social danger (being the center of attention, being rejected), or losing important things (job, competition, sports match).	• Safety-zone • Detachment • Control	Creates a heightened state of awareness with intense physiological arousal—racing heart, adrenaline rush, and sharpened senses. Time perception often slows; each moment is experienced with unusual clarity. The action tendency is vigilance and focused attention on the source of danger, with readiness for quick movement or escape if needed. The experience feels vivid and memorable, and creates a powerful sense of being alive.
The Challenging Frustration + Determination ---- *An obstacle that requires effort to overcome.* Instances include physical obstacles (lifting a heavy object, climbing a steep hill), cognitive challenges (puzzles, complex problems), skill-based hurdles (mastering an instrument, learning a language), or social barriers (convincing a skeptical audience, negotiating a contract).	• Control (Required)	Generates a state of heightened focus and engagement with the obstacle. The person experiences an irresistible pull to solve the problem, creating a "just one more try" mentality. The action tendency is to apply effort, creative thinking, and a willingness to experiment with different approaches. The experience may combine moments of pure frustration with periods of satisfaction when progress is made.

Rich experience, emotions & appraisal	Protective frames	Resulting experience & action tendency
The Grotesque Disgust + Fascination ---- *Something repulsive yet compelling.* Instances include physically disgusting elements (bodily fluids, decay, unusual textures), conceptually repulsive ideas (moral violations, taboo topics), or aesthetic violations (distorted forms, unnatural colors in familiar objects).	• Safety-zone • Detachment • Control	Creates a conflicting, push-pull dynamic wherein initial revulsion competes with curiosity. The action tendency begins with withdrawal (averting the eyes, physical distancing) but transforms into approach behavior (cautious examination, extended attention). The experience has an inherent ambivalence—simultaneously wanting to look away and being unable to do so—resulting in heightened attentiveness and strong memory formation.
The Scandalous Indignation + Fascination ---- *Witnessing the violation of a social norm.* Instances include violating informal conventions (etiquette, code of conduct), trust (betrayal, revealing secrets), purpose (misappropriating charity funds), rights (impeding freedom of speech), or breaking actual laws.	• Safety-zone • Detachment • Control	Produces moral alertness combined with intense interest. The action tendency is to investigate further, form judgments, and actively share the transgression with others. Creates a sense of insider knowledge while satisfying curiosity about normally hidden aspects of social life.
The Mysterious Confusion + Enchantment ---- *Encountering something ambiguous or unexplained.* Often characterized by incomplete information (partial revelations, obscured views), seemingly impossible situations (uncanny events, inexplicable phenomena), contradictory elements (simultaneously familiar and strange objects), or deliberately maintained uncertainty (withheld conclusions, open-ended narratives).	• Safety-zone • Detachment • Control	Generates a state where uncertainty becomes intriguing rather than frustrating. The action tendency is to explore, investigate, and seek explanations—often in supernatural or transcendental realms when conventional explanations fall short. Involves sustained attention as the mind generates multiple interpretations and possibilities, creating engagement that feels dreamlike or significant beyond ordinary understanding.

Rich experience, emotions & appraisal	Protective frames	Resulting experience & action tendency
The Wistful Longing + Affection ---- *Perceiving something valuable as unattainable or lost.* Often characterized by temporal distance (past experiences, bygone eras), spatial separation (far-away places, inaccessible locations), social distance (estranged relationships, unrequited feelings), or hypothetical alternatives (paths not taken, missed opportunities).	• Detachment • Control	Creates a bittersweet emotional state combining gentle sadness with appreciation. The action tendency is toward reflection, reminiscence, and seeking connections to what is absent or lost. The experience feels contemplative and meaningful, often leading to a heightened awareness of personal values and deeper emotional connections. Time often seems temporarily suspended as present reality blends with memory or imagination.
The Absolving Guilt + Determination ---- *Recognizing harmful personal actions.* Instances include acknowledging direct harm (damage caused to others, broken promises), indirect harm (environmental impact, unintended consequences), social transgressions (betrayed trust, neglected obligations), or personal failures (abandoned principles, compromised values).	• Perspective (Required) • Control	Produces a journey from negative self-assessment toward purposeful action. The action tendency is to acknowledge wrongdoing, make amends, and change future behavior. The experience progresses from uncomfortable self-awareness through active reparation to eventual relief and renewed self-respect. This cycle creates a powerful sense of moral growth and often strengthens social bonds that may have been damaged.
The Self-Sacrificing Reluctance + Pride ---- *Voluntarily accepting discomfort for a larger purpose.* Instances include physical hardship (strenuous exercise, physical labor), temporal sacrifice (waiting, delaying gratification), resource allocation (donating money, sharing limited supplies), or foregoing pleasures (abstaining from indulgences, accepting austere conditions).	• Perspective (Required) • Control	Fosters meaningful endurance of hardship in service of larger purpose. The action tendency is to persist despite discomfort, with increased seriousness and discipline. The experience involves a certain austerity or harshness, redirecting attention from personal comfort toward principled action. Generates satisfaction derived not from pleasure but from living according to deeper convictions.

Rich experience, emotions & appraisal	Protective frames	Resulting experience & action tendency
The Teasing Annoyance + Amusement ---- *Being subject to harmless transgressions or mild provocations.* Instances include playful mockery (gentle ribbing, inside jokes), practical jokes (pranks, inconveniences), social boundary-testing (friendly challenges, ritual embarrassment), or deliberate subversion of expectations (absurd situations, incongruous experiences).	• Safety-zone • Detachment • Control • Perspective	Generates a playful state where minor irritation becomes a source of shared enjoyment. The action tendency is to engage with the provocation through reciprocal banter, amused tolerance, or good-natured retaliation. The experience builds social connections through the mutual acknowledgment of boundaries being harmlessly tested. If done well, the initial annoyance transitions to an appreciation for the creativity or affection behind the teasing.

T&T 11 — CREATING A RICH EXPERIENCE BLUEPRINT

This procedure is similar to the positive emotion blueprint method described on page 252, with some key differences.

Step 1. Choose a negative emotion to design for: Your starting point is a specific negative emotion. While the final rich experience will incorporate positive emotions—otherwise, it wouldn't be "rich"—the negative emotion is your target. You can start from two different angles. One is the experience you want to create: Do you want the user to feel riveted, reflective, edgy, moved? The other is the action tendency you want to elicit: Do you want the user to slow down, become more alert, act more boldly, or reflect on their behavior?

For instance, if you want to grab attention in a busy environment, disgust (the Grotesque) might be a good fit. If you want to engage users on a task, some frustration (the Challenging) might work well. If you want to create a moment of reflection or emotional weight, sadness (the Wistful) could be the right choice.

Step 2. Find the emotional trigger: Next, consider how to evoke the emotion by considering the way people interpret a situation that leads to a specific emotion: its appraisal structure. Keep in mind that the product doesn't have to explicitly elicit the emotion. It can facilitate an interaction or situation that does, by provoking a certain behavior in the user or in others or revealing something hidden. The product can act as a mirror, a guide, a stage, a lens, or a trigger.

Take indignation (the Scandalous). It arises from the perception that a *rule or norm is being violated.* Which norm is being broken, and by whom? How is this norm connected to the product or context? Does your design break a norm by existing? Does it reveal that someone else is breaking one? Does it invite the user to break a norm? Or consider fear (the Thrilling), which is triggered by *danger.* Danger comes in many forms: physical (heights), psychological (the impression of being followed), or social (public speaking). Frame different fears specifically, as in "the fear of suddenly becoming the center of attention in a group" or "the fear of losing your balance." Also consider what the source of danger is in your concept. Does your product present a danger? Does it expose danger in the world? Or does it push the user to do something risky?

Similar to a positive emotion blueprint, it is important that you gather specific insights about the context and your user group. While some emotional triggers are nearly universal, such as a fear of falling or disgust toward bodily fluids, others are much more culturally or personally defined. Your design will only work if you understand the context in which the emotion will be experienced and the meanings users attach to it.

Step 3. Construct a protective frame: Here lies the biggest difference with the positive emotion blueprint: your design must include a protective frame. Use the different protective frames as thinking tools. Which type or types fit your concept best? Remember that you can use a combination of protective frames to make sure the experience is enjoyable.

Suppose you want to evoke the Thrilling through "the fear of suddenly becoming the center of attention in a group." How do you ensure this will actually be enjoyable for the user? Do you give them control over how, where, or with whom it happens (control frame)? Is it not a real audience but a representation (detachment frame)? Or do you frame the ordeal as an act of courage or personal growth (perspective frame)?

Even though we describe the protective frame as a separate step, in practice you will often go back and forth between the emotional trigger and the protective frame, as they are two aspects of the same outcome: how the rich experience is evoked.

Further Reading

Key Concepts Across Experience Layers

This section offers an overview of influential concepts from emotional design research, organized according to the four experience layers of perceiving, using, doing, and becoming (see Chapter 8). We've selected twenty concepts in total—five for each layer. Each concept is presented with a brief description of its focus and key research questions, followed by four key references that provide entry points into its academic foundations.

This collection provides a starting point for further exploration of what design research has to offer. The field is vast and evolves constantly, drawing insights from psychology, sociology, anthropology, neuroscience, philosophy, and many other disciplines. Each concept presented here opens the door to a body of knowledge that designers can draw upon to create more meaningful and emotionally resonant products. We encourage you to use these references as entry points into deeper investigations that may inform and inspire your design practice, research, and teaching.

This section concludes with ten foundational books that offer overarching perspectives on designing for emotion, experience, and well-being. These works provide valuable frameworks for integrating individual concepts into coherent design approaches.

The Perceiving Layer

Design Aesthetics: Examines how visual properties like form, proportion, color, and composition prompt immediate affective responses. Researchers investigate which aesthetic principles transcend cultural boundaries, how visual preferences evolve over time, and why aesthetic judgments can differ between individuals. Key references: Behrens (1998); Hekkert (2006); Hekkert and Leder (2008); Pye (1978).

Sensory Design: Investigates the deliberate orchestration of multisensory stimuli beyond visual elements to include sound, touch, smell, and taste. Researchers ask how different sensory channels reinforce or contrast with each other and how multisensory integration creates more compelling experiences. Key references: Haverkamp (2012); Lupton and Lipps (2018); Schifferstein and Spence (2008); Spence and Gallace (2011).

Product Semantics: Studies how product forms communicate functional meaning and usage cues through their physical attributes. Central questions explore how shapes, controls, and organization intuitively signal operation methods and why some semantic cues are immediately understood while others require learning. Key references: Crilly, Moultrie, and Clarkson (2004); Karana, Hekkert, and Kandachar (2009); Krippendorff (2005); Krippendorff and Butter (1984).

Symbolic Meaning: Explores the cultural and personal associations users attribute to products beyond their utilitarian functions. Researchers investigate how products become vessels for values, status, or memories and why these symbolic dimensions often prove more enduring than functional considerations in product attachment. Key references: Casais, Mugge, and Desmet (2018); Csikszentmihalyi and Halton (1981); Kleine,

Kleine, and Allen (1995); Van Rompay, Pruyn, and Tieke (2009).

Product Personality: Examines how products embody human-like character traits through design elements. Researchers investigate which design attributes consistently evoke specific character impressions across different user groups and how personality alignment influences emotional connection and purchase decisions. Key references: Aaker (1997); Govers, Hekkert, and Schoormans (2003); Govers and Schoormans (2005).

The Using Layer

Usability: Investigates how product design supports effective, efficient, and satisfying task completion. Key questions include how and why specific design features influence user performance, cognitive load, behavior, and subjective experience across different contexts and user populations. Key references: Jordan (2020); Nielsen (1994); Norman (2013); Shackel (2009).

Affordances: Studies how products communicate possible actions through their design properties. Central questions explore what makes affordances immediately intuitive versus requiring learning and how mismatched affordances create emotional breakdowns during interaction. Key references: Gaver (1991); Gibson (1979); Hartson (2003); Norman (1999).

Service Quality: Examines how service interactions meet user expectations across dimensions of reliability, responsiveness, and empathy. Central questions focus on how service touchpoints create emotional moments of truth and why gaps between expected and experienced qualities trigger particularly strong emotional responses. Key references: Asubonteng, McCleary, and Swan (1996); Cronin and Taylor (1992); McDougall and Levesque (1995); Parasuraman, Zeithaml, and Berry (1985).

Physical Ergonomics: Explores how products accommodate human physical capabilities and limitations. Researchers explore how body-object relationships create comfort or strain during extended use and how ergonomic refinements can shift emotional responses during extended use. Key references: Guastello (2023); Helander (2005); Salvendy (2012); Stanton et al. (2017).

Cognitive Ergonomics: Studies how products accommodate mental capabilities and limitations regarding memory, attention, and decision-making. Researchers ask how cognitive load affects user experience and which information presentation strategies best support different mental processes. Key references: Hollnagel (1997); Norman (2014); Vicente (1999); Wickens et al. (2021).

The Doing Layer

Motivational Design: Investigates how products can activate and sustain user engagement through supporting psychological needs. Key questions examine how designs can foster Autonomy, Competence, and Relatedness and why these needs predict long-term engagement and satisfaction. Key references: Deterding et al. (2011); Ertmer and Newby (1993); Keller (2009); Peters, Calvo, and Ryan (2018).

Activity Theory: Examines goal-directed actions mediated by tools within social and organizational systems. Researchers explore how tools transform the activities they support and why understanding broader activity contexts is essential for successful emotional design. Key references: Kaptelinin and Nardi (2009); Nardi (1996); Raeithel (1992); Verbeek (2006).

Practice Theory: Studies how products become elements in socially shared routines and habits. Central questions address how established practices shape product adoption and use and why disruptive innovations often succeed or fail based on their relationship to existing practice patterns. Key references: Bourdieu (1977); Giddens (1984); Kuijer (2014); Nicolini (2012).

Co-experience: Explores the social dimensions of product use and shared interactions. Researchers investigate how collective engagement transforms individual emotional experiences and why products can serve as powerful mediators of social connection or disconnection. Key references: Battarbee and Koskinen (2005); Koskinen and Battarbee (2003); Lee (2009); Strokosch and Osborne (2020).

Empathic Design: Investigates methods for deeply understanding users' experiences, needs, and emotions. Key questions address how designers can genuinely access others' emotional worlds and which research approaches reveal implicit needs that users themselves may not articulate. Key references: Bollen (2024); Kouprie and Visser (2009); Leonard and Rayport (1997); Van Rijn et al. (2011).

The Becoming Layer

Design for Behavior Change: Studies how products can systematically influence specific habits and actions over time. Researchers examine which intervention strategies most effectively support sustained behavior change and how to align product influence with users' personal values and goals. Key references: Fogg (2003); Michie, Van Stralen and West (2011); Niedderer, Clune, and Ludden (2017); Tromp, Hekkert, and Verbeek (2011).

Design for Well-Being: Explores how products actively support psychological flourishing beyond momentary pleasure. Key questions address how design can enhance positive emotions, engagement, relationships, meaning, and accomplishment, and what distinguishes hedonic from eudaemonic product experiences. Key references: Calvo and Peters (2014); Desmet and Pohlmeyer (2013); Hassenzahl et al. (2013); Jimenez, Pohlmeyer, and Desmet (2015).

Identity and Design: Examines how products help users express, construct, and transform their self-concept over time. Researchers investigate why certain products become powerful identity markers and how design can support positive identity development or reinforce problematic self-perceptions. Key references: Ahuvia (2005); Belk (1988); Dittmar (1992).

Technological Domestication: Studies how new technologies become normalized in everyday life through distinct adoption phases. Key questions explore why some innovations integrate seamlessly while others remain perpetually novel or alien and how emotional responses evolve throughout domestication. Key references: Berker et al. (2006); Silverstone and Hirsch (1992); Silverstone and Mansell (1996); Verbeek (2005).

Life-Centered Design: Investigates products' impacts beyond individual users, considering social systems, communities, and ecosystems. Researchers ask how designs affect indirect stakeholders and future generations and why considering these broader impacts increasingly influences user satisfaction. Key references: Bendor (2018); Borthwick, Tomitsch, and Gaughwin (2022); Fry (2009); Lau (2004).

Foundational Books

Affective Computing by Rosalind Picard (1997). Establishes the fundamental concepts of computing that can recognize, interpret and simulate human emotions, and examines the technical challenges and ethical implications of creating emotionally aware machines.

Design for Wellbeing: An Applied Approach by Ann Petermans and Rebecca Cain (eds.) (2019). Explores practical approaches to designing for human well-being through theoretical frameworks and case studies, offering actionable strategies for creating products, services, and environments that enhance quality of life.

Designing Pleasurable Products: An Introduction to the New Human Factors by Patrick Jordan (2000). Proposes the "Four Pleasures" framework—physio-pleasure, socio-pleasure, psycho-pleasure, and ideo-pleasure—as a structure for addressing different dimensions of user enjoyment, advocating for design beyond usability to include emotional and hedonic aspects.

Emotional Design: Why We Love (or Hate) Everyday Things by Don Norman (2004). Introduces the three levels of emotional design—visceral (appearance), behavioral (pleasure and effectiveness of use), and reflective (personal satisfaction and memories)—and examines how emotions influence product relationships.

Emotionally Durable Design: Objects, Experiences and Empathy (2nd ed.) by Jonathan Chapman (2015). Explores how emotional attachment can lead to product longevity and sustainability and presents strategies for designing products that maintain meaningful relationships with users over time.

Experience Design: Technology for All the Right Reasons by Marc Hassenzahl (2010). Introduces a framework centered on psychological needs as drivers of user experience and presents the concept of "experience patterns" as a practical approach to designing technologies that fulfill fundamental needs like Autonomy, Competence, and Relatedness.

Funology 2: From Usability to Enjoyment by Mark Blythe and Andrew Monk (eds.) (2018). Examines how playfulness, pleasure, and fun can be incorporated into interactive systems and explores methods for evaluating enjoyment beyond traditional usability metrics.

Positive Computing: Technology for Wellbeing and Human Potential by Rafael Calvo and Dorian Peters (2014). Introduces positive computing as an interdisciplinary approach combining psychology, design, and technology to support psychological well-being and provides frameworks for integrating well-being determinants like autonomy, compassion, and gratitude into technology design.

Product Experience by Rick Schifferstein and Paul Hekkert (eds.) (2008). Compiles interdisciplinary research to explain how people experience products through various senses, cognition, and emotion, addressing both practical applications and theoretical perspectives.

Technology as Experience by John McCarthy and Peter Wright (2004). Examines technology use as a holistic experience with emotional, sensual, compositional, and spatio-temporal threads, showing how technological interactions are woven into everyday life.

References

Aaker, J. L. (1997). Dimensions of brand personality. *Journal of Marketing Research, 34*(3), 347–356.

Ahuvia, A. C. (2005). Beyond the extended self: Loved objects and consumers' identity narratives. *Journal of Consumer Research, 32*(1), 171–184.

Andrade, E. B., & Cohen, J. B. (2007). On the consumption of negative feelings. *Journal of Consumer Research, 34*(3), 283–300.

Apter, M. J. (2007). *Reversal theory: The dynamics of motivation, emotion, and personality* (2nd ed.). Oneworld.

Aristotle. (1909). *On the art of poetry* (I. Bywater, Trans.). Oxford University Press. (Original work published 4th century B.C.E.).

Aristotle. (1954). *Rhetoric* (W. R. Roberts, Trans.). Modern Library. (Original work published 4th century B.C.E.).

Arnold, M. B. (1960). *Emotion and personality: Volume I – Psychological aspects.* Columbia University Press.

Arnous, J. (Ed.). (2023). *Prediction: The future of customer experience.* McKinsey Global Institute.

Asch, S. E. (1951). Effects of group pressure upon the modifications and distortion of judgments. In H. S. Guetzkow (Ed.), *Groups, leadership, and men: Research in human relations* (pp. 177–190). Carnegie Press.

Asubonteng, P., McCleary, K. J., & Swan, J. E. (1996). SERVQUAL revisited: A critical review of service quality. *Journal of Services Marketing, 10*(6), 62–81.

Averill, J. R. (1980). A constructivist view of emotion. In R. Plutchik and H. Kellerman (Eds.), *Emotion: Theory, research, and experience: Vol. 1. Theories of emotion* (pp. 305–339). Academic Press.

Barrett, L. F. (2006). Are emotions natural kinds? *Perspectives on Psychological Science, 1*(1), 28–58.

Barrett, L. F. (2017). *How emotions are made: The secret life of the brain.* Pan Macmillan.

Barrett, L. F., & Satpute, A. B. (2019). Historical pitfalls and new directions in the neuroscience of emotion. *Neuroscience Letters, 693*, 9–18.

Battarbee, K., & Koskinen, I. (2005). Co-experience: User experience as interaction. *CoDesign, 1*(1), 5–18.

Behrens, R. R. (1998). Art, design and gestalt theory. *Leonardo, 31*(4), 299–303.

Belk, R. W. (1988). Possessions and the extended self. *Journal of Consumer Research, 15*(2), 139–168.

Bendor, R. (2018). *Interactive media for sustainability.* Palgrave Macmillan.

Berker, T., Hartmann, M., Punie, Y., & Ward, K. (Eds.). (2006). *Domestication of media and technology.* McGraw-Hill Education.

Berlyne, D. E. (1960). *Conflict, arousal and curiosity.* McGraw-Hill.

Bjørnland, D. F., Ditzel, C., Visser, J., Knox, S., Sánchez-Rodríguez, V., & Esquivias, P. (2015). *What really shapes the customer experience.* Boston Consulting Group.

Blythe, M., & Monk, A. (Eds.). (2018). *Funology 2: From usability to enjoyment.* Springer.

Bollen, C. J. M. (2024). *Empathy 2.0: What it means to be empathetic in a diverse and digital world.* [Doctoral dissertation]. Delft University of Technology.

Boon, B. (2020). *Playscapes: Creating space for young children's physical activity and play.* [Doctoral dissertation]. Delft University of Technology.

Borg, J., & Khasnabis, C. (2008). *Guidelines on the provision of manual wheelchairs in less-resourced settings.* World Health Organization.

Borthwick, M., Tomitsch, M., & Gaughwin, M. (2022). From human-centred to life-centred design: Considering environmental and ethical concerns in the design of interactive products. *Journal of Responsible Technology, 10*, 100032.

Bourdieu, P. (1977). *Outline of a theory of practice* (R. Nice, Trans.). Cambridge University Press.

Brosnan, S. F., & De Waal, F. B. M. (2003). Monkeys reject unequal pay. *Nature, 425*, 297–299.

Brown, N. J., & Rohrer, J. M. (2020). Easy as (happiness) pie? A critical evaluation of a popular model of the determinants of well-being. *Journal of Happiness Studies, 21*, 1285–1301.

Calvo, R. A., & Peters, D. (2014). *Positive computing: Technology for wellbeing and human potential*. The MIT Press.

Casais, M., Mugge, R., & Desmet, P. M. A. (2018). Objects with symbolic meaning: 16 directions to inspire design for well-being. *Journal of Design Research, 16*(3–4), 247–281.

Chapman, J. (2015). *Emotionally durable design: Objects, experiences and empathy* (2nd ed.). Routledge.

Crilly, N., Moultrie, J., & Clarkson, P. J. (2004). Seeing things: Consumer response to the visual domain in product design. *Design Studies, 25*(6), 547–577.

Cronin Jr, J. J., & Taylor, S. A. (1992). Measuring service quality: A reexamination and extension. *Journal of Marketing, 56*(3), 55–68.

Csikszentmihalyi, M., & Halton, E. (1981). *The meaning of things: Domestic symbols and the self*. Cambridge University Press.

Cunningham, W. A., & Zelazo, P. D. (2007). Attitudes and evaluations: A social cognitive neuroscience perspective. *Trends in Cognitive Sciences, 11*(3), 97–104.

Cunningham, W. A., Zelazo, P. D., Packer, D. J., & Van Bavel, J. J. (2007). The iterative reprocessing model: A multilevel framework for attitudes and evaluation. *Social Cognition, 25*(5), 736–760.

D'Olimpio, L. (2024). What's wrong with wishful thinking? "Manifesting" as an epistemic vice. *Educational Theory*, 75(2), 260–275.

Damasio, A. (1994). *Descartes' error: Emotion, reason, and the human brain*. G.P. Putnam's Sons.

Deci, E. L., & Ryan, R. M. (2000). The "what" and "why" of goal pursuits: Human needs and the self-determination of behavior. *Psychological Inquiry, 11*, 227–268.

Dehaene, S., Changeux, J. P., Naccache, L., Sackur, J., & Sergent, C. (2006). Conscious, preconscious, and subliminal processing: A testable taxonomy. *Trends in Cognitive Sciences, 10*(5), 204–211.

Desmet, P. M. A. (2002). *Designing emotions*. [Doctoral dissertation]. Delft University of Technology.

Desmet, P. M. A. (2003). Measuring emotion: Development and application of an instrument to measure emotional responses to products. In M.A. Blythe, A.F. Monk, K. Overbeeke, & P.C. Wright (Eds.), *Funology: From usability to enjoyment* (pp. 111–123). Springer.

Desmet, P. M. A. (2012). Faces of product pleasure: 25 positive emotions in human-product interactions. *International Journal of Design, 6*(2), 1–29.

Desmet, P. M. A., & Fokkinga, S. F. (2020). Beyond Maslow's pyramid: Introducing a typology of thirteen fundamental needs for human-centered design. *Multimodal Technologies and Interaction, 4*(38), 2–22.

Desmet, P. M. A., & Hekkert, P. (2007). Framework of product experience. *International Journal of Design, 1*(1), 57–66.

Desmet, P. M. A., & Pohlmeyer, A. E. (2013). Positive design: An introduction to design for subjective well-being. *International Journal of Design, 7*(3), 5–19.

Desmet, P. M. A., & Sääksjärvi, M. C. (2016). Form matters: Design creativity in positive psychological interventions. *Psychology of Well-Being, 6*, 1–17.

Desmet, P. M. A, Sauter, D. A., & Shiota, M. N. (2021). Apples and oranges: Three criteria for positive emotion typologies. *Current Opinion in Behavioral Sciences*, 39, 119–124.

Desmet, P. M. A., & Schifferstein, H. N. J. (2022). Emotion research as input for product design. In K. Lopetcharat, D. Paredes, & J. H. Beckley (Eds.), *Product innovation toolbox: A field guide to consumer understanding and research* (pp. 149–175). John Wiley & Sons.

Deterding, S., Dixon, D., Khaled, R., & Nacke, L. (2011). From game design elements to gamefulness: Defining "gamification". In *Proceedings of the 15th international academic MindTrek conference: Envisioning future media environments* (pp. 9–15). ACM.

Dittmar, H. (1992). *The social psychology of material possessions: To have is to be.* St. Martin's Press.

Dupré, D., Krumhuber, E. G., Küster, D., & McKeown, G. J. (2020). A performance comparison of eight commercially available automatic classifiers for facial affect recognition. *PLOS ONE, 15*(4), e0231968.

Ehrenreich, B. (2009). *Bright-sided: How the relentless promotion of positive thinking has undermined America.* Metropolitan Books.

Ekman, P. (1999). Basic emotions. In T. Dalgleish & M. Power (Eds.), *Handbook of cognition and emotion* (pp. 45–60). John Wiley & Sons.

Ekman, P., & Friesen, W. V. (1978). *Facial action coding system: A technique for the measurement of facial movement.* Consulting Psychologists Press.

Ellsworth, P. C., & Scherer, K. R. (2003). Appraisal processes in emotion. In: R. J. Davidson, K. R. Scherer & H. H. Goldsmith (Eds.). *Handbook of affective sciences* (pp. 572–595). Oxford University Press.

Emmons, R. A., & McCullough, M. E. (2003). Counting blessings versus burdens: An experimental investigation of gratitude and subjective well-being in daily life. *Journal of Personality and Social Psychology, 84*(2), 377–389.

Epstein, S. (1992). Coping ability, negative self-evaluation, and overgeneralization: Experiment and theory. *Journal of Personality and Social Psychology, 62*(5), 826–836.

Ertmer, P. A., & Newby, T. J. (1993). Behaviorism, cognitivism, constructivism: Comparing critical features from an instructional design perspective. *Performance Improvement Quarterly, 6*(4), 50–72.

Fiske, S. T. (2004). *Social beings: A core motives approach to social psychology.* Wiley.

Fogg, B. J. (2003). *Persuasive technology: Using computers to change what we think and do.* Morgan Kaufmann.

Fokkinga, S. F. (2015). *Design –|+ Negative emotions for positive experiences.* [Doctoral dissertation]. Delft University of Technology.

Fokkinga, S. F., & Desmet, P. M. A. (2013). Ten ways to design for disgust, sadness, and other enjoyments: A design approach to enrich product experiences with negative emotions. *International Journal of Design, 7*(1), 19–36.

Ford, D. H. (2013). *Humans as self-constructing living systems: A developmental perspective on behavior and personality. Second edition.* The Pennsylvania State University.

Ford, M. E., & Nichols, C. W. (1987). A taxonomy of human goals and some possible applications. In M. E. Ford & D. H. Ford (Eds.), *Humans as self-constructing living systems: Putting the framework to work* (pp. 289–311). Lawrence Erlbaum.

Fredrickson, B. L. (1998). What good are positive emotions? *Review of General Psychology, 2*(3), 300–319.

Fredrickson, B. L., & Branigan, C. (2005). Positive emotions broaden thought-action repertoires: Evidence for the broaden and-build model. *Cognition and Emotion, 19*(3), 313–332.

Fredrickson, B. L., & Cohn, M. A. (2008). Positive emotions. In M. Lewis, J. M. Haviland-Jones, & L. F. Barrett (Eds.), *Handbook of emotions* (3rd ed., pp. 777–798). Guilford Press.

Frijda, N. H. (1994). Varieties of affect: Emotions and episodes, moods, and sentiments. In P. Ekman & R. J. Davidson (Eds.), *The nature of emotion, fundamental questions* (pp. 59–67). Oxford University Press.

Frijda, N. H. (2007). *The laws of emotion.* Lawrence Erlbaum.

Fry, T. (2009). *Design futuring: Sustainability, ethics and new practice.* Berg Publishers.

Ganapati, P. (2010, January 27). Would you buy an iPad? Wired readers weigh in. *Wired.* https://www.wired.com/2010/01/apples-ipad-muted-response/

Gaver, W. W. (1991, March). Technology affordances. In *Proceedings of the SIGCHI Conference on Human Factors in Computing Systems* (pp. 79–84). ACM.

Gibson, J. J. (1979). *The ecological approach to perception.* Lawrence Erlbaum.

Giddens, A. (1984). *The constitution of society: Outline of the theory of structuration.* University of California Press.

Goldenberg, A., Garcia, D., Halperin, E., & Gross, J. J. (2020). Collective emotions. *Current Directions in Psychological Science, 29*(2), 154–160.

Govers, P. C., Hekkert, P., & Schoormans, J. P. (2003). Happy, cute and tough: Can designers create a product personality that consumers understand. In D. McDonagh, P. Hekkert, J. Van Erp, & D. Gyi (Eds.), *Design and emotion: The experience of everyday things* (pp. 345–349). Taylor & Francis.

Govers, P. C., & Schoormans, J. P. (2005). Product personality and its influence on consumer preference. *Journal of Consumer Marketing, 22*(4), 189–197.

Gross, J. J. (1998). The emerging field of emotion regulation: An integrative review. *Review of General Psychology, 2*(3), 271–299.

Guastello, S. J. (2023). *Human factors engineering and ergonomics: A systems approach.* CRC Press.

Gutman, J. (1982). A means-end chain model based on consumer categorization processes. *Journal of Marketing, 46*(2), 60–72.

Hartson, R. (2003). Cognitive, physical, sensory, and functional affordances in interaction design. *Behaviour & Information Technology, 22*(5), 315–338.

Hassenzahl, M. (2010). *Experience design: Technology for all the right reasons.* Morgan & Claypool.

Hassenzahl, M., Eckoldt, K., Diefenbach, S., Laschke, M., Lenz, E., & Kim, J. (2013). Designing moments of meaning and pleasure: Experience design and happiness. *International Journal of Design, 7*(3), 21–31.

Haverkamp, M. (2012). *Synesthetic design: Handbook for a multi-sensory approach.* Walter de Gruyter.

Hebb, D. O. (1955). Drives and the CNS (conceptual nervous system). *Psychological Review, 62*(4), 243–254.

Hekkert, P. (2006). Design aesthetics: Principles of pleasure in design. *Psychology Science, 48*(2), 157–172.

Hekkert, P., & Leder, H. (2008). Product aesthetics. In H. N. J. Schifferstein & P. Hekkert (Eds.), *Product experience* (pp. 259–285). Elsevier.

Helander, M. (2005). *A guide to human factors and ergonomics.* CRC press.

Hirschman, E. C., & Holbrook, M. B. (1982). Hedonic consumption: Emerging concepts, methods and propositions. *Journal of Marketing, 46*(3), 92–101.

Hoemann, K., Nielson, C., Yuen, A., Gurera, J. W., Quigley, K. S., & Barrett, L. F. (2021). Expertise in emotion: A scoping review and unifying framework for individual differences in the mental representation of emotional experience. *Psychological Bulletin, 147*(11), 1159–1183.

Hollnagel, E. (1997). Cognitive ergonomics: It's all in the mind. *Ergonomics, 40*(10), 1170–1182.

Hornsey, M. J., & Jetten, J. (2004). The individual within the group: Balancing the need to belong with the need to be different. *Personality and Social Psychology Review, 8*(3), 248–264.

Howard, T. (2014). Journey mapping: A brief overview. *Communication Design Quarterly Review, 2*(3), 10–13.

Huang, S., Desmet, P. M. A., & Mugge, R. (2025). Introducing the Fundamental User Needs (FUN) scales: Assessing need satisfaction and frustration in design-mediated interactions. *International Journal of Human-Computer Interaction, 1–18.*

Izard, C. E. (1977). *Human emotions.* Springer.

James, W. (1884). What is an emotion? *Mind, 9*(34), 188–205.

Jimenez, S., Pohlmeyer, A. E., & Desmet, P. M. A. (2015). *Positive design reference guide.* Delft University of Technology.

Jordan, P. W. (2000). *Designing pleasurable products: An introduction to the new human factors.* Taylor & Francis.

Jordan, P. W. (2020). *An introduction to usability.* CRC Press.

Kahneman, D. (2011). *Thinking, fast and slow.* Penguin Books.

Kahneman, D., & Tversky, A. (1979). Prospect theory: An analysis of decision under risk. *Econometrica, 47,* 263–291.

Kaptelinin, V., & Nardi, B. A. (2009). *Acting with technology: Activity theory and interaction design.* The MIT press.

Karana, E., Hekkert, P., & Kandachar, P. (2009). Meanings of materials through sensorial properties and manufacturing processes. *Materials & Design, 30*(7), 2778–2784.

Keller, J. M. (2009). *Motivational design for learning and performance: The ARCS model approach.* Springer Science & Business.

Kleine, S. S., Kleine, R. E., & Allen, C. T. (1995). How is a possession "me" or "not me"? Characterizing types and an antecedent of material possession attachment. *Journal of Consumer Research, 22*(3), 327–343.

Koskinen, I., & Battarbee, K. (2003). Defining co-experience. In *Proceedings of the 2003 International Conference on Designing Pleasurable Products and Interfaces* (pp. 269–273). ACM.

Kouprie, M., & Visser, F. S. (2009). A framework for empathy in design: Stepping into and out of the user's life. *Journal of Engineering Design, 20*(5), 437–448.

Krippendorff, K. (2005). *The semantic turn: A new foundation for design.* CRC Press.

Krippendorff, K., & Butter, R. (1984). Product semantics: Exploring the symbolic qualities of form. *Innovation, 3*(40), 4–9.

Kuijer, L. (2014). *Implications of social practice theory for sustainable design.* Delft University of Technology.

Kuppens, P., & Verduyn, P. (2017). Emotion dynamics. *Current Opinion in Psychology, 17,* 22–26.

Lange, C. G. (1922). The emotions (I. A. Haupt, Trans.). In C. G. Lange & W. James (Eds.), *The emotions* (Vol. 1, pp. 33–90). Williams & Wilkins. (Original work published 1885).

Lapate, R. C., Samaha, J., Rokers, B., Hamzah, H., Postle, B. R., & Davidson, R. J. (2017). Inhibition of lateral prefrontal cortex produces emotionally biased first impressions: A transcranial magnetic stimulation and electroencephalography study. *Psychological Science, 28*(7), 942–953.

Larsen, J. T., McGraw, A. P., & Cacioppo, J. T. (2001). Can people feel happy and sad at the same time? *Journal of Personality and Social Psychology, 81*(4), 684–696.

Lau, A. (2004). Life-centered design: A paradigm for engineering in the 21st century. In *Proceedings of the American Society for Engineering Education Annual Conference & Exposition* (session 3261). ASEE.

Lazarus, R. S. (1991). *Emotion and adaptation.* Oxford University Press.

LeDoux, J. E. (2012). Rethinking the emotional brain. *Neuron, 73*(4), 653–676.

Lee, J. J. (2009). Culture and co-experience: Cultural variation of user experience in social interaction and its implications for interaction design. In N. Aykin (Ed.). *Internationalization, Design and Global Development. Third International Conference* (Vol. 5623, pp. 39–48). Springer.

Leonard, D., & Rayport, J. F. (1997). Spark innovation through empathic design. *Harvard Business Review, 75*(6), 102–115.

Lupton, E., & Lipps, A. (Eds.). (2018). *The senses: Design beyond vision.* Chronicle Books.

Lyubomirsky, S., King, L., & Diener, E. (2005). The benefits of frequent positive affect: Does happiness lead to success? *Psychological Bulletin, 131*(6), 803–855.

Lyubomirsky, S., Sheldon, K. M., & Schkade, D. (2005). Pursuing happiness: The architecture of sustainable change. *Review of General Psychology, 9*(2), 111–131.

Magids, S., Zorfas, A., & Leemon, D. (2015). The new science of customer emotions. *Harvard Business Review, 76*(11), 66–74.

Marks, L. V. (2001). *Sexual chemistry: A history of the contraceptive pill.* Yale University Press.

Maslow, A. H. (1987). *Motivation and personality* (3rd ed.). Addison-Wesley.

Mason, M. C., Oduro, S., Umar, R. M., & Zamparo, G. (2023). Effect of consumption values on consumer behavior: A meta-analysis. *Marketing Intelligence & Planning, 41*(7), 923–944.

Mauss, I. B., & Robinson, M. D. (2009). Measures of emotion: A review. *Cognition and Emotion, 23*(2), 209–237.

McCarthy, J., & Wright, P. (2004). *Technology as Experience.* The MIT Press.

McDougall, G. H., & Levesque, T. J. (1995). A revised view of service quality dimensions: An empirical investigation. *Journal of Professional Services Marketing, 11*(1), 189–210.

McDougall, W. (1908). *An introduction to social psychology.* John W. Luce & Co.

Merritt, J. (Ed.) (2018). *Experience is everything: Here's how to get it right.* PricewaterhouseCoopers.

Mesquita, B. (2022). *Between us: How cultures create emotions.* WW Norton & Company.

Michie, S., Van Stralen, M. M., & West, R. (2011). The behaviour change wheel: A new method for characterising and designing behaviour change interventions. *Implementation Science, 6,* 1–12.

Miller, D. T. (1999). The norm of self-interest. *American Psychologist, 54*(12), 1053–1060.

Miller, M., Kiverstein, J., & Rietveld, E. (2022). The predictive dynamics of happiness and well-being. *Emotion Review, 14*(1), 15–30.

Moors, A., Ellsworth, P. C., Scherer, K. R., & Frijda, N. H. (2013). Appraisal theories of emotion: State of the art and future development. *Emotion Review, 5*(2), 119–124.

Murray, H. A. (1938). *Explorations in personality.* Oxford University Press.

Nardi, B. A. (Ed.). (1996). *Context and consciousness: Activity theory and human-computer interaction.* The MIT Press.

Nicolini, D. (2012). *Practice theory, work, and organization: An introduction.* Oxford University Press.

Niedderer, K., Clune, S., & Ludden, G. (Eds.). (2017). *Design for behaviour change: Theories and practices of designing for change.* Routledge.

Nielsen, J. (1994). *Usability engineering.* Morgan Kaufmann.

Norman, D. A. (1999). Affordance, conventions, and design. *Interactions 6*(3), 38–43.

Norman, D. A. (2004). *Emotional design: Why we love (or hate) everyday things.* Basic Books.

Norman, D. A. (2013). *The design of everyday things.* Basic books.

Norman, D. A. (2014). *Things that make us smart: Defending human attributes in the age of the machine.* Diversion Books.

Ochsner, K. N., & Gross, J. J. (2005). The cognitive control of emotion. *Trends in Cognitive Sciences, 9*(5), 242–249.

Ortony, A., Clore, G. L., & Collins, A. (1988). *The cognitive structure of emotions.* Cambridge University Press.

Ortony, A., Clore, G. L., & Foss, M. A. (1987). The referential structure of the affective lexicon. *Cognitive Science, 11*(3), 341–364.

Özkaramanlı, D. (2017). *Me against myself: Addressing personal dilemmas through design.* [Doctoral dissertation]. Delft University of Technology.

Özkaramanlı, D., Desmet, P. M. A., & Özcan, E. (2016). Beyond resolving dilemmas: Three design directions for addressing intrapersonal concern conflicts. *Design Issues, 32*(3), 78–91.

Özkaramanlı, D., Desmet, P. M. A., & Özcan, E. (2017). From teatime cookies to rain-pants: Resolving dilemmas through design using concerns at three abstraction levels. *International Journal of Design Creativity and Innovation, 5*(3–4), 195–215.

Özkaramanlı, D., Özcan, E., & Desmet, P. M. A. (2017). Long-term goals or immediate desires? Introducing a toolset for designing with self-control dilemmas. *The Design Journal, 20*(2), 219–238.

Pakman, M. (2006). Microflow and the emotional spillover effect: An interpretation of daily stress interacting with habitual patterns. *Nonlinear Dynamics, Psychology, and Life Sciences, 10*, 427–464.

Parasuraman, A., Zeithaml, V. A., & Berry, L. L. (1985). A conceptual model of service quality and its implications for future research. *Journal of Marketing, 49*(4), 41–50.

Petermans, A., & Cain, R. (Eds.). (2019). *Design for wellbeing: An applied approach.* Routledge.

Peters, D., Calvo, R. A., & Ryan, R. M. (2018). Designing for motivation, engagement and wellbeing in digital experience. *Frontiers in Psychology, 9*, 300159.

Picard, R. W. (1997). *Affective computing.* The MIT Press.

Pittman, T. S., & Zeigler, K. R. (2007). Basic human needs. In A. W. Kruglanski & E. T. Higgins (Eds.), *Social psychology: Handbook of basic principles* (2nd ed., pp. 473–489). Guilford Press.

Pye, D. (1978). *The nature and aesthetics of design.* Van Nostrand Reinold.

Pyszczynski, T., Greenberg, J., & Solomon, S. (1997). Why do we need what we need? A terror management perspective on the roots of human social motivation. *Psychological Inquiry, 8*, 1–20.

Raeithel, A. (1992). Activity theory as a foundation for design. In C. Floyd, H. Züllighoven, R. Budde, & R. Keil-Slawik (Eds.), *Software development and reality construction* (pp. 391–415). Springer.

Reynolds, T. J., & Gutman, J. (1988). Laddering theory, method, analysis, and interpretation. *Journal of Advertising Research, 28*(1), 11–31.

Ricciardi, L., Demartini, B., Fotopoulou, A., & Edwards, M. J. (2015). Alexithymia in neurological disease: A review. *The Journal of Neuropsychiatry and Clinical Neurosciences, 27*(3), 179–187.

Rokeach, M. (1973). *The nature of human values.* The Free Press.

Rokeach, M. (2000). *Understanding human values: Individual and societal.* Simon & Schuster.

Russell, J. A. (1980). A circumplex model of affect. *Journal of Personality and Social Psychology, 39*(6), 1161–1178.

Ryff, C. D. (1989). Happiness is everything, or is it? Explorations on the meaning of psychological well-being. *Journal of Personality and Social Psychology, 57*(6), 1069–1081.

Sahebi, S., & Formosa, P. (2022). Social media and its negative impacts on autonomy. *Philosophy & Technology, 35*(3), 70.

Salvendy, G. (Ed.). (2012). *Handbook of human factors and ergonomics.* John Wiley & Sons.

Sauter, D. (2010). More than happy: The need for disentangling positive emotions. *Current Directions in Psychological Science, 19*(1), 36–40.

Schifferstein, H. N. J., & Hekkert, P. (Eds.). (2008). *Product experience*. Elsevier.

Schifferstein, H. N., & Spence, C. (2008). Multisensory product experience. In H. N. J. Schifferstein & P. Hekkert (Eds.), *Product experience* (pp. 133–161). Elsevier.

Schimmack, U. (2001). Pleasure, displeasure, and mixed feelings: Are semantic opposites mutually exclusive? *Cognition & Emotion, 15*(1), 81–97.

Schwartz, S. H. (1994). Are there universal aspects in the structure and contents of human values? *Journal of Social Issues, 50*(4), 19–45.

Seligman, M. E. P., & Csikszentmihalyi, M. (2000). Positive psychology: An introduction. *American Psychologist, 55*(1), 5–14.

Shackel, B. (2009). Usability: Context, framework, definition, design and evaluation. *Interacting with Computers, 21*(5–6), 339–346.

Shaver, P., Schwartz, J., Kirson, D., & O'connor, C. (1987). Emotion knowledge: Further exploration of a prototype approach. *Journal of Personality and Social Psychology, 52*(6), 1061–1086.

Sheldon, K. M., Elliot, A. J., Kim, Y., & Kasser, T. (2001). What is satisfying about satisfying events? Testing 10 candidate psychological needs. *Journal of Personality and Social Psychology, 80*, 325–339.

Sheldon, K., & Niemiec, C. (2006). It's not just the amount that counts: Balanced need satisfaction also affects well-being. *Journal of Personality and Social Psychology, 91*, 331–341.

Shiota, M. N., Campos, B., Oveis, C., Hertenstein, M. J., Simon-Thomas, E., & Keltner, D. (2017). Beyond happiness: Building a science of discrete positive emotions. *American Psychologist, 72*(7), 617.

Shiota, M. N., Neufeld, S. L., Danvers, A. F., Osborne, E. A., Sng, O., & Yee, C. I. (2014). Positive emotion differentiation: a A functional approach. *Social and Personality Psychology Compass, 8*(3), 104–117.

Silverstone, R. & Hirsch, E. (Eds.). (1992). *Consuming technologies: Media and information in domestic spaces*. Routledge.

Silverstone, R. & Mansell R. (Eds.). (1996). *Communication by design: The politics of information and communication technologies*. Oxford University Press.

Solomon, R. L., & Corbit, J. D. (1974). An opponent-process theory of motivation: I. Temporal dynamics of affect. *Psychological Review, 81*(2), 119.

Spence, C., & Gallace, A. (2011). Multisensory design: Reaching out to touch the consumer. *Psychology & Marketing, 28*(3), 267–308.

Stanton, N. A., Salmon, P. M., Rafferty, L. A., Walker, G. H., Baber, C., & Jenkins, D. P. (2017). *Human factors methods: A practical guide for engineering and design*. CRC Press.

Sternberg, R. J., & Grajek, S. (1984). The nature of love. *Journal of Personality and Social Psychology, 47*(2), 312–329.

Strokosch, K., & Osborne, S. P. (2020). Co-experience, co-production and co-governance: An ecosystem approach to the analysis of value creation. *Policy & Politics 48*(3), 425–442.

Tangney, J. P., Stuewig, J., & Mashek, D. J. (2007). Moral emotions and moral behavior. *Annual Review of Psychology, 58*(1), 345–372.

Tay, L., & Diener, E. (2011). Needs and subjective well-being around the world. *Journal of Personality and Social Psychology, 101*(2), 354–365.

Tamir, M. (2009). What do people want to feel and why? Pleasure and utility in emotion regulation. *Current Directions in Psychological Science, 18*(2), 101–105.

Tamir, M., & Ford, B. Q. (2009). Choosing to be afraid: Preferences for fear as a function of goal pursuit. *Emotion, 9*(4), 488–497.

Tamir, M., Mitchell, C., & Gross, J. J. (2008). Hedonic and instrumental motives in anger regulation. *Psychological Science, 19*(4), 324–328.

Tong, E. M. (2015). Differentiation of 13 positive emotions by appraisals. *Cognition and Emotion, 29*(3), 484–503.

Tooby, J., & Cosmides, L. (2008). The evolutionary psychology of the emotions and their relationship to internal regulatory variables. In M. Lewis, J. M. Haviland-Jones, & L. F. Barrett (Eds.), *Handbook of emotions* (3rd ed., pp. 114–137). Guilford Press.

Trampe D., Quoidbach J., & Taquet M. (2015). Emotions in Everyday Life. *PLOS ONE 10*(12), e0145450.

Tromp, N., Hekkert, P., & Verbeek, P. P. (2011). Design for socially responsible behavior: A classification of influence based on intended user experience. *Design Issues, 27*(3), 3–19.

Tulving, E. (1972). Episodic and semantic memory. In E. Tulving & W. Donaldson (Eds.), *Organization of memory* (pp. 381–403). Academic Press.

UNICEF (2022). *Appropriate and quality wheelchairs.* UNICEF.

Van Rijn, H., Sleeswijk Visser, F., Stappers, P. J., & Özakar, A. D. (2011). Achieving empathy with users: The effects of different sources of information. *CoDesign, 7*(2), 65–77.

Van Rompay, T. J. L., Pruyn, A. T., & Tieke, P. (2009). Symbolic meaning integration in design and its influence on product and brand evaluation. *International Journal of Design, 3*(2), 19–26.

Verbeek, P. P. (2005). *What things do: Philosophical reflections on technology, agency, and design.* Pennsylvania State University Press.

Verbeek, P. P. (2006). Acting artifacts: The technological mediation of action. In P. P. Verbeek & A. Slob (Eds.), *User behavior and technology development: Shaping sustainable relations between consumers and technology* (pp. 53–60). Springer.

Vicente, K. J. (1999). *Cognitive work analysis: Toward safe, productive, and healthy computer-based work.* CRC press.

Villmoare, B., Klein, D., Liénard, P., & McHale, T. S. (2024). Evolutionary origins of temporal discounting: Modeling how time and uncertainty constrain optimal decision-making strategies across taxa. *PLOS ONE, 19*(11), e0310658.

Watermark Consulting (2023). *The 2023 customer experience ROI study: Quantifying the impact of great—and poor—customer experiences on stock performance.* Retrieved from https://watermarkconsult.net

Watkins, E. S. (1998). *On the pill: A social history of oral contraceptives, 1950–1970.* Johns Hopkins University Press.

Watson, D., & Tellegen, A. (1985). Toward a consensual structure of mood. *Psychological Bulletin, 98*(2), 219–235.

Wickens, C. D., Helton, W. S., Hollands, J. G., & Banbury, S. (2021). *Engineering psychology and human performance.* Routledge.

Williams, P., & Aaker, J. L. (2002). Can mixed emotions peacefully coexist? *Journal of Consumer Research, 28*(4), 636–649.

Woods, A. T., Poliakoff, E., Lloyd, D. M., Kuenzel, J., Hodson, R., Gonda, H., ... & Thomas, A. (2011). Effect of background noise on food perception. *Food Quality and Preference, 22*(1), 42–47.

Yih, J., Kirby, L. D., & Smith, C. A. (2020). Profiles of appraisal, motivation, and coping for positive emotions. *Cognition and Emotion, 34*(3), 481–497.

Yoon, J. K, Pohlmeyer, A., & Desmet, P. M. A. (2016). When 'feeling good' is not good enough: Seven key opportunities for emotional granularity in product development. *International Journal of Design, 10*(3), 1–15.

Zheng, J., & Meister, M. (2025). The unbearable slowness of being: Why do we live at 10 bits? *Neuron, 113*(2), 192–204.

Zillmann, D. (1980). The anatomy of suspense. In P. H. Tannenbaum (Ed.), *The Entertainment Function of Television (pp. 133–163).* Lawrence Erlbaum.

Zuckerman, M. (1979). *Sensation seeking: Beyond the optimal level of arousal.* Lawrence Erlbaum.

Acknowledgements

This book exists because remarkable people shared their wisdom, offered their support, and believed in ideas before they were fully formed.

Frances Philips and Jianne Whelton were our editors. Their roles were vital—Frances helped us discover what we were actually trying to say, and Jianne ensured we said it with precision and grace.

The graphic team brought a second layer of authorship to this work. Through design, illustration, and production, they helped make our ideas accessible and engaging. Yvo Zijlstra handled the typography, layout and DTP for the book. Markus Eberhard's vibrant cartoons brought warmth and humor to concepts that would have otherwise remained abstract. Jort Nijhuis captured the essence of complex products and concepts in illustrations so clear they often explain things better than our words could.

Delft University of Technology has been our intellectual home throughout this journey. The Faculty of Industrial Design Engineering is one of the most vibrant design research environments in the world—a place that gives researchers space to explore, question, experiment, and collaborate.

Our ideas didn't emerge in isolation. They evolved from years of working sessions and hallway conversations with many of our Delft colleagues. Particular thanks go to Paul Hekkert, Anna Pohlmeyer, Rick Schifferstein, Haian Xue, and the late Kees Overbeeke. Much of the thinking we now take for granted took root in conversations with them.

Over the years, we've had the privilege of working with a remarkable group of PhD candidates—each one sharpening our thinking. Several contributed directly to the ideas in this book: Erdem Demir on emotional appraisals, Gael Laurans on measuring emotions, Değer Özkaramanlı on dilemmas, and Jay Yoon on positive emotions. Postdoctoral researchers Tjaša Kermavnar and Siyuan Huang helped us refine the framework of fundamental needs. To all of you, named and unnamed: it's been a joy to think alongside you.

Our greatest teachers have been the hundreds of Delft design students we've worked with over the years. We're grateful to all of them for shaping our thinking, especially those whose projects appear in the book. Their enthusiasm is infectious, their curiosity relentless, and their tolerance for academic jargon refreshingly low. If the ideas in this book make sense, it's because our students trained us to explain ourselves clearly.

Academic theories about design mean little until someone risks real money on them. When we decided to test our ideas beyond university walls, we found industry leaders brave enough to experiment with approaches that existed only on paper. These collaborations launched Emotion Studio and transformed our thinking from academic theory into practical method. Many of the people who placed their trust in us early on became partners in discovery, helping us understand not just what worked, but why it mattered. We wish to acknowledge Robert Ehrencron, Steffen Ristau, Sabine Boesen, Marie-Agnès Beetschen, Hyejin Byun, Esmeralde Marsman, Gijs Ockeloen, and the late Eapen George, without whose efforts our theories and approach would have remained an academic exercise.

We thank all our Emotion Studio colleagues who have helped bring emotional design into practice. Leonie Houwen, Sophie Kelder, and Mariette Klunder deserve special recognition for joining when our office furniture consisted of upturned boxes and our business plan was mostly ambition and hope. You took a leap of faith when we were still figuring out what emotional design actually looked like in the wild.

While we were busy writing about emotions and needs, others were busy supporting ours. Each of us adds our personal thanks:

Charlotte, thank you for being the first reader, the wisest critic, and the most patient supporter. Your love and encouragement carried me through every doubt. Isaac and Marie, watching you discover the world with pure and unfiltered emotions has taught me something new about wonder and joy every single day. You three are living proof that happiness emerges when your deepest needs are fulfilled. — Steven

Johan, thank you for creating the home I could always return to. Through the long hours and the occasional crisis of confidence, you made room not just for this book but for the person writing it. —Pieter

Writing about emotions and needs has reminded us that meaningful work emerges from meaningful relationships. To everyone who supported this journey: we thank you.

COLOPHON

Publisher
BIS Publishers
Timorplein 46
1094 CC Amsterdam
The Netherlands
bis@bispublishers.com
www.bispublishers.com

ISBN 978 90 636 9970 3

Authors: Pieter Desmet and Steven Fokkinga
Developmental editor: Frances Phillips
Copy editor: Jianne Whelton
Typography, layout and DTP: Yvo Zijlstra
Cartoons: Markus Eberhard – Markilus
Drawings: Jort Nijhuis – Jort Design

Image credits
Cover Photo: Miss Sissi table lamp, designed by Philippe Starck in 1991, produced by FLOS (Italy) until 2020. Depicted with permission from Philippe Starck and FLOS.

Page 4, 176, 211: Pexels; Page 10: Pixabay; Page 13, 16, 51, 56, 93, 99, 105: Emotion Studio; Page 19, 20, 67, 96, 120, 140, 169, 194: Adobe Stock; Page 33: Body chair photo by Aava Anttinen; Page 33: Harp Chair photo by MassModernDesign; Page 34: Terra! photo by Studio Nucleo & Twinpixelvideo (Carlo Mossetti + Jacopo Gallitto); Page 34: Luxor Tech photo by Vismara Design; Page 35: Hush Pod from Huus by Freyja Sewell; Page 35: Ku-dir-ka photo by Darius Petrulaitis; Page 40, 43, 70, 142, 228: Istock; Page 45: Public domain via Wikimedia Commons; Page 47: Pxhere; Page 67, 163: Shutterstock; Page 114, 138, 139: Unsplash; Page 116, 132: NOS; Page 138, 139: Stockcake; Page 139: Farmery Pods; Page 158: Light & Shadow Chandelier photo by Stijn Bollaert; Page 160: AV1 Avatar Robot photo by Christian Sinibaldi; Page 189: Oatly "Ditch Milk" photo by Alice Schoolcraft (NB. the photo shows claims from a 2019 campaign which are no longer accurate); Page 207: Harley-Davidson, Unsplash; Page 222: Fang Hung, Unsplash.

This book was supported by The Netherlands Organization for Scientific Research (NWO), through VIDI grant 452-10-011 and VICI grant 453-16-009, both awarded to P.M.A. Desmet by the Division for the Social and Behavioural Sciences.